The
Carolina
Curriculum
for Handicapped Infants
and Infants At Risk

The Carolina Curriculum for Handicapped Infants and Infants At Risk

by

Nancy Johnson-Martin, Ph.D.

*Carolina Institute for Research on Early Education for
  the Handicapped and
Division for Disorders of Development and Learning
University of North Carolina at Chapel Hill*

Kenneth G. Jens, Ph.D.

*Carolina Institute for Research on Early Education for
  the Handicapped and
Division for Disorders of Development and Learning
University of North Carolina at Chapel Hill*

and

Susan M. Attermeier, M.A., LPT

*Division for Disorders of Development and Learning
  and
Division of Physical Therapy
Department of Medical Allied Health Professions
University of North Carolina at Chapel Hill*

·P A U L·H·
BROOKES
PUBLISHING CO

Baltimore • London

Paul H. Brookes Publishing Co.
Post Office Box 10624
Baltimore, Maryland 21285-0624

Typeset by Brushwood Graphics Studio, Baltimore, Maryland.
Manufactured in the United States of America.

The Carolina Curriculum for Handicapped Infants and Infants At Risk was produced under the auspices of the Carolina Institute for Research on Early Education for the Handicapped, a division of the Frank Porter Graham Child Development Center at the University of North Carolina, Chapel Hill.

This work was developed under a contract with Special Education Programs, U.S. Department of Education (originally awarded by The Bureau of Education for the Handicapped, U.S. Office of Education, DHEW, Contract Number 300-77-0309). The content, however, does not necessarily reflect the position or policy of ED/SEP and no official endorsement of these materials should be inferred.

Sketches in text by Sandy Brooks, LPT.

Also available as a companion volume is: *The Carolina Curriculum for Preschoolers with Special Needs,* by Nancy Johnson-Martin, Susan M. Attermeier, and Bonnie Hacker. It may be ordered from Paul H. Brookes Publishing Co., P.O. Box 10624, Baltimore, Maryland 21285-0624 (1-800-638-3775).

Library of Congress Cataloging in Publication Data

Martin, Nancy Johnson, 1934–
    The Carolina curriculum for handicapped infants and infants at risk.

    Bibliography: p.
    Includes index.
    1. Handicapped children—Rehabilitation—Methodology.   I. Jens, Kenneth G., 1935–   II. Attermeier, Susan M., 1942–   III. Title.
RJ138.M368   1986   618.92   85-9725
ISBN 0-933716-52-4

Contents

Acknowledgments

W E ARE GRATEFUL to the Division for Disorders of Development and Learning, University of North Carolina at Chapel Hill, for allowing us to divert our priorities to the curriculum project and for the support of its many staff members in both the development of these curricular materials and in the operation of the Infant Treatment Group (ITG). We are particularly grateful to the infants in the ITG and their parents. Without them, there would have been no project and no reason to develop the materials.

We are also indebted to many individuals who contributed to the development of these materials. Judy Burke, Pat Gallagher, Karen O'Donnell, Joan Anderson, Peggy Ogle, Jerri Moore, Mary Lou Lyon, and Connie Kasari helped in developing items and in the myriad of other tasks inherent in the curriculum development process. Pat Porter took primary responsibility for reviewing aspects of the curriculum related to language development. Barbara Dixon, Julie Brigdon, Amy Glass, and Barbara Wagner took barely legible draft materials and turned them into a manuscript, working without complaint through the many revisions. Tom Mates traveled many miles collecting field-test data.

Finally, we give special thanks to the many staff members in the field-test sites who gave unselfishly of their time and energy to collect data for us, to make constructive suggestions, and to pass on their experience to others. We are especially appreciative of Virginia Bishop, whose efforts exceeded all that was asked of her. The workshop materials she prepared for her staff and the many suggestions she made for improving the curriculum for visually impaired children helped make this second edition a marked improvement over the first.

The Carolina Curriculum for Handicapped Infants and Infants At Risk

chapter *1*

Introduction

T HE PAST DECADE has witnessed rapid growth in the number of programs available
to handicapped infants in the United States. Laws such as PL 94-142 (the Education for All Handicapped Children Act of 1975) and increasing evidence of the
pliability and readiness for learning demonstrated by infants shortly following birth
have interacted to bring about this program growth. Evolving programs vary greatly
in their characteristics. Many are closely associated with university, medical, or
rehabilitation centers and are staffed by professionals from a variety of special
areas—most commonly physical and occupational therapy, special education, and
communicative disorders. Other programs, however, are outgrowths of community-
based day care programs for older handicapped individuals and are staffed primarily
by volunteers, parents, or paraprofessionals who have had relatively little formal
training in infant development. It is probably safe to say that neither personnel in the
most up-to-date centers nor those in the community feel fully confident of their ability
to provide appropriate and comprehensive programs for the infants entrusted to their
care, given the extreme variability in the characteristics of handicapped infants. In
general, caregivers probably cope adequately with the mild to moderately handicapped child whose development proceeds along a relatively normal course, but at a
slower rate. These youngsters do not frequently present major problems either in
assessment or intervention. Assuming responsibility for intervention with the
severely/multiply handicapped child is another matter, though. It is much more
difficult to assess and develop programs for youngsters who show markedly atypical
patterns of development. Thus, programmatic materials—for example, curricula—
are in greater need and are more difficult to produce for this latter group.

OBSERVATIONS ON CURRICULA

Curricula have been developed for use with children at risk for socioculturally
induced developmental delays, as well as for children with specific etiological
conditions and, in some cases, a broad range of handicapping conditions. Although
few curricula have been empirically tested and validated (Bailey & Wolery, 1984),

1

procedures appropriate to the validation process are available (Wolery, 1983), and the value of the process to consumers is acknowledged. A review of curriculum materials available for use with handicapped infants has been provided by Bailey, Jens, and Johnson (1983).

Curricula developed for children perceived as being at risk tend to be experiential in nature and generally provide play and interactional activities to be fostered at various developmental stages (e.g., Karnes, 1979, 1981; Sparling & Lewis, 1981) and aimed at the development of positive parenting behaviors (Bromwich, 1981). Materials of this nature, as well as some developed for children with Down syndrome (e.g., Hanson, 1977), assume that development will follow a relatively normal course, with motor, language, cognitive, and social skills emerging relatively evenly—something we know is not generally true for young severely/ multiply handicapped children. As is generally acknowledged by their authors, these curricula would require extensive revision and expansion, in order to be considered for use with a severely handicapped population.

Materials developed for children with fairly specific developmental problems usually focus on those aspects of development most obviously affected. For example, the materials concentrate on the development of language for hearing-impaired children (Northcott, 1977), a specific mode of therapy for autistic-like children (Bachrach, Mosley, Swindle, & Wood, 1978), handling physically handicapped children (Finnie, 1975), and sensory stimulation for visually impaired children (Bortner, Jones, Simon, & Goldblatt, 1978).

A number of curricula, or assessment tools used as curricular sequences, have also been developed for use with a broad range of handicapped children. These curricula are essentially restructured lists of items taken from existing assessment instruments, with items typically sequenced according to the mean ages at which normal children master skills. Examples of curricular sequences developed in this manner are the *Learning Accomplishment Profile* (Griffin & Sanford, 1975), and the *Portage Guide to Early Education* (Bluma, Shearer, Frohman, & Hillard, 1976). The atypical development of many handicapped youngsters makes it unlikely that they will master skills in the sequences provided, and it is frequently necessary to modify the sequences to fit the unique sensory and motor capabilities of individual children.

McCormick and Noonan (1984) have pointed out that it is unlikely that the needs of severely or multiply handicapped children can be met by a curriculum intended for at-risk or moderately delayed children. Handicapped children may not have the integrated attending and motor responses assumed for the nonhandicapped population. In addition, a significant number of severely handicapped youngsters will never either develop verbal language, walk, or acquire other desirable skills included in "normal" developmental sequences; thus, attention must be directed to teaching those skills that might provide alternative adaptive behaviors when normal behaviors are unachievable (e.g., shaping the minimal motor and discrimination skills necessary for an alternative communication system, should speech not prove a viable means of communication).

THE CCHI APPROACH

Based on these observations and on our experience working with handicapped infants, we have incorporated the following characteristics into *The Carolina Curriculum for Handicapped Infants and Infants At Risk* (CCHI).

1. The curriculum is based on normal sequences of development but does *not* assume there will be relatively even development across all spheres (e.g., a child may exhibit normal cognitive development with very delayed motor development). Thus, the curriculum can be used with both the mildly delayed child who is developing slowly but in a normal pattern, and the multiply handicapped child whose patterns of development are markedly atypical.

2. The curriculum is based on logical teaching sequences; that is, item order is determined by how skills should be taught, *not* by the mean age levels at which normal children learn a skill.

3. The curriculum is based on the recognition that most seriously handicapped infants will never be "normal" in spite of intervention efforts. Thus, in treating the infant, consideration must be given to teaching nonnormal but highly adaptive skills that replace normal skills *when necessary*. For example, should the development of speech prove impossible or nonfunctional for communication, and a decision is made to implement an aided augmentation communication system, attention will have to be directed to building appropriate prerequisite behaviors to facilitate the system's use.

4. The curriculum makes explicit the values and assumptions the authors have chosen to emphasize in selecting items for inclusion in the curriculum.

WHEN IS IT APPROPRIATE TO USE THE CCHI?

The CCHI was designed to provide curricular intervention strategies appropriate for use with handicapped youngsters functioning in the birth to 24-month developmental age range. Items are included in an easy-to-use format, with materials necessary for teaching, teaching strategies, and criterion measures for evaluating performance, along with special notes and cautions, provided for all items. Thus, the CCHI is designed for use by any program involved in providing direct services to handicapped children and their families. It is appropriate for, and has been pilot tested in, home intervention programs, center-based infant stimulation programs, and developmental day care centers.

WHO IS THE CCHI DESIGNED TO BE USED BY?

The CCHI was designed to be used by both professionals and paraprofessionals. It has been used successfully by educators, psychologists, day care and church school workers, public health nurses, physical and occupational therapists, and speech and language specialists. To encourage broad use of the curriculum, a major effort has been made to avoid professional jargon in the wording of its materials.

Although the CCHI is appropriate for use in both center- and home-based training programs, it is anticipated that parents will use the CCHI only with professional consultation and guidance. Despite this, the role of parents in using the curriculum materials should not be minimized. The importance of incorporating teaching into the daily routines of the youngsters' homes cannot be overstated.

WHAT DO I NEED TO KNOW BEFORE USING THE CCHI?

An academic degree in child development or special education is neither necessary nor sufficient to intervene appropriately with handicapped infants. However, the

CCHI does assume that the user will be familiar with basic principles of learning and assessment appropriate for working with handicapped populations. Caregivers should be aware, however, that the materials included here do not prepare them completely for intervening with youngsters functioning in the birth–2-year developmental range.

Many problems that caregivers may confront in using the CCHI can be solved on the basis of common sense. For example, not all items will work for every child. The caregiver will have to consider the nature of the item and the characteristics of the child (i.e., sensory handicaps, muscle tone, state of the child, and the like) when planning an individual intervention program. Caution is particularly appropriate when working with items from the motor areas of the curriculum. *Do not begin using the motor items without first thoroughly reading Chapter 5, "Motor Development," and then reading individual sequence items (sequences 19–24) completely. It is particularly important that attention be paid to the notes and cautions provided with items in these sequences.*

One important function of a curriculum is to alert caregivers to the need for consultation regarding individual youngsters. If, for example, after your best intervention efforts, a child does not appear to be making reasonable progress, you should arrange for another child development professional to evaluate the youngster from the viewpoint of his or her area of expertise. This may be especially important when only a few disciplines are represented on a staff. We all operate within the limitations of our professional training and assumptions. In so doing, we sometimes fail to note all of the appropriate possibilities for intervention. Interaction with other professionals responsible for the health and developmental care of youngsters in intervention programs improves planning and communication, resulting in a more effective program and better parent satisfaction.

HOW WERE ITEMS CHOSEN FOR THE CCHI?

Basic content for the curriculum was selected in the same manner that it has been selected for most other infant curricula. That is, the developmental skills listed on a variety of norm-referenced tests of development were reviewed (Bayley, 1969; Cattell, 1940; Knobloch & Pasamanick, 1974). To these were added skills defined by one of the better-known tests of development based on Jean Piaget's theory—the Uzgiris and Hunt *Ordinal Scales of Psychological Development* (Uzgiris & Hunt, 1975), skills in the tactile integration area compiled by Callier and Azusa in the *Callier-Azusa Scale* (Stillman, 197 7), skills judged to be alternatives to "normal" skills for children with specific handicaps, and a few other skills considered important by the authors for social development and motivation. Specialists in speech and language, occupational therapy, physical therapy, nursing, psychology, education, and nutrition reviewed the skills and contributed to the final selection process.

REFERENCES

Bachrach, A., Mosley, A., Swindle, F., & Wood, M. (1978). *Developmental therapy for young children with autistic characteristics*. Baltimore: University Park Press.
Bailey, D. B., Jens, K. G., & Johnson, N. (1983). Curricula for handicapped infants. In R. Fewell & S. G. Garwood (Eds.), *Educating handicapped infants*. Germantown, MD: Aspen Systems Corp.

Bailey, D. B., & Wolery, M. (1984). *Teaching infants and preschoolers with handicaps.* Columbus, OH: Charles E. Merrill Publishing Co.

Bayley, N. (1969). *Bayley Scales of Infant Development.* New York: Psychological Corp.

Bluma, S., Shearer, M., Frohman, S., & Hillard, J. (1976). *Portage Guide to Early Education* (rev. ed.). Portage, WI: C.E.S.A., #12.

Bortner, S., Jones, M., Simon, S., & Goldblatt, S. (1978). *Sensory stimulation kit: A teacher's guidebook.* Louisville: American Printing House for the Blind.

Bromwich, R. (1981). *Working with parents and infants: An interactional approach.* Baltimore: University Park Press.

Cattell, P. (1940). *The measurement of intelligence of infants and young children.* New York: Psychological Corp.

Finnie, N. R. (1975). *Handling the young cerebral palsied child at home* (2nd ed.). New York: E. P. Dutton & Co.

Griffin, P. M., & Sanford, A. R. (1975). *Learning accomplishment profile for infants (CAP-I).* Winston-Salem, NC: Kaplan School Supply Corp.

Hanson, M. (1977). *Teaching your Down's syndrome infant: A guide for parents.* Baltimore: University Park Press.

Karnes, M. B. (1979, 1981). *Small wonder.* Circle Pines, MN: American Guidance Service.

Knobloch, H., & Pasamanick, B. (1974). *Gesell and Amatruda's developmental diagnosis* (3rd ed.). New York: Harper & Row.

McCormick, L., & Noonan, M. J. (1984). A responsive curriculum for severely handicapped preschoolers. *Topics in Early Childhood Special Education, 4*(3), 79–96.

Northcott, W. H. (1977). *Curriculum guide: Hearing-impaired children birth to three years and their parents.* Washington, DC: Alexander Graham Bell Association for the Deaf.

Sparling, J., & Lewis, I. (1981). *Learning games for the first three years: A program for a center/home partnership.* New York: Walker Educational Book Corp.

Stillman, R. (Ed.). (1977). *The Callier-Azusa Scale.* Dallas: Callier Center for Communication Disorders, University of Texas.

Uzgiris, I. C., & Hunt, J. McV. (1975). *Assessment in infancy: Ordinal Scales of Psychological Development.* Urbana, IL: University of Illinois Press.

Wolery, M. (1983). Evaluating curricula: Purposes and strategies. *Topics in Early Childhood Special Education, 2*(4), 15–24.

chapter **2**

Teaching Suggestions

Karen O'Donnell and Peggy Ogle

THE GOAL OF *The Carolina Curriculum for Handicapped Infants and Infants At Risk* (CCHI) is to provide assistance to teachers and caregivers in optimizing the handicapped child's positive interactions with the world and the people in it. Assuming that children's basic physical needs are met, teachers and caregivers have the unique and exciting opportunity to arrange experiences that will allow children to know that what they do, indeed, makes a difference in their surroundings.

Several basic principles of teaching young children are fundamental to all of the items included in this curriculum. This chapter presents these principles in a highly condensed form. A selected reading list is provided at the end of Chapter 5 for readers who desire further elaboration on any of these points.

CONSEQUENCES COUNT

One of the most fundamental precepts of teaching is that consequences are important in maintaining or changing behavior. A consequence is merely an act that follows another act as an effect or a result of the former. Consequences can be powerful in strengthening or weakening specific behaviors. Stated simply, this means that when a child does something that is followed by a desirable or interesting action, he or she will be more likely to repeat or continue that behavior. For example, if Mary pulls a string on a mobile and the mobile moves, Mary is more likely to pull the string again than if there were no effect. Likewise, when Johnny and his teacher play a "tickle game" after he sits up on his own for 1 minute, Johnny will probably struggle to sit on his own again very soon.

A behavior that is followed by an unpleasant event or experience or one that appears to have no effect at all, on the other hand, will probably decrease in frequency. This is the principle underlying the fact that some behaviors are best

Karen O'Donnell, Ph.D., Frank Porter Graham Child Development Center, University of North Carolina at Chapel Hill.

Peggy Ogle, Ph.D., Department of Special Education, University of Maryland, College Park, Maryland.

changed by ignoring them, by providing a mild reprimand, or by isolating a youngster for a very short period (timing him or her out). If, for instance, Paul is removed from the presence of all other youngsters for 2 minutes each time he tries to bite another child, it is possible that the biting behavior will be eliminated.

MAKE YOUR CONSEQUENCES EFFECTIVE

Promoting learning through the use of consequences sounds simple—and it is. However, some crucial things must be remembered if your consequences are to be used effectively.

1. Naturally occurring consequences are the most effective in teaching a child about his or her ability to bring about change in the world. This is especially true for the young, or developmentally young, child. Consider the difference between Mary's effect on the mobile and Johnny's earning a tickle by sitting alone. The mobile turning with Mary's pull is a naturally occurring consequence, and this type of experience is much more likely to affect her behavior than a consequence artificially instituted by her caregivers (i.e., hugging her for pulling the mobile string). By using naturally occurring consequences, a caregiver can "set up" learning situations for a child so that interesting and desirable things happen when the child interacts with his or her environment.
2. Remember that the same consequences will not be effective with all children. Children enjoy many different types of stimulation. Mary may be more interested in her mobile, while Robbie would rather play with a musical toy. Some children will respond more readily and positively to a tangible reward like food or the chance to play with a special toy. Others are quite pleased to receive a hug, a smile, or a tickle. One of your first tasks will be to *test* different positive and negative consequences to see which get the best response from each child.
3. Effective positive consequences must be changed often. Like adults, children become bored, too, and previously desired events or experiences become less exciting and less useful in teaching. Mary, for example, will only pull the mobile string so long as the motion is somewhat new and different from what it has been the past 2 weeks.
4. For a particular consequence to work in promoting or reducing behaviors, it must follow the target behavior *immediately*. This helps the child to perceive the relationship between what he or she does and what happened in the environment.
5. Further, if a child is to understand this relationship between what he or she does and what happens in the environment, the consequence must occur *consistently*. In providing "undesirable" consequences for negative behaviors, the consequence must be employed *every time* the behavior occurs. For instance, Paul would become very confused if he were "timed out" of group activities only some of the times he tried to bite others.

    In providing pleasant and desirable consequences for positive behaviors, it is best to begin by providing the consequence each time the behavior occurs. Studies have shown us, however, that it is appropriate to gradually begin to provide the reward or consequence less often, but regularly. Eventually, for example, it may be helpful to tickle Johnny after he sits alone for the designated time every two, three, or four times, rather than every time.

6. With children who can understand, you can explain the consequence situation to the child. In this way the child receives an additional clue about the way he or she affects the world. Examples are: "Pull the knob . . . see the TV come on"; "Give me your hands, and I will pick you up"; "Eat lunch, and we will go outside."

BREAK A TASK INTO SMALL STEPS

After deciding what you want to teach, the behavior usually needs to be broken down into smaller steps. After that, the small steps can be arranged into a logical teaching sequence. Andy, for example, smiles and claps when a toy radio plays. If you would like to help Andy learn that he can make the radio work, you may begin by rewarding Andy with the music as he touches the radio near the knob. The next step would involve the reward (teacher turns the radio on) as Andy touches the knob. As a final step, Andy turns the knob for himself.

Each teaching task of this curriculum is organized into small steps according to a logical teaching sequence. There will be times, however, when the steps are not small enough for a particular child; you may have to break the task down into even smaller steps then so the child can slowly but consistently approach the desired behavior. There will also be times when you will find the sequence does not work for a particular child, and you will have to alter it. Andy, for example, may need to have his caregiver or teacher begin by physically guiding his hand to touch and turn the knob on the toy television.

PROVIDE SAMENESS AND CHANGE

Although it sounds contradictory, children seem to need both sameness and change in their surroundings. Sameness gives the child a sense of security. The teacher or caregiver should provide order and routine in the child's life; this helps the child learn that the world is, in part, predictable. The child learns what to expect from specific people and in what order daily routines such as bathing, feeding, and dressing occur. Of course, routines are altered sometimes, but a sense of sameness helps the child learn to feel safe in the world and trust in his or her caregivers. It is after the child comes to view the world as safe, predictable, and secure, that he or she becomes interested in things in the environment that bring about action or change. Only then will the child explore his or her role in bringing about change.

"SET UP" SUCCESS

To ensure a child's continued willingness to interact with the environment and make things happen in it, it is vital that he or she have continued successes at each of the small steps you teach. Once a child wants to make things happen, make sure he or she *can* make them happen. For instance, if you are teaching a child to reach for an object such as a ball, begin with the ball close enough for the child to grasp without any difficulty. As you move the ball farther and farther away, make sure the ball *can* be reached. Children frustrate easily and may "turn off." The activity should be a challenge, but not an impossibility.

BUILD LEARNING EXPERIENCES INTO DAILY ROUTINES

Learning occurs in all areas for the child at all times. Although development may be relatively advanced in some areas and more delayed in others, each activity has possibilities for learning in a number of areas. Playing pat-a-cake, for instance, involves gross motor, fine motor, cognitive, and social skills.

Similarly, teachers and caregivers have the opportunity to encourage learning in every interaction with the child, whether it be during a specific "learning time" or during routine caregiving and play activities. In fact, there is good evidence that experiences that take place as a part of daily routines are more effective for teaching than those that are isolated in a specific teaching activity. A child who is learning to improve his or her grasp, for example, has many opportunities to practice this skill during the day—upon getting up and getting dressed in the morning, during feeding times, and in free play activities.

ALLOW QUIET TIMES

Like adults, all children need time to themselves—time to play by themselves or time to play with adults without the adults making demands. Parents and teachers have learned that a good adjunct to therapeutic intervention is to provide special times with children in which the interaction is without constant direction by the adult.

Use curricular materials such as those provided in this book consistently and regularly, but keep in mind that the activities featured here constitute only a few of the important things you and your youngster will do on a daily basis.

chapter **3**

Using the Curriculum

Traditionally, curricula for young handicapped children have been divided into six developmental areas: Cognition, Communication/Language, Social Skills/Adaptation, Self-Help, Fine Motor, and Gross Motor. Within each area, however, the items have not been arranged in a logical teaching sequence. Rather, the sequence has been based upon the mean ages at which normal children master the skills. As noted in Chapter 1, this procedure creates some major problems in planning intervention programs for children whose development is atypical.

In an attempt to deal with this problem, *The Carolina Curriculum for Handicapped Infants and Infants At Risk* (CCHI) has identified 24 areas of development, as well as logical sequences for teaching the skills within each. Table 1 lists these areas alongside the more traditional areas identified by other curricula.

In choosing the 24 areas of development and the sequence of skills within each, we have assumed the following:

1. The ability of a child to exert some control over his or her physical and social environment is crucial for the development and maintenance of motivation for learning. One primary goal of the curriculum must be to enhance the child's potential for bringing about changes in his or her environment.

2. Communication should also be a major focus of an infant curriculum. Clearly, communication is the most effective way to bring about changes in the social environment, and, for the most physically handicapped children, it may also be the primary means of changing the physical environment (by causing other people to make changes for them). Communication can and does take place without speech (through gestures, signs, and augmentative communication aids). Thus, every avenue available for communication should be explored in the earliest phases and throughout the course of intervention.

3. An infant curriculum should be as complete as possible, with every effort made to enhance the child's strengths and to remedy his or her weaknesses. The child should be allowed and encouraged to develop rapidly in one or more areas, even though others are far behind. It is particularly important not to neglect cognitive and communication skills in children with massive motor problems, even though physical therapy or training for motor functions may seem to be the most pressing need.

Table 1. Areas of development in *The Carolina Curriculum for Handicapped Infants and Infants At Risk*

Traditional areas	CCHI areas
Cognition	Tactile Integration and Manipulation Auditory Localization and Object Permanence Visual Pursuit and Object Permanence Object Permanence (Visual-Motor) Spatial Concepts Functional Use of Objects and Symbolic Play Control over Physical Environment "Readiness" Concepts
Communication/Language	Responses to Communication from Others Gestural Imitation Gestural Communication Vocal Imitation Vocal Communication
Social Skills/Adaptation	Social Skills Self-Direction
Self-Help	Feeding Grooming Dressing
Fine Motor	Reaching and Grasping Object Manipulation Bilateral Hand Activity
Gross Motor	Gross Motor Activities: Stomach Gross Motor Activities: Back Gross Motor Activities: Upright

4. The sequences of cognitive development described by Jean Piaget have been substantiated by a sizable volume of literature and can, therefore, logically form the basis of the cognitive portions of an infant curriculum.
5. The methods of teaching contributed by behaviorism are the most effective methods currently known for teaching severely handicapped individuals.

ASSESSING A YOUNGSTER FOR CURRICULUM ENTRY

The first step in planning any intervention program must necessarily be to carefully assess the current developmental abilities of youngsters for whom the materials are intended. For this purpose, items from the 24 sequences of the CCHI (as identified in Table 1) have been incorporated into the Assessment Log (pp. 46–60) with space for scoring several assessments. (Additional copies of this checklist, available as a 20-page pamphlet in packages of 10 may be obtained from Paul H. Brookes Publishing Company.) Each of the curricular sequences represents a significant area of development. Thus, it is important that each child using this curriculum be evaluated in all 24 areas of development except when this is precluded by a particular handicapping condition (e.g., totally blind children will not be evaluated on items requiring vision).

It is also crucial to remember that the numbers assigned to the curricular sequences are not related in any way to the importance of a given sequence, nor are they related to the order in which these sequences develop in normal infants; the numbers and ordering of the curricular areas are purely arbitrary. However, an attempt has been made to list the items within each curricular area in the order of their expected development. That is, item *a* is generally expected to be learned before item *b,* item *b* before item *c,* and so forth.

Although every effort has been made to achieve this ordinal structure, the authors are well aware that moderately and severely handicapped infants, who manifest unusual developmental patterns, will undoubtedly show erratic patterns of achievement within the sequences on occasion. It is also true that some of the sequences are not ordinal for all normal youngsters. Often a child practices several related skills at once, and there is little consistency as to which one is mastered first. For example, a child practices getting to a sitting position and sitting when placed during the same time period. There is little consistency as to which skill will emerge first.

Before evaluating a youngster and beginning work with the CCHI, the caregiver should assemble the few toys described in Table 2 and then use them while getting acquainted with the infant and his mother or father. Find out what things they enjoy doing together and how the mother or father elicits attending and responding. After you become familiar with the curriculum sequences, you will find this brief informal observation period will allow you to check off many of the items in the sequences without further assessment as well as to establish a comfortable relationship with the infant and his or her mother or father.

Generally, evaluation begins with item *a* in each sequence and continues until the child fails to accomplish three successive items. It is not necessary, however, to observe directly the skills of the first items in a sequence if you know from other evaluations (e.g., the *Bayley Scales of Infant Development* [Bayley, 1969]) or from your informal observation that the youngster easily does some of the items in a given sequence. For example, if you observe initially that a youngster readily picks up two blocks and bangs them together, you will not need to assess items *a–h* in sequence 19 (Reaching and Grasping).

Table 2. Assessment materials

The following materials have been found to be useful when implementing the CCHI. Many of them are listed on the individual item descriptions. These are merely suggestions. Feel free to modify the materials, provided you maintain the intent of the item.

Scraps of fabric or toys with different textures
Box of sand, beans, rice, or other textured material
Bells, rattles, and other noisemakers
A variety of small, brightly colored toys
Several small cloths (handkerchief size)
Spoon, cup, bottle, and a variety of foods
Mirror
Crayons
Large (¾″–1″) and small (¼″) pegboards and pegs
Tub of water
Finger paints
Play-dough or clay
A variety of containers, some with holes in the lids

A selection of "early-day" objects: feeding utensils, toothbrush, hairbrush, shoe, ball, and so forth
Small broom, dustpan, dustcloth, and the like—things the child would use in the home
Dolls, doll furniture, stuffed animals
Square blocks of various sizes
Simple form boards with circles, squares, and triangles
Several short dowels of different diameters
Gum or candy in wrappers
Pop beads
Keg beads for stringing (¾″–1″)
Small jars with lids (baby food jars)

Most items listed in the sequences in the Assessment Log (pp. 46–60) are self-explanatory. If, however, it is unclear how a given skill should be assessed, simply turn to the corresponding curriculum item and read the instructions for teaching it; assessment will then become clear. For initial assessment purposes, the child does not have to reach the teaching criterion (e.g., three of five trials). The child only has to demonstrate the skill one time. If, however, you must try an item many times before getting a correct response, it should probably be counted as an emerging skill and given only half-credit. If it is difficult to assess a particular item in the intervention setting, ask a parent for his or her assessment, making your question as clear as possible. Items may be credited on the basis of the parental report, but every attempt should be made to carefully check them out during the intervention process. For the gross motor sections of the curriculum, it is important to have the motor development chart (Figure 3, pp. 34–35) readily available. The chart illustrates a normal motor pattern from birth to 12 months, since development in this period is more apt to be misunderstood than that in the 12–24-month period. An item should not be scored as passed if it is accomplished in an abnormal fashion.

CHARTING ASSESSMENT RESULTS

Once all items on the Assessment Log have been assessed, a Developmental Progress Chart (p. 61) can be completed to reveal a profile of skills. (Additional copies of the chart, available with the Assessment Log, may be procured from Paul H. Brookes Publishing Company.) Each item on the log is represented by a blank on the chart. If an item is passed, the corresponding space should be colored in completely. If the skill in question appears to be inconsistent or emerging, the space should be colored in only partially (e.g., ▬▬▭). Physical and occupational therapists will often find that simply recording a skill as ''emerging'' does not satisfy record-keeping needs, and they therefore supplement this system with more complex scoring codes. Further assessments in areas such as range of motion, muscle testing, skin sensitivity, and respiratory function can be carried out as required. If this charting procedure is employed regularly, using different colors to complete the charting with each new assessment, a visual display is provided of the youngster's progress through the curriculum sequences.

SELECTING CURRICULAR ITEMS FOR
INDIVIDUAL YOUNGSTERS' INTERVENTION PROGRAMS

Within the body of the CCHI, there is a teaching activity that corresponds to each item in a sequence, as depicted in the Developmental Progress Chart (p. 61). Caregivers should select activities for a given child on the basis of the first item the child failed or the item that was judged to be just emerging in each sequence, unless a particular handicapping condition makes this strategy inappropriate. However, this will produce an intervention plan including up to 24 items, which may be unwieldy for some children and some programs. Therefore, a decision must be made regarding which activities (and which sequences) will be worked on at any given time. In making this decision it must be reemphasized here that all 24 sequences represent important areas of development. It is essential to promote development in areas in which youngsters show strengths, as well as in areas in which they show weaknesses. In fact, it is by being able to enhance strengths that most people learn to compensate for their weaknesses.

The following guidelines may be helpful in selecting particular activities for given youngsters' programs. 1) Since motor behaviors provide such a vital link between the infant and his or her world, items should be selected from all of the motor sequences (sequences 19 through 24). The motor development chart (Figure 3) on pages 34 and 35 shows sequential development in "on tummy," "on back," and "upright" positions. It is important, however, to observe the vertical clustering of items in the three sequences. You will notice that particular skills in upright position cannot be expected to be achieved before skills in the other positions. 2) The other curricular sequences should be rank-ordered according to the level of skills demonstrated by a youngster. It is recommended that you choose half of the nonmotor sequences to work on for the first treatment period, representing equally areas of both strength and weakness. 3) As you develop the first intervention plan, decide how much time to allot to a treatment period before reevaluation. When children are developing rapidly, the treatment period may be as short as 2 months; for slowly developing children, it may be as long as 6 months. 4) For the second treatment period, the sequences initially omitted should form the basis of the program in nonmotor areas. 5) Subsequent periods should continue to alternate groupings of nonmotor sequences. This will provide ongoing documentation of the effectiveness of intervention, similar to the process used in field-testing the curriculum (see Chapter 4).

IMPLEMENTING THE PROGRAM

When the assessment and item selection have been completed, the intervention process can begin. In order not only to maintain continuity but to measure progress and make program modifications, it is essential that careful records be kept for each child. Though methods of record keeping vary from program to program, we offer the following three general guidelines:

1. Each *item* selected should be written on an individual activity sheet. Figure 1 is an example of a sheet that has proved helpful. Figure 2 gives instructions for its use. In addition to describing the criterion performances, each item on the CCHI has been broken down into steps. Begin with Step 1. Record the child's progress on that step. When the child is able to demonstrate three or more times the skill defined by that step, move on to Step 2. There will be times when the child catches on so quickly that he or she skips a step. In such cases, it is not necessary to proceed through all of the steps. There will also be times when progress is so slow that you will need to break these steps down further. In addition, some children will require significant modification of steps because of the nature of their handicap. Feel free to do this, provided you maintain the intent of the item.

   When working with a child, it is often desirable to be working on more than one item at a time. For example, it makes sense to combine a gross motor activity, such as back extension, with a cognitive activity, such as pointing to pictures. For record-keeping purposes, however, each of these skills needs to be evaluated separately. Initially, you may want to have a second observer assist you in data collection, but with practice you will be able to do it alone.

Individual Activity Sheet

Student _____ Date begun _____

Teacher _____ Curriculum number _____

Target behavior (goal)

Training method (description of positioning, materials, and toys needed, etc.)

Steps

Step 1 _____

Step 2 _____

Step 3 _____

Criterion

State of the child																						

| Trials | 5 5 5 5 5
 4 4 4 4 4
 3 3 3 3 3
 2 2 2 2 2
 1 1 1 1 1 | | 5 5 5 5 5
 4 4 4 4 4
 3 3 3 3 3
 2 2 2 2 2
 1 1 1 1 1 | | 5 5 5 5 5
 4 4 4 4 4
 3 3 3 3 3
 2 2 2 2 2
 1 1 1 1 1 | | 5 5 5 5 5
 4 4 4 4 4
 3 3 3 3 3
 2 2 2 2 2
 1 1 1 1 1 |

Step

Date

State of the child																						

| Trials | 5 5 5 5 5
 4 4 4 4 4
 3 3 3 3 3
 2 2 2 2 2
 1 1 1 1 1 | | 5 5 5 5 5
 4 4 4 4 4
 3 3 3 3 3
 2 2 2 2 2
 1 1 1 1 1 | | 5 5 5 5 5
 4 4 4 4 4
 3 3 3 3 3
 2 2 2 2 2
 1 1 1 1 1 | | 5 5 5 5 5
 4 4 4 4 4
 3 3 3 3 3
 2 2 2 2 2
 1 1 1 1 1 |

Step

Date

Comments:

Figure 1.   Example of an individual activity sheet.

Using the Individual Activity Sheet

(Student)	Record the student's name.
(Date begun)	Record the date the curriculum item is started.
(Teacher)	Record the person who will be teaching the item.
(Curriculum number)	Record the number and letter of the item (e.g., 20a).
(Target behavior [goal])	State the item goal, the Behavior found centered above each curriculum item.
(Training method)	Generally describe the item procedures (e.g., positioning, arrangement of materials, toys needed) in simple terms so as to avoid constant referral to the curriculum book.
(Steps)	List the steps in the curriculum item. Additional steps may be derived through task analysis if necessary.
(Criterion)	State the standard on which the decision is made to progress to the next step.

(State of the child)	Describe the state of the child during the programming (e.g., drowsy, fussy, alert).
(Trials)	Five trials should be run on each item, if at all possible. Starting with 1 and moving vertically, mark each trial using a slash (/) for a correct response or a cross (X) for an incorrect response. After 5 trials have been run, circle the number out of a total of 5 that the child got correct. If no correct responses are obtained, add a zero below the column and circle it. After 5 sets of 5 trials have been run, connect the circled numbers. This will give a visual trend of the child's progress and the program's effectiveness. (See example of data below.)
(Example of data)	On the 1st set of trials (1st column), the child got 1 correct— circle the 1; 2nd set (2nd column), 3 correct—circle the 3; 3rd set (3rd column), 3 correct—circle the 3; 4th set (4th column), 4 correct—circle the 4; 5th set (5th column), 5 correct—circle the 5.
(Step and date)	Under each set of 5 trials, record the Step the child is working on and the Date the trials are run. (Please note that 5 or 40 trials can be done on one day; while data is collected in sets of five, more than five trials may be done at one time.)
(Comments)	Add information that enhances the program, such as suggested toys for variety, or the time of day the child is most alert.

Figure 2.   Instructions for using individual activity sheet (Figure 1).

2. Careful record keeping must be utilized if developmental progress is to be documented and intervention modified appropriately for individual infants. It is not necessary to record every response a child makes to a curriculum item, because any item may be incorporated into daily care and tried many times each day. However, it is vital that specific times be designated for recording responses to each curriculum item that is included in a youngster's intervention plan. In well-staffed centers and in some homes, such record keeping should take place every day at agreed-upon times. In other settings it may only be possible to collect the needed data once or twice a week. In no case should data collection be neglected altogether, since the information the data provide is necessary to make appropriate instructional decisions.

3. Most centers establish a set of goals to be achieved within a 3- or 6-month period. Nevertheless, it is important to remember that you want to maintain steady progress within each sequence. Therefore, if a child masters a particular item before the reevaluation date, go on immediately to the next item in the sequence.

USING THE CCHI WITH OLDER STUDENTS

Although the CCHI has been designed primarily for use with infants and young children, the field-testing population did include some older retarded and multiply handicapped individuals. Caregivers who want to use the CCHI with these groups will need to make appropriate adaptations in the items and materials used. Generally, the sequences can be maintained, but the overriding concern should be to teach behaviors that are adaptive for the individual. For example, it is appropriate to use blocks when teaching matching to a young child. With a teenager, however, more benefit would be derived by constructing a prevocational task using nuts and bolts or different-sized envelopes.

DEVELOPING AN INDIVIDUALIZED EDUCATION PROGRAM

What? An individualized education program (IEP) for infants and others functioning below the 1-year level? An IEP is required, is it not, only for youngsters enrolled in special programs in the public schools. True, Public Law 94-142 mandated the IEP only for "exceptional" youngsters enrolled in public school programs. But, gradually, states have been lowering the age level at which exceptional children are included in school programs, and it is anticipated that in the near future many school systems will be serving handicapped individuals from birth through 20 years of age. It is also true that as more severely and multiply handicapped youngsters are being admitted to the public schools, there are increasing numbers of youngsters in programs who are functioning within the developmental range extending from birth to 1 year. Thus, it is important that individuals who provide services to very young handicapped children be aware of the basic requirements of an IEP and be prepared to develop them.

The IEP is not a new concept. For years teachers, therapists, and other caregivers have been developing lesson and treatment plans and individual objectives for youngsters in educational and treatment programs. The IEP merely provides a systematic way of ensuring that those working with handicapped individuals will work from a plan that 1) is focused on the individual child, 2) emphasizes careful planning, implementation, and assessment of instruction and treatment, and 3) enumerates specific changes that are expected to occur in development and behavior as a result of intervention. It is generally expected that an adequate IEP will contain at least the following:

1. A statement about a youngster's present level of performance/development;
2. Long-term goals (e.g., 6 months) and short-term objectives (e.g., 1 month);
3. A description of specific developmental and treatment services that are to be provided;
4. The date on which programmatic services are expected to be initiated and the expected duration of services;

5.   A statement of the extent to which a youngster will be worked with in proximity to normal youngsters;
6.   Evaluation procedures to be used; and
7.   A schedule of and procedures for review.

The Carolina Curriculum for Handicapped Infants and Infants At Risk lends itself readily to supplying information necessary for several components of the IEP. When the curriculum sequences are used as a developmental checklist and the information is transferred to the Developmental Progress Chart, the child's level of development is well described. The criterion performance specified with each item indicates short-term objectives, while long-term goals may be identified from items further ahead in each curriculum sequence.

The specificity of the curriculum items defines some of the services to be provided, although additional information will have to be included with regard to other treatment services (e.g., physical therapy, medical follow-up). Evaluation procedures are also defined in the curriculum and are a part of the data collection procedures previously described. Standardized measures (e.g., the Denver Developmental Screening Test or the Bayley scales) may be utilized to provide additional indicators of progress. However, it must be recognized that these instruments will be particularly insensitive to changes in youngsters with significant sensory or motor impairments.

Although PL 94-142 only requires that a child's IEP be reviewed annually, there is general agreement among practitioners that, when working with handicapped infants, it is imperative that review occur more frequently. With this population a review is desirable every 2 or 3 months, and should include sufficient assessment to update the Developmental Progress Chart in all areas of development. If progress is not occurring, or if it is occurring more slowly than anticipated, decisions must be made as to whether the procedures being utilized remain appropriate. Concerns about health and physical development should also be dealt with in these review sessions, and appropriate plans made to provide the necessary services.

REFERENCES

Bayley, N. (1969). *Bayley Scales of Infant Development*. New York: Psychological Corp.
Frankenburg, W. K., Dodds, J., & Frankel, A. (1975). *Denver Developmental Screening Test*. Denver: LADOCA Project & Publishing Foundation.

chapter **4**

Field-Test Results

THIS CHAPTER REPORTS the results of field-testing of the first version of *The Carolina Curriculum for Handicapped Infants and Infants At Risk* (CCHI), the version developed for infants functioning in the birth to 12-month range. The current, birth to 24-month, version of the CCHI was not field tested; it is an extension of the original birth to 12-month curriculum and it incorporates suggestions obtained while field testing the first version of the curriculum. In addition to expanding the curriculum to include material for the 12- to 24-month developmental period, the sequences were reorganized, a few items were deleted or reordered, and revisions were made in individual curriculum items to reflect the recommendations of those who participated in the field-testing.

Adequate field-testing of any curriculum involves looking at three important characteristics: the curriculum's usefulness to service providers in their attempts to develop appropriate programs for children; the ability of interventionists to use the curriculum in the way intended by the authors; and the effect of the curriculum on the learning progress of children. Field-test results in each of these areas are discussed in the sections following.

HOW USEFUL IS THE CCHI?

In order to assess usefulness, individuals receiving the curriculum were asked to review it and fill out a brief form containing 11 items to be rated on a 5-point scale, from *agree* to *disagree*. These 11 items related to the curriculum's comprehensiveness, understandability, usefulness in individualized education program (IEP) preparation, applicability to children with a broad range of handicapping conditions, and ease of procedures for monitoring child progress. These ratings were identified as the ''perceived usability'' of the curriculum, since the assessment was taking place prior to its actual use.

Individuals who then participated in the field-testing were asked to fill out a second rating form after 6 to 8 months of using the curriculum and collecting data on children. This rating scale tapped the same content as the perceived usability rating, but added items related to the extent the curriculum had been useful in understanding individual children and in explaining children's programs to their parents, as well as an item asking if data collection procedures interfered with optimal therapist-child interaction.

A total of 61 perceived usability and 10 actual usability forms were returned. Several of the field-test sites chose to write extensive evaluative comments rather than fill out the usability forms. These comments were more useful in guiding the authors in making changes for the 0- to 24-month version of the curriculum than were the rating forms. The total mean rating of the items on the perceived usability forms was 1.49 (1 = agree; 5 = disagree) with a mean rating range from 1.25 to 1.71 on individual items. It was anticipated that users would rate the curriculum less favorably than reviewers, since the former would have had the opportunity to discover its shortcomings through use. The total mean rating on the actual usability forms was 2.27, with a range of mean ratings from 2.0 to 3.0. The item rated least favorably was the one stating that data collection procedures were clear. Efforts were made in the revised curriculum to improve both procedures and the explanation of them.

As noted, evaluative comments provided by some users in place of the usability forms were useful in modifying the curriculum. Those who filled out the forms also made many such comments. Of these comments, the most common positive statement was that the assessment system was useful whether one faithfully used the curriculum items or generated activities of one's own. The only concern occurring repeatedly was that the curriculum did not have a sufficient number of items at the lowest levels (0–3 months) to provide good programming for severely and profoundly handicapped infants and profoundly handicapped older children. We recognize this problem but have not made major changes in the curriculum to accommodate it.

We do not believe that a developmental curriculum can meet all of the programming needs of severely and profoundly handicapped young children. Most of the curriculum sequences begin with skills observed in normally developing infants between birth and 2 weeks of age. At this level, normal infants are able to make visual and auditory discriminations and to modify their behavior on the basis of the effect of that behavior. For example, a newborn can discriminate between the sound of his or her mother's native language and the sound of a foreign language; an infant 2 weeks old will change his or her sucking pattern in order to change visual stimulation. As yet, how to develop these basic discrimination and learning skills in individuals who do not have them is not known. Probably the most effective intervention is to provide these children with systematically varied auditory, visual, and tactile stimulation, always allowing time for them to show some response to the stimulation. Only when it is possible to determine that an infant reacts to stimulation more than to no stimulation or prefers one kind of stimulation to another is it possible to enter this or any other developmental curriculum.

After a profoundly handicapped child is ready to enter the curriculum, however, the steps between some items may seem too large. We believe that modifications of the curriculum need to be relatively child specific. The interventionist should assess thoroughly the response capabilities of a child, determine which curriculum items are appropriate given the child's limitations, and use a task-analysis approach to identify steps sufficiently small to allow the child to progress and master the items.

CAN THE CCHI BE USED AS INTENDED?

To address curriculum use and child progress, arrangements were made for field-testing in 22 programs serving approximately 150 children estimated to be functioning in the 0- to 12-month developmental range. Seventeen of the programs were chosen to represent different sections of the United States and 5 were selected in North Carolina that were within driving distance of the authors, to allow monitoring of data collection. No extensive workshops were provided for curriculum users, although telephone contact was maintained to answer questions. Because of a variety of problems including extensive staff turnover, loss of staff due to curtailed budgets in some centers, the deaths of several children, and the fact that many children simply "outgrew" the curriculum in a 6-month period, usable data were available on only 96 children from 4 North Carolina sites and 10 national sites representing Texas, Pennsylvania, Alaska, Oregon, Maryland, Louisiana, Michigan, Arizona, and Wisconsin. The characteristics of the field-test sample are summarized in Table 3.

Throughout field-testing, we were concerned to know whether the curriculum could be used by interventionists in the manner intended, in a variety of settings, and without prior specific training. A research assistant made bimonthly visits to the four local programs, two of which were center-based and two home-based, to observe the use of the curriculum. After observing treatment sessions, the research assistant completed a checklist for each item used, indicating whether appropriate materials were used, whether each item was begun at the correct step, whether the instructions and/or demonstrations were as specified, whether prompting and scoring procedures

Table 3. Characteristics of field-test population

Characteristic	Number	Characteristic	Number
Primary diagnosis		Age at initial assessment	
Mental retardation or		0 to 2 years	68
developmental disability	27	2 to 4 years	15
Cerebral palsy	18	4 years or older	13
Known genetic disorder	21		
Seizure disorder	12	Sex	
Hydro- or microcephaly	8	Male	44
Other	10	Female	52
Additional problems		Education of mother	
Vision	40		
Hearing	18	0 to 8 years	7
Seizures	58	8 to 10 years	8
Congenital defects	6	10 to 12 years	33
Heart defect	7	Over 12 years	34
Autistic features	2	Unknown	14
Abnormal reflexes	47		
Feeding	4	Occupation of household head	
Other	11	Professional	27
Level of handicap		Clerical	20
Mild	17	Labor	21
Moderate	19	Unemployed	18
Severe/profound	60	Other	10

were followed, and whether an appropriate number of trials was done. In addition, he, along with the interventionist, scored the children's performance on each trial and computed the percentage of agreement. In 88 observations of individual items there were 14 instances of an incorrect number of trials (usually stopping prior to reaching criteria), one instance where prompting procedures were not followed, and one instance of the interventionist beginning on the wrong step in view of the child's previous performance. Percentage of agreement in scoring the child's responses was 96.9. These descriptive data suggest that the curriculum can be used in the manner intended by the authors with no extensive training.

DOES THE CCHI PROMOTE DEVELOPMENTAL PROGRESS?

The effectiveness of the curriculum in promoting developmental changes was assessed by a procedure similar to that described by Barrerra, Routh, Johnson, Parr, Goolsby, and Schroeder (1976). Curriculum users were instructed to assess each child carefully and to record his or her skills on the progress chart. The curriculum sequences were then ordered from strongest to weakest according to the skills the child demonstrated. The child's program for the first 3 months of field-testing consisted of items from all of the fine and gross motor sequences and from *half* of the others, chosen to include a relatively equal number of sequences representing strengths and weaknesses. This was done both as a control, since there is evidence that more rapid progress can be expected in strong areas, and in response to the authors' belief that intervention must involve building on strengths as well as remediating weaknesses.

The first item failed in each selected sequence was chosen for the intervention program, but as soon as the child reached criterion performance on that item, the next item in the sequence was begun. At the end of 3 months, each child was reassessed, his or her progress recorded, and a new 3-month intervention plan developed. The new plan included continued work in all of the motor sequences but suspended work on the nonmotor sequences chosen for the first 3 months, picking up those sequences initially omitted. With this procedure, it was possible to compare progress in sequences worked on with progress in sequences not worked on during each 3-month period. It was recognized that this procedure was problematic from a scientific viewpoint, in that there are not equal numbers of items within the sequences, the items are not of equal difficulty, and the selection of sequences was not done on the basis of random assignment. It was felt, however, that the approach would provide a rough estimate of differential progress and would be reasonably scientific, provided there was no systematic bias in the sequences chosen to be included in the first intervention period. Indeed, no systematic bias could be identified.

Table 4 presents the child progress data during the first and second field-test periods. Note that fewer subjects are included in the second half of field-testing. This is because one program collected data only for 3 months, a few children left their programs, and a few children aged out of the curriculum after the first 3 months.

As might be expected, the children who were moderately or mildly handicapped made the most progress. Severely and profoundly handicapped children made minimal progress. Interventionists using the curriculum with these children noted both the limitations of the curriculum for children who are very unresponsive to normal environmental stimuli and the fact that 3 months is too short a time to

Table 4.   Child progress data: Differences in numbers of items passed between assessments in sequences worked on and not worked on during first and second field-test periods

Degree of handicapping conditions	W_1	NW_1	W_2	NW_2
Mild	N = 15 M = 10.07 SD = 6.23	N = 15 M = 5.37 SD = 4.63	N = 11 M = 10.95 SD = 4.95	N = 11 M = 6.14 SD = 3.81
	$t = 3.16^a$		$t = 2.84^a$	
Moderate	N = 19 M = 9.26 SD = 6.72	N = 19 M = 5.42 SD = 4.79	N = 15 M = 10.00 SD = 8.45	N = 15 M = 6.13 SD = 4.34
	$t = 2.77^a$		$t = 0.84^a$	
Severe/profound	N = 58 M = 3.84 SD = 4.51	N = 58 M = 2.58 SD = 4.88	N = 39 M = 2.42 SD = 4.38	N = 39 M = 1.99 SD = 4.13
	$t = 2.77^a$		$t = 0.84^a$	

Note: W refers to the sequences worked on; NW to sequences not worked on; numerical subscripts denote whether the data come from the first or the second field-test period.

[a]Differences between means are significant at the .01 level (one-tailed t-test).

document much progress in these youngsters. Indeed, 12 of the children made no progress in 6 months of curriculum use. All but one of these children were over 4 years of age, and four were adolescents, indicating especially profound handicapping conditions.

Table 5 presents the progress data on the motor sequences. These are purely descriptive data, since no effort was made to alternate treatment in the various motor sequences, as was done in the other sequences. It was not felt that such a procedure was workable, given that the motor skills are so interrelated and that they are vitally important to the other sequences in the curriculum. Again, it is evident that progress is related to the extent of the handicap, with severely and profoundly retarded children making little or no measurable progress over a 6-month period.

SUMMARY

The field-testing of the 0- to 12-month curriculum indicated that interventionists could use it as intended and found it useful both for assessing handicapped infants and developing programs for them. Interventionists' major reservations had to do with the curriculum's limitations for more severely and profoundly handicapped children. The data collected on the children suggest that the curriculum is effective in promoting developmental progress in children with mild to moderate handicaps in a relatively short time period (3 to 6 months). It is not effective as a whole in promoting measurable progress during such short periods for many children with severe and profound handicaps, particularly in children who are past 4 years of age. It should be noted that the curriculum was not intended for children over 4 years of age, although it

Table 5.   Child progress data in motor sequences

Level of handicap	GM$_1$	GM$_2$	FM$_1$	FM$_2$
Mild	N = 17 M = 4.18 SD = 3.59	N = 10 M = 4.10 SD = 2.14	N = 14 M = 3.61 SD = 3.53	N = 10 M = 4.90 SD = 1.88
Moderate	N = 19 M = 2.26 SD = 2.67	N = 17 M = 2.50 SD = 3.19	N = 19 M = 3.55 SD = 4.24	N = 17 M = 3.74 SD = 4.30
Severe/profound	N = 57 M = 0.63 SD = 1.10	N = 39 M = 0.51 SD = 1.00	N = 57 M = 0.94 SD = 1.59	N = 39 M = 0.62 SD = 1.41

Note: GM, gross motor; FM, fine motor; numerical subscripts denote whether the data come from the first or second field-test period.

is unclear at this point what the upper age should be. It is also unclear whether parts of the curriculum may be more appropriate to older populations than others. Considerably more data are necessary before such conclusions may be drawn.

REFERENCE

Barrerra, M., Routh, D., Johnson, N., Parr, C., Goolsby, E., & Schroeder, S. (1976). Early intervention with biologically handicapped infants and young children. A preliminary study using multiple baseline procedures. In T. J. Tjossem (Ed.), *Intervention strategies with young children*. Baltimore: University Park Press.

chapter 5

Motor Development

THE MOTOR SECTION of *The Carolina Curriculum for Handicapped Infants and Infants At Risk* (CCHI) presents a normal developmental sequence to be used as a guideline for gross motor programming with developmentally handicapped children. Based on the work of Margaret Rood (as interpreted by Shirley Stockmeyer, 1967, 1972), Lois Bly (1980), and Emmi Pikler (1971), and the authors' clinical experiences, the CCHI incorporates the following principles:

1. Development of trunk stability in prone and supine positions is a prerequisite to adequate functioning in upright positions.
2. Mobilizing and stabilizing functions must be balanced in all positions.
3. Rotational movements represent the highest level of skill in each position.

The items in the gross motor section are divided into three separate sequences—prone, supine, and upright—as depicted in Figure 3 on pages 34 and 35. In order to maintain appropriate sequencing of skill development, attention should be paid not only to the horizontal order of items but also to the vertical clustering.

Handicapped children, by definition, show deficits in their performance of items as compared to the development of normal children, and for this reason the services of a physical therapist are critical in individualizing each child's program. The therapist will demonstrate appropriate techniques for working on items and may also modify items, break them down into smaller steps, or present alternate methods of working on a particular motor skill.

Example: Item *g* in the prone sequence of Figure 3 consists of supporting on hands with the head lifted to 90°. A spastic diplegic child may be supporting on extended arms but at the same time showing the undesirable patterns of pulling forward at the shoulders and flexing the hips. The therapist would demonstrate proper techniques for keeping the hips and shoulders well positioned during the activity and may add other exercises, such as wheelbarrow walking, to improve shoulder stability.

Although the general sequence of items in the CCHI curriculum should be followed, many children will never achieve the "criterion" level of function on some items. Notations on the instructions for each item will help the caregiver decide when to emphasize work on subsequent items, but this decision should be made jointly with the physical therapist.

CHARACTERISTICS OF NORMAL MOTOR DEVELOPMENT

Motor development occurring in the first year of life is dramatic, and culminates in the ability to rise to a standing position and move through space. In order to provide a basis for planning motor programs, an understanding of the basic principles of motor development is essential. These principles are delineated in the following paragraphs (*1–5*). The terminology used in the description is commonly employed by therapists to describe motor activity.

1. Normal development takes place on a background of normal muscle tone. The term *muscle tone* refers essentially to the background resting state of the muscles. Normal muscle tone provides a basis for posture and movement on a moment-to-moment basis. The best way to understand what is meant by "normal tone" is to handle normal babies—feel how their muscles react under your hands and how easy it is to move their arms, legs, and heads.

2. The ability to work against gravity emerges gradually.

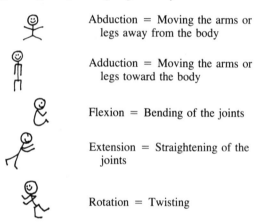

Newborn infants are incapable of effectively resisting the pull of gravity. Their postures and movements are characterized by *flexion*, with varying degrees of *abduction* and *adduction*, depending on their position.

Abduction = Moving the arms or legs away from the body

Adduction = Moving the arms or legs toward the body

The development of *extension* in the spine and extremities allows the child to pull up against gravity and move into upright positions.

Flexion = Bending of the joints

Extension = Straightening of the joints

The ability for *rotation* appears gradually in lying, sitting, standing, and walking, and is crucial for developing smooth, skilled transition from one position to another.

Rotation = Twisting

3. Motor development proceeds in a cephalo-caudal direction.

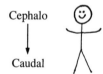

Cephalo

Caudal

The head and upper trunk develop strength before the lower trunk.

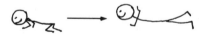

The arms are used for weight-bearing and locomotion before the legs.

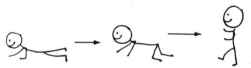

4. Primitive reflexes gradually fade out as postural reflexes develop. This is described in more detail below.

Primitive ⟷ Postural

Primitive Reflexes

The term *reflex,* when applied to motor development, refers to a specific movement or posture that occurs when a particular stimulus is given.

A group of reflexes are present at the time of birth and for this reason are called *primitive reflexes.* Their influence gradually fades, and by 6 months of age they should no longer significantly influence motor behavior.

The major primitive reflexes are:

1. *Moro reflex*

    Stimulus: The baby's head is allowed to fall backward into the examiner's hand.
    Response: The arms move suddenly up and back, then are brought forward across the chest. As the reflex fades out, you may see only slight arm movements.
    Significance: To the degree that this reflex is present, the baby cannot use the arms for protection during sudden loss of balance, and therefore should not be left unattended while sitting without support.

    Present: ± Birth to 4 months

2. *Asymmetric tonic neck reflex (ATNR)*

    Stimulus: The baby's head is turned to the side.
    Response: There is a tendency for the arm and sometimes the leg on the face side (the side to which the head is turned) to extend, and for the arm and sometimes the leg on the opposite side to flex.
    Significance: This reflex may assist a baby in reaching out for an object in back-lying position. In a normal baby, the reflex is never "obligatory"; that is, he or she can easily break out of the pattern. The reflex fades out at the time the baby starts to roll from back to stomach by first turning the head.

    Present: ± 1 to 4 months

3. *Symmetric tonic neck reflex (STNR)*

    Stimulus: Flexion or extension of the neck.
    Response: With flexion, the arms tend to flex and the legs tend to extend. With extension, the arms tend to extend and the legs tend to flex.
    Significance: This reflex is thought to provide assistance to the child who is starting to assume an all-fours position. As with the ATNR, the patterns are never obligatory in a normal child.

    Present: ± 6 to 8 months

4. *Hand grasp reflex or palmar grasp reflex*

    Stimulus: The examiner's finger is placed across the infant's palm.
    Response: The infant's fingers close tightly and remain closed.
    Significance: This reflex initially supports the baby's ability to grasp objects, but must fade before objects can be released.

    Present: ± Birth to 3 months

5. *Foot grasp reflex or toe grasp*

Present: ± Birth to 12 months

Stimulus: A slight pressure is given over the ball of the
   foot, *or* the baby is placed in standing position.
Response: The toes curl in flexion and stay curled.
Significance: This reflex must fade before the child will
   have good balance in the standing position.

Postural Reflexes

The postural reflexes begin to appear a few months after birth and continue their development through the first 5 years of life, although the greatest development takes place in the first 12–18 months. These reflexes persist throughout life, providing an automatic support for voluntary actions. They can be grouped, according to their function, into righting, tilting, and protective extension.

Righting Reactions   This group of reactions assures the alignment of body parts to each other and the alignment of the body as a whole in space.

1. *Head righting reflexes*

Onset: 2 to 4 months

Stimulus: The baby is held at the shoulders and tilted
   forward or sideways.
Response: The baby brings his or her head back to an
   upright position with eyes parallel to the horizon.
Significance: The ability to right the head in space is the
   first phase of the cephalo-caudal development of
   postural control. A child with this ability requires
   less support when being carried and has greater
   freedom to visually inspect the environment.

2. *Landau response*

Onset: 4 to 6 months

Stimulus: The child is suspended horizontally in the air
   with support under the stomach.
Response: Initially the child lifts only the head; later on,
   the back and legs extend as well. In the full-blown
   response, the back is seen to arch upward.
Significance: The ability to use the postural extensors
   against gravity is essential for developing good upright postures (sitting and standing). The reflex supports the ability of the child to push up on elbows and
   later to push up on hands in prone position.

3. *Neck righting*

Onset: 4 to 6 months

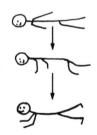

Stimulus: With the child lying supine (on back), the
   examiner turns the child's head to one side.
Response: The child turns first the shoulders, then the
   hips in the same direction, and rolls into prone (on
   stomach).
Significance: This sequence of activities promotes a
   rolling pattern initiated at the head. After the child is
   able to roll easily, he or she may voluntarily inhibit
   the rolling pattern when the head is turned.

4. *Body righting*   Onset: 4 to 6 months

   Stimulus: With the child lying supine, the examiner
        bends one of the child's legs and draws it up and
        across to the opposite side.
   Response: The child turns shoulders, then head, in the
        direction of the leg movement, completing a roll into
        prone.
   Significance: This reflex supports development of a
        rolling pattern initiated from the legs and subsequent
        assumption of sitting position. After the child is able
        to roll well, he or she will voluntarily inhibit the
        rolling pattern when the leg is flexed.

Tilting Reactions   These are movements of the spine that allow the child to maintain
balance while moving.

Tilting reactions   Onset:

   Stimulus: The child is placed on a tilt board and rocked
        slowly from side to side.
   Response: As the tilting of the surface occurs, the child's
        spine curves away from the direction of the tilt so that
        balance is regained. The responses appear in the
        following order:
        Prone
        Supine
        Sitting
        All fours
        Standing
   Significance: Tilting reactions are a fundamental pro-
        tective balancing system. If a child lacks brisk tilting
        reactions in sitting or standing, he or she should not
        be left unattended in that position.

Prone: ± 6 Months
Supine: 7 to 8 Months
Sitting: 7 to 8 Months
All fours: 9 to 12 Months
Standing: 12 to 24 Months

Protective Extension Reactions   Sometimes called "parachute" reactions,
these consist of automatic movements of the extremities to catch oneself after balance
has been lost. Protective extension reactions develop in the following order:

1. *Downward extension reactions* (response seen in legs)   Onset of downward: 4 to 6 Months

   Stimulus: The child, suspended vertically in the air, is
        suddenly lowered toward a supporting surface, with-
        out letting the feet actually contact the surface.
   Response: The legs extend quickly, moving slightly
        apart; the toes are brought up in preparation for
        weight-bearing.

2. *Forward extension reactions* (response seen in arms)   Onset of forward: 6 to 7 Months

   Stimulus: The child is suspended horizontally in the air,
        face down, then moved suddenly toward a support-
        ing surface.
   Response: The arms are brought quickly forward and
        weight is taken on open hands.

3. *Sideways extension reactions* (response seen in arms)   Onset of sideways: 7 to 8 Months

   Stimulus: The child, placed in sitting position, is
        pushed gently but firmly to either side.
   Response: The arm on the side to which the child is
        pushed moves quickly outward to that side and
        weight is taken on an open hand.

4. *Backward extension reactions* (response seen in arms)
   Stimulus: The child, in sitting position, is pushed
   quickly backward at the shoulder.
   Response: On the side pushed, the arm extends behind
   the body and weight is taken on an open hand.
   Significance: The protective extension reactions function to prevent falling when movement is too sudden
   or extreme to be handled by tilting reactions.

Onset of backward: 9 to 10 Months

5. *Motor milestones appear in an orderly fashion.* The attainment of
functional motor skill is based on the integrated processes just described. Although
there is considerable variety in rate and some variety in order of milestone attainment,
infants gain skills in a similar manner. These milestones are depicted in Figure 3. The
process is not a strictly stepwise one however. At any given point in development,
babies will alternate between using established skills and experimenting with new
ones. If left on their own, and not placed in positions that they cannot independently
assume, they will generally stay within the limit of their motor ability. Their
exploration of movement, then, is continually self-reinforcing.

CHARACTERISTICS OF ABNORMAL MOTOR DEVELOPMENT

Abnormal motor development can result from a great variety of conditions including
prenatal problems, birth trauma, chromosomal disorders, accidents, and severe
illness. Many of these conditions can be given specific diagnoses such as cerebral
palsy, Down syndrome, and postmeningitis. The diagnosis, however, does not
describe motor function. Children with dissimilar diagnoses can show similar motor
patterns. For purposes of assessment and intervention, it is more useful to think in
terms of the basic characteristics of abnormal motor development, as described in the
following list.

1. *Abnormal muscle tone.* Normal tone can be felt by bending and straightening the
   arm of a normal person and feeling the amount of resistance you encounter. The
   muscles of a normal person will feel the same throughout the body. Abnormal
   muscle tone can occur in a number of different patterns. For any given child,
   abnormal tone is described in terms of three parameters: type, distribution, and
   severity. Table 6 summarizes the most commonly seen types of neuromuscular
   disorders in terms of type and distribution. In addition to these combinations, it is
   common to find a "mixed" type of involvement, e.g., "spastic athetoid." The
   different combinations of type and distribution of muscle tone are seen in varying
   degrees of severity, and the terms *mild, moderate,* and *severe* are used to
   describe this spectrum. These terms, in fact, refer not only to muscle tone itself
   but also to the accompanying abnormal reflex development and disruption of
   functional activity. In addition to describing current status, they carry im-
   plications for ease of intervention and expectations for the future. Severity of
   involvement is a reflection of the extent to which the nervous system has been
   damaged.
       Mildly involved children often respond well to intervention and can be
   expected to achieve motor milestones at a normal or slightly delayed rate and to
   become functionally independent in ambulation and self-care.

Moderately involved children respond more slowly to intervention and therefore gain motor skills at a considerably delayed rate. There is a good chance that these children will be ambulatory at some point, with or without assistive devices. They can be nearly independent in self-care activities.

Severely involved children have a much bleaker prospect for attaining motor skills. They respond very slowly to treatment and cannot be expected to progress through the sequence of motor milestones. Functional ambulation is not likely, and assistance will be required for all self-care. At the extreme of this range is a group of children for whom prevention of deterioration is the major goal. This does not mean that ongoing efforts at improving head control and postural stability should not be made; over a long period of time, improvement may be seen. These children are at great risk, though, for orthopaedic problems and progressive deformity. They must be handled and positioned very carefully, and passive range of motion exercises may be required. Your therapist will show you how to carry out these procedures correctly.

2. *Abnormal reflex activity.* Children with cerebral palsy show deviations from the normal pattern of reflex development described in the previous section. Persistence of the primitive reflexes is frequently seen and may range from a subtle to a strong influence:

A *Moro reflex* will cause a child's arms to move suddenly up and back in response to a sudden noise, movement, or visual stimulus. This reflex can be strong in severely involved children, and, as a result, they are unable to use their arms for protection against falling. These children should not be left unattended in sitting positions.

An *asymmetric tonic neck reflex* will interfere with moving the arms independently from the head, rolling to prone, and mouthing of the hand or objects when the head is turned.

A *symmetric tonic neck reflex* will also interfere with moving the arms independently from the head. Children with a strong STNR will inspect objects by pulling the head toward the chest. They will have difficulty crawling and may "bunny-hop" instead.

A *hand grasp reflex* will interfere with a child's ability to release objects from the hand. Children with a strong palmar grasp in combination with an ATNR often get into the predicament of painfully pulling the hair on the back of their head.

A *foot grasp reflex* will make it more difficult for a child to attain a good weight-bearing position on flat feet.

While the primitive reflexes dominate, the postural reflexes are absent or delayed. Children with cerebral palsy show absent or deficient righting, tilting, and protective extension responses. Appropriate positioning and therapeutic handling can improve a child's ability to use these postural reflexes.

Compounding the picture is the presence of postures and reflexes that are never seen in normal children.

Entrapped thumbs ("cortical thumbs") In spastic children the thumbs are pulled under the fingers and the tip of the thumb will appear between the fingers.

34

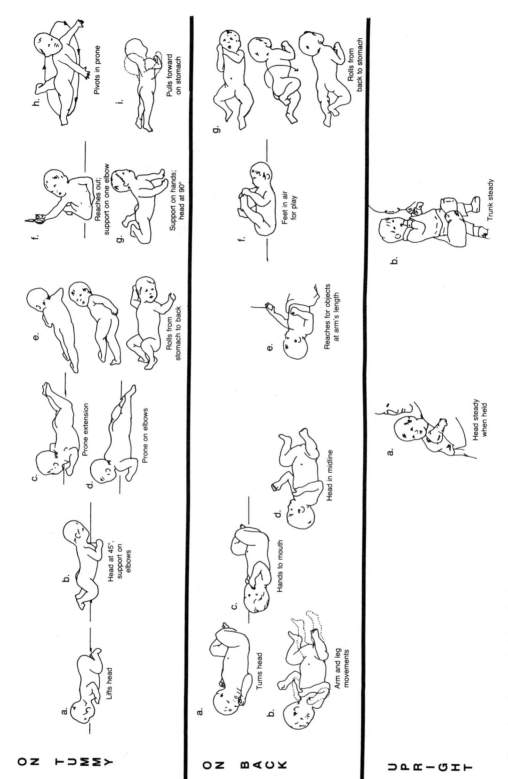

Figure 3. Motor milestones in infant development, birth to 12 months.

ON TUMMY

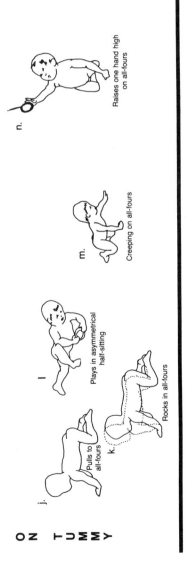

j. Pulls to all-fours

k. Rocks in all-fours

l. Plays in asymmetrical half-sitting

m. Creeping on all-fours

n. Raises one hand high on all-fours

UPRIGHT

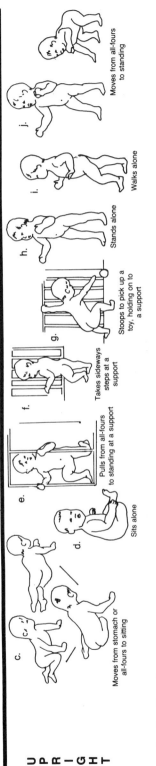

c. Moves from stomach or all-fours to sitting

d. Sits alone

e. Pulls from all-fours to standing at a support

f. Takes sideways steps at a support

g. Stoops to pick up a toy, holding on to a support

h. Stands alone

i. Walks alone

j. Moves from all-fours to standing

Figure 3. *(continued)* .

35

Table 6. Characteristics of the most common types of cerebral palsy

TYPE:	Spastic	Athetoid	Hypotonic	Ataxic
MUSCLE TONE:	Increased	Fluctuating between low and high	Decreased	Normal or slightly decreased
DISTRIBUTION:	1. *Hemiplegia:* Only one side is involved (right arm and leg or left arm and leg), but the arm is more involved. 2. *Quadriplegia:* All four extremities and trunk are involved. 3. *Diplegia:* All four extremities are involved, but the legs are more involved.	Whole body is involved.	Generally the whole body is involved, but there may be differences between arms and legs, trunk and extremities.	Whole body is involved.
CHARACTERISTICS:	Movements are carried out in stereotypic patterns; freedom of movement is restricted; child is "stiff."	Movements are large and difficult to control. Head control is a major problem, as are speech and feeding. Some athetoid children are very tense ("tension athetosis"); others are very hypotonic. When reaching for objects, the fingers overextend.	Movements themselves are fairly normal but lack holding power. Child is "floppy." Hypotonic infants frequently develop spasticity or athetosis.	Child may have good movements in prone, but will look "wobbly" in sitting and standing. Reaching patterns show poor directionality.

Relaxation of the entire arm or light stroking of the tops of the fingers may release the thumb. One may also pull the thumb out gently by grasping the *lowest* part of the thumb. *Never* pull the thumb out by grasping the tip, as this can damage the joints.

Strong arching of the back in supine position ("opisthotonus") Very severely involved children may assume this position, and it can be prevented only by not placing them in supine position.

3. *Delay in development of motor skills or abnormal performance of motor skills.* Due to the interplay of the conditions just described, appearance of motor milestones is delayed and abnormal in quality. Intervention by therapists is geared toward changing those underlying conditions.
4. *Associated disorders.* A number of additional impairments can occur in children with neuromuscular disorders:

Seizure disorders are fairly common. Indications of seizure activity include episodes of "staring," during which eye contact cannot be obtained, jerking movements of the arms and/or legs, and sudden loss of head control. For children with known seizure disorders, make sure you know what their seizures look like and keep track of their occurrence; if seizures are increasing, the child's medication may need adjusting. When a child is having a seizure, simply position him or her comfortably and let the seizure run its course.

Visual problems are common, and can consist of inability to focus the eyes together, inability to stabilize the eyes in midline, nearsightedness or blindness. The term *cortical blindness* is used when the eye and optic nerve appear to be intact but the child does not seem to be processing visual stimuli.

Hearing deficits can also occur, and can range from mild loss of high-frequency sounds to total deafness. There are two kinds of hearing impairments. "Conductive" losses occur when there is some problem with the outer or middle ear; this type of impairment can be helped with hearing aids, medication, "ear tubes," or surgery. "Sensorineural" losses are the result of damage to the auditory nerve itself. Hearing aids sometimes help these children, but surgery and "ear tubes" cannot help the condition. If you have children in your class who wear hearing aids, check the devices daily to make sure they are functioning properly. Any child whose hearing status you question should be checked by an audiologist or an ear, nose, and throat doctor.

MOTOR PROGRAMMING IN THE CLASSROOM

General Guidelines

The following general statements are offered here to help put motor programming into perspective.

It is helpful to spend time periodically with normal infants to reacquaint yourself with their response patterns and motor capabilities. This will give you a basis of comparison with your students and help prevent overestimation of their abilities.

Bear in mind that motor development is not a strictly stepwise process. At any given time a child will have some skills at a proficient level of development and other skills at lower stages of development. The motor program should include a variety of activities in different positions.

In general, it is important to gear motor activities to the child's developmental level rather than chronological age. This will allow the child to develop the basic motor capabilities needed to function at higher levels. Developmentally disabled

children have a slower rate of development and should not, for example, be
expected to show a 6-month gain in a 6-month period. A physical or occupational therapist can make judgments as to whether a child is ready to work in
more advanced patterns.

As much as possible, let movement be its own reward. Avoid excessive use of social
praise or tangible reinforcers for performance of motor skills. The child's motor
skills should be used primarily for independent exploration and play rather than
to gain the approval of the caregivers.

Normal children do not "think" about how they are moving; rather, their actions fall
into place automatically to achieve a particular goal. This situation should be
maintained as much as possible with abnormal children. Instructions for movement should be goal-directed (e.g., "Hit the balloon") rather than motion-
directed (e.g., "Straighten your arm"). Likewise, it does no good to instruct a
child repeatedly to sit up straight or to hold his or her head up. Deficiencies in
posture are indicators that exercises need to be done in more elementary
patterns.

Improving Motor Skills

For best results, the motor program will include two major components. One is the
specific exercise program. The other is the manner in which the child is handled and
positioned throughout the day—at home as well as at school. Incorporating motor
goals into the daily routine speeds progress and prevents or forestalls the development
of physical deformities. Neuromuscular disorders are not curable conditions, and the
more severely a child is involved, the poorer are the odds for smooth motor
functioning. It remains true, however, that postures and movements are established
through repetition. If a child practices abnormal patterns, these quickly become
habitual and difficult to change. For this reason it is important that motor experiences
be as normal as possible.

The overall procedure for training is:

1. Based on the motor evaluation, decide on the activity you want the child to do.
2. Get the child's muscle tone to an appropriate state through handling and
   positioning.
3. Have the child perform and repeat the activity.
4. Gradually make it more challenging for the child to perform the activity, by
   changing position, placing objects higher, and so forth.

Handling

Implementing a motor program involves skill in physically handling the child. The
most important points to consider are:

1. Always give the child the opportunity to perform as much of the movement as
   possible. This usually means doing things more slowly so that the child is given
   the chance to organize a response. For example, when bringing a child from
   back-lying to sitting, roll the child slowly to the side and give the child time to
   push up on his or her arm, even if he or she can only do this partially.

2. When carrying the child, allow for as much independent head and trunk control as possible. Carrying a child over a shoulder or hip rather than nestling a child in your arm helps build strength while allowing more visual inspection of the environment.

3. With *spastic* children, it is important not to pull against their tightness, as this tends to increase tightness. The proper methods of relaxation are:

    Gently moving the shoulders (to release the arms) and pelvis (to release the legs)
    Slowly and gently extending the arms and legs

4. Many severely involved children, especially those with *athetoid* features, show hypersensitivity to tactile, auditory, and visual stimuli. They startle easily and withdraw from contact on the mouth, hands, and feet. These children should be approached slowly and quietly. They should be encouraged to keep their heads, hands, and visual focus in midline. Tolerance to rougher textures may be improved by firm pressure on the sensitive skin areas. Weight-bearing on hands and feet is an important activity for these children.

5. Low-tone children need a more vigorous approach, but are likely to require frequent rest periods. Back-lying (supine) positions should be avoided, as they do not help the child learn to function against gravity. Stomach-lying (prone) positions should be emphasized for strengthening back muscles, and abdominal muscles should be exercised in semireclining postures. To encourage arm use and provide opportunity for visual learning, infant seats can be used for infants. For the older child an adapted corner chair is helpful.

Specific discussions of handling techniques can be found in Finnie (1975) or Haynes (1983).

Positioning

The primary purpose of good positioning is to place the child appropriately for optimum *functioning* in a given activity. A second and important purpose is to prevent *contractures* (permanent shortening) of muscles in spastic children. The muscle groups most prone to contractures are:

Elbow flexors (biceps)
Hip flexors (iliopsoas)
Knee flexors (hamstrings)
Ankle downward flexors (gastrocnemius)

The major goal in positioning children with low tone is to provide adequate support while allowing for visual inspection of the environment. Infant carriers, which place the baby in a semiupright position, are an excellent choice for the young child. At home, the baby can be propped in a semiupright position on a chair or couch by using pillows. For the older child, adapted chairs (see Figure 4) are useful. Nonambulatory children should spend a good deal of time on their stomach, as this builds strength in the extensor muscles.

Figure 5 describes sitting and lying positions commonly assumed by handicapped children. Because handicapped children cannot move easily into the most optimal positions for various activities, it is essential that they be placed and secured by their caregivers. Several types of equipment are available commercially and some support systems can be improvised.

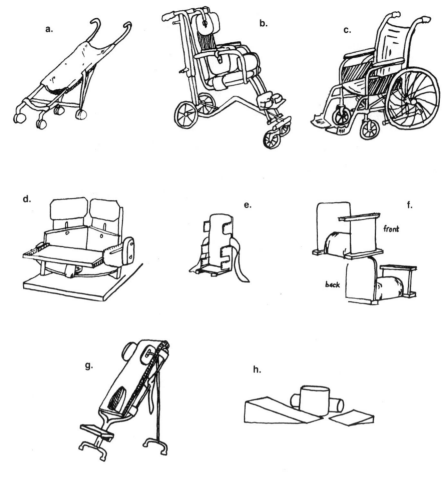

Figure 4.   Special-purpose chairs.
    a. *Folding strollers* are inexpensive, lightweight, collapsible, and convenient for transportation.
    b. *Upholstered wheeled chairs* provide good support at the head, trunk, hips, and feet. Trays can be attached for feeding and play. The back wheels retract so that the chair can be placed into an automobile without moving the child. These chairs are suitable for children with poor control of head and trunk. They cannot be propelled by the child, however, and are intended only for severely handicapped children. When used in cars or schoolbuses, additional safety restraints *must* be used.
    c. *Standard wheelchairs* come in a variety of sizes and can be used with trays and head supports. A child who has use of the upper extremities can propel the chair independently. These chairs are more cumbersome in terms of automobile transportation because the child has to be removed and the chair folded.
    d. *Corner chairs* provide some support at the shoulders and hips. An extension to the back portion can provide support at the head, and wedges on the seat control hip position. A tray can be attached. This type of seating places spastic children with low-trunk tone in a functional position with shoulders forward and hips apart. Hypotonic children also make good use of corner chairs.
    e. *Seat inserts* can be used to support small children in chairs that would otherwise be too large or would not offer enough support.
    f. *Bolster chairs,* to which a tray can be attached, require some head and trunk control on the part of the child. The straddle seat ensures good separation of the legs for a spastic child.
    g. *Prone-standers* can be adjusted to accommodate virtually any child, and are used to provide activity in upright positions while maintaining good body alignment. Arm use, head/trunk control, and social interaction are all facilitated in this position. Care should be taken in placement to make sure the feet are flat and the entire body is properly aligned.
    h. *Bolsters and wedges* of various sizes allow play in prone position for children with poor control of head, trunk, and arms. Care should be taken to make sure the child's legs are not thrusting stiffly. If necessary, place a towel between the knees or keep them turned slightly outward.

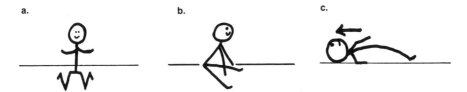

Figure 5.   Sitting and lying positions commonly assumed by handicapped children.
   a. *W-sitting (reverse tailor).* Many children will want to sit like this because it affords them more sideways balance. They should not be permitted to do so, however, because of the strain this position imposes on knee ligaments and the improper pressure exerted on the hips and ankles. This is especially true for spastic children whose muscle tone tends to make their legs turn in to begin with.
   b. *Prop sitting.* If a child consistently sits in this position, it is an indication that his or her back muscles are too weak to support the trunk in an upright position with the hands free for play. Such children should have more support in sitting for classroom activities. Toys can be elevated to shoulder level to encourage straighter backs.
   c. *Supine position.* Some severely involved children lie on their backs and push themselves backward in an arched position. This is a highly abnormal pattern and should be discouraged. It may be possible for the child to use a prone scooter board.

Safety Precautions

One result of securing children well into adaptive equipment is that it takes time to get them freed. Caregivers are strongly advised to practice emergency procedures so that if a fire occurs, or if a child chokes, proper measures can be taken. Caregivers should practice taking children out of equipment quickly, removing children from the building while still in the equipment, and turning a child upside-down while still fastened in a chair. There should always be at least one person available who is trained in basic first-aid procedures, including cardiopulmonary resuscitation.

Precautions

Avoid encouraging a child to walk before he or she is motorically ready for it. A physical or occupational therapist is the most appropriate person to make the judgment. If a child has poor trunk-balancing reactions, habitually stands on the toes, or cannot extend the arms for protection, walking should not be encouraged. Parallel bars (walking bars) are not helpful in teaching walking. If a young child needs parallel bars in order to walk, then he or she is not yet ready to walk but needs further work on lower-level motor skills. Wheeled baby walkers should be used very cautiously and only after consultation with a therapist. Some blind or retarded infants who need to "get the idea" of walking can benefit, but as a rule infants should be encouraged to move on their own.

Creeping is frequently an inappropriate activity for children with spasticity and/or athetosis, unless closely supervised by a therapist. There is a strong tendency to use abnormal reflex patterns, which may inhibit the child's future ability to walk. Bunny-hopping utilizes abnormal reflex patterns, and should be discouraged.

Ice cubes are sometimes used to promote better oral-motor function, but this should be done only under a therapist's supervision.

Spinning is a therapeutic technique that is used selectively by occupational therapists and physical therapists. However, it can produce undesirable side-effects and should not be used unless the child is supervised by a well-trained therapist.

Body Mechanics

If you do a lot of lifting and carrying during the day, you may be in danger of injuring your back. A few simple rules of body mechanics, if incorporated into your daily routine, will reduce the risks to a minimum.

1. When lifting a child or piece of equipment, bend your knees to get a firm grasp. Never lean over with your legs straight to lift or put down a child.

2. During lifting and carrying, hold the load close to your body. The closer you hold something to your center of gravity, the less muscle power you need to carry it.

REFERENCES

Bly, L. (1980). The components of movement during the first year of life. In *Development of movement in infancy*. Chapel Hill, NC: University of North Carolina, Division of Physical Therapy.

Finnie, N. (1975). *Handling the young cerebral palsied child at home*. New York: E. P. Dutton & Co.

Haynes, U. (1983). *Holistic health care for children with developmental disabilities*, pp. 13–84. Baltimore: University Park Press.

Pikler, E. (1971). Learning of motor skills on the basis of self-induced movements. In J. Helmuth (Ed.), *Exceptional infant, Vol. 2. Studies in abnormalities*. New York: Brunner Mazel.

Stockmeyer, S. (1967). An interpretation of the Rood approach to the treatment of neuromuscular dysfunction. *American Journal of Physical Medicine, 46*, 900–955.

Stockmeyer, S. (1972). A sensorimotor approach to treatment. In P. Pearson and C. Williams (Eds.), *Physical therapy in the developmental disabilities*. Springfield, IL: Charles C Thomas.

RECOMMENDED READING

Bleck, E., & Nagel, D. (Eds.). (1975). *Physically handicapped children: A medical atlas for teachers*. New York: Grune & Stratton.

Connor, F., Williamson, G., & Siepp, J. (Eds.). (1978). *Program guide for infants and toddlers with neuromotor and other developmental disabilities*. New York: Teachers College Press, Columbia University.

Fraiberg, S. (1977). *Insights from the blind*. New York: Basic Books.

Sontag, E. (Ed.). (1977). Educational programming for the severely and profoundly handicapped. Reston, VA: Division on Mental Retardation, Council for Exceptional Children.

Wilmot, M. E. (1977). Motor development, posture, and physiotherapy. In E. Jan, R. Freeman, & E. Scott (Eds.), *Visual impairment in children and adolescents*. New York: Grune & Stratton.

Assessment Log
and
Developmental Progress Chart

ASSESSMENT LOG

Insert the date of your assessment at the top of the column and insert a + in the box for each mastered item.

Age (Months)	Curriculum Sequences	Date:	Date:	Date:	Date:
	1. Tactile Integration and Manipulation				
(3)	a. Responds differently to warm/cold, rough/smooth				
	b. Permits soft, smooth textures to be rubbed on hands, feet, or body; or moves own body over such textures				
(6)	c. Reacts to tactile stimulation with movement				
	d. Permits hands, feet, or body to be moved over rough-textured surfaces; or moves them over these surfaces spontaneously				
	e. Explores objects with fingers				
(9)	f. Plays in water				
	g. Finds object hidden in textured material				
(12)	h. Plays with soft-textured materials				
(15)	i. Spreads soft materials with fingers				
(18)	j. Spreads firmer materials with hands				
(21)	k. Pokes or plays with clay				
	2. Auditory Localization and Object Permanence				
	a. Quiets when noise is presented				
	b. Visually searches for sound				
(3)	c. Turns head and searches or reaches for ear-level sound while lying down				
	d. Turns head or reaches toward source of sound while sitting; sound at ear or shoulder level				
(6)	e. Turns head toward sound and looks or reaches directly at noisemaker when noise presented at ear or shoulder level				
	f. (1) Looks directly at noisemaker when sound presented to the side and at waist level				
(9)	(2) *Alternate for visually impaired children* Reaches in the right direction when sound presented below ear level				
	g. (1) Turns head and looks back and forth to 2 sounds				
(9)	(2) *Alternate for visually impaired children* Reaches to either side for noisy object				

Age (Months)		Curriculum Sequences	Date: ___	Date: ___	Date: ___	Date: ___
		Omit the following for children physically able to do sequence 4.				
(12)	h.	*For visually impaired children* Reaches for object after it no longer makes noise				
(18)	i.	*For visually impaired children* Reaches for object that no longer makes noise, at midline and on both sides, above and below shoulder level				
(21)	j.	*For visually impaired children* Reaches correctly for object that has made noise in several places				
	3.	**Visual Pursuit and Object Permanence**				
	a.	Visually fixates for at least 3 seconds				
	b.	Visually tracks object from side to side				
	c.	Visually tracks object from forehead to chest				
	d.	Visually tracks object moving in a circle				
(3)	e.	Gaze lingers where object disappears				
(6)	f.	Continues to look at caregiver when caregiver's face is covered with a cloth				
(9)	g.	Looks at cover under which object has disappeared.				
		Omit the following for children physically able to do sequence 4.				
(12)	h.	Looks to the correct place when object is hidden in 1 of 2 places				
(15)	i.	Looks to the correct place when object is hidden in 1 of 3 places				
(18)	j.	Looks at correct place for toy after seeing it covered in 3 places successively				
(21)	k.	Looks successively at 2 different covers until toy is found that was hidden from the child's view (invisible displacement)				
(24)	l.	Looks systematically at 3 different covers until toy is uncovered that was hidden from the child's view				
	4.	**Object Permanence (Visual-Motor)**				
	a.	Pulls cloth from face				
	b.	Pulls cloth from caregiver's face				
(6)	c.	Uncovers partially hidden toy				
	d.	Removes cover from fully hidden toy				
	e.	Finds toy hidden under a cover when 2 covers are present				

Age (Months)		Curriculum Sequences	Date:	Date:	Date:	Date:
	f.	Finds toy when it is hidden under 2 covers, alternately				
(9)	g.	Removes cover when object is hidden under 1 of 3 covers				
(12)	h.	Finds toy hidden under 3 superimposed covers				
	i.	Finds toy after seeing it covered in 3 places successively				
(15)	j.	Finds object after searching under 2 covers (invisible displacement)				
(18)	k.	Finds object after systematic search under 3 covers (invisible displacement)				
	5.	**Spatial Concepts**				
	a.	Shifts attention (visual fixation or body orientation) from 1 object to another				
(3)	b.	Looks for or reaches toward objects in sight that touch the body (omit for visually impaired children)				
	c.	Looks for or reaches toward objects out of sight that touch the body				
(6)	d.	Looks for or reaches for objects that fall from view while making a noise				
	e.	Looks for or reaches for objects that fall quietly from view				
(9)	f.	Looks or moves in the right direction for objects that fall and roll or bounce to new location				
(12)	g.	Searches for objects moved out of visual field or (for visually impaired children) away from midline				
	h.	Retrieves toys from a container when they have been dropped through a hole in the top				
(15)	i.	Pulls string to get object from behind barrier				
	j.	Reaches object from behind barrier				
(18)	k.	Moves self around barrier to get object				
	l.	Retrieves objects from usual locations in another room				
(21)	m.	Puts objects away in correct places				
(24)	n.	Uses "tools" to deal with spatial problems (extends reach with a stick, extends height with a stool, etc.) (same as item 7i)				
	6.	**Functional Use of Objects and Symbolic Play**				
	a.	Moves hand to mouth				
(3)	b.	Explores objects with mouth				

Age (Months)		Curriculum Sequences	Date: ___	Date: ___	Date: ___	Date: ___
	c.	Plays with (e.g., shakes or bangs) toys placed in hand				
	d.	Commonly performs 4 or more activities with objects				
(6)	e.	Explores toys and responds to their differences				
	f.	Demonstrates appropriate activities with toys having obviously different properties				
(9)	g.	Combines 2 objects in a functional manner				
(12)	h.	Imitates activities related to the function of objects				
(15)	i.	Plays spontaneously with variety of objects, demonstrating their functions				
(18)	j.	Imitates adult behavior with props				
(21)	k.	Spontaneously engages in adult activities with props				
(24)	l.	"Talks" to dolls or animals or makes them interact with one another				
	7.	**Control over Physical Environment**				
(3)	a.	Repeats activity that produces an interesting result				
(6)	b.	Persists in effort to obtain something				
	c.	Uses simple "tool" to obtain an object or effect				
(9)	d.	Overcomes obstacles to get toys				
(12)	e.	Plays with variety of toys to produce effects				
(15)	f.	Uses adults to solve problems (work on items 7f and 7g simultaneously)				
(18)	g.	Imitates adult action to solve problems				
(21)	h.	Solves simple problems without adult assistance				
(24)	i.	Uses "tools" to solve problems (same as item 5n)				
	8.	**"Readiness" Concepts**				
	a.	Matches simple geometric shapes				
(18)	b.	Matches objects to pictures				
	c.	Matches colors				
(21)	d.	Matches "big" and "little"				
	e.	Identifies circle and square when they are named				
	f.	Understands "same"				
(24)	g.	Understands "big"				

Age (Months)	Curriculum Sequences	Date:	Date:	Date:	Date:
	9. Responses to Communication from Others				
	a. Quiets to voice				
(3)	b. Smiles to person talking and gesturing				
	c. Turns to name being called				
	d. Responds to intonation or attitudes expressed by intonation				
	e. Stops activity when name is called				
	f. Vocalizes when talked to				
(6)	g. Does previously learned task on verbal or gestural cue				
	h. Responds with correct gesture to "Up" and "Bye-bye"				
(9)	i. Responds to "No"				
	j. Points to or looks at 3 objects or people named or signed				
(12)	k. Responds to "Give me" (word and/or gesture) (same as 14k)				
	l. Follows simple commands (signed and/or spoken)				
(15)	m. Points to or looks at most common objects when they are named and/or signed				
	n. Indicates "Yes" or "No" appropriately in response to questions (signed or spoken)				
	o. Points to or otherwise indicates 2 body parts when they are named or signed				
(18)	p. Retrieves visible object on verbal or signed request				
	q. Points to at least 4 animals in pictures when they are named or signed				
	r. Points to or otherwise indicates 15 or more pictures of common objects				
(21)	s. Responds to simple questions correctly				
	t. Understands 2 or more "category" words (e.g., "animals")				
	u. Points to or otherwise indicates 5 body parts				
	v. Correctly follows 3 different 2-part commands involving 1 object				
(24)	w. Follows 3 different 3-part commands				

50

Age (Months)	Curriculum Sequences	Date:	Date:	Date:	Date:
	10. Gestural Imitation				
(3)	a. Looks at person talking and gesturing				
	b. Continues a movement if it is imitated by caregiver				
(6)	c. Will begin a movement already in repertoire if same activity is begun by caregiver				
	d. Tries to imitate unfamiliar movement; child's own action is visible to himself or herself				
(9)	e. Imitates unfamiliar movement that is not visible to himself or herself				
(12)	f. Imitates new activities, including use of materials				

Stop here if child is progressing well with spoken words.

Age (Months)	Curriculum Sequences	Date:	Date:	Date:	Date:
	g. Imitates 1 sign that stands for a word (e.g., "Daddy," "all gone," "more," "eat," "drink," etc.)				
(15)	h. Imitates 2 signs that stand for words				
(18)	i. Imitates 3 signs that stand for words				
(21)	j. Imitates sequence of 2 signs that stand for words				
	11. Gestural Communication				
	a. Shows anticipation of regularly occurring events in everyday care				
(3)	b. Responds to being shifted from mother or caregiver to another person				
	c. Anticipates frequently occurring events in "games" (nursery rhymes, etc.)				
	d. Repeats acitivity that gets interesting reaction from others				
	e. Gets adult to continue activity by starting body movements				
(6)	f. Initiates activity by starting movement				
	g. Raises arms to be picked up				
	h. Consistently indicates desire to "get down"				
(9)	i. Reaches toward something to indicate "Get it" or "Give it"				
(12)	j. Uses gestures for word concepts ("all gone," "more," "eat," "drink," etc.)				

Stop here if child is progressing well with spoken words.

Age (Months)		Curriculum Sequences	Date:	Date:	Date:	Date:
(15)	k.	Uses gestures or signs for 5 words or concepts				
(18)	l.	Uses signs for 7 or more words				
	m.	Uses signs to communicate wants				
(21)	n.	Uses 15 signs consistently				
(24)	o.	Combines signs to communicate				
	12.	**Vocal Imitation**				
	a.	Vocalizes in response to person talking				
	b.	Repeats sounds just made when they are imitated by caregiver				
	c.	Shifts sounds—imitates sound in repertoire when made by caregiver				
(6)	d.	Imitates inflection (pitch)				
	e.	Attempts to match new sounds				
(9)	f.	Imitates familiar 2-syllable words like "baba," "Dada," or "Mama"				
(12)	g.	Imitates 2-syllable words with syllable changes ("baby," "uh-oh," "all gone," etc.)				
	h.	Imitates familiar words overheard in conversation				
(15)	i.	Imitates novel 2-syllable words				
(18)	j.	Imitates environmental sounds during play				
(21)	k.	Imitates 2-word sentences				
(24)	l.	Imitates 3-syllable words				
	13.	**Vocal Communication**				
	a.	Differentiates cries				
	b.	Stops crying when sees (or touches) bottle or breast				
	c.	Vocalizes to get attention				
(3)	d.	Vocalizes 5 or more consonant and vowel sounds				
	e.	Laughs appropriately				
	f.	Vocalizes 3 or more feelings				
	g.	Repeats vocalizations that get reactions				
(6)	h.	Vocalizes to get return of object				
	i.	Vocalizes repetitive consonant-vowel combinations				
(9)	j.	Indicates wants by vocalizing				

Age (Months)		Curriculum Sequences	Date:	Date:	Date:	Date:
(12)	k.	Uses 2 or more word labels				
	l.	Uses 3 or more word labels				
	m.	Indicates wants with words				
(15)	n.	Uses 1 or more exclamations				
	o.	Uses inflection pattern when vocalizing (babbling); no understandable words				
(18)	p.	Greets familiar people with some appropriate vocalization				
	q.	Says "No" meaningfully				
	r.	Names 5 or more familiar objects				
(21)	s.	Uses inflection pattern(s) in a sentence with 1 or 2 understandable words				
	t.	Says familiar greetings and farewells at appropriate times				
	u.	Names 3 or more pictures of familiar objects				
(24)	v.	Combines 2 or more words in sentences				
	14.	**Social Skills**				
	a.	Can be comforted by talking to, holding, or rocking				
	b.	Smiles reciprocally				
(3)	c.	Smiles to auditory or tactile stimulation				
	d.	Smiles at a familiar person				
	e.	Smiles at mirror image (omit for significantly visually impaired children)				
(6)	f.	Tries to attract attention through smiling and eye contact or (if visually impaired child) through other body language				
	g.	Responds differently to strangers versus familiar people				
(9)	h.	Participates in games				
	i.	Repeats activity that is laughed at				
	j.	Initiates game playing				
(12)	k.	"Gives" things to others upon request (same as 9k)				
	l.	Shares spontaneously with adults				
(15)	m.	Shows affection (hugs, kisses)				
	n.	Tries to please others				

Age (Months)		Curriculum Sequences	Date:	Date:	Date:	Date:
(18)	o.	Plays alongside other children—some exchange of toys				
	p.	"Helps" in simple household tasks—imitates				
(21)	q.	"Performs" for others				
	r.	Tries to comfort others in distress				
(24)	s.	Shares spontaneously with peers				
	15.	**Self-Direction**				
(12)	a.	Moves away from Mom in same room				
	b.	Moves away from Mom to nearby area				
(15)	c.	Makes choices—has preferred toys, foods, and so forth				
(18)	d.	Plays alone with toys for 15 minutes				
(21)	e.	Explores different areas of own home				
(24)	f.	Explores unfamiliar places with mother present				
	16.	**Feeding**				
	a.	Sucks from nipple smoothly				
(3)	b.	"Roots" toward food or objects infrequently				
	c.	Bites down on spoon infrequently				
	d.	Gags infrequently, only when appropriate				
	e.	Munches food (chewing up and down)				
	f.	Development of tongue movements				
(6)	g.	Pulls food off spoon with lips				
	h.	Holds own bottle (omit for breast-fed babies)				
	i.	Drinks from cup held by adult				
	j.	Tolerates junior or mashed table foods without gagging				
	k.	Cleans lower lip with teeth				
(9)	l.	Chews with a rotary/side-to-side action				
(12)	m.	Finger feeding				
	n.	Holds and drinks from cup				
(15)	o.	Brings spoon to mouth, gets food off				
	p.	Scoops food from dish onto spoon				
(18)	q.	Chews well				

Age (Months)		Curriculum Sequences	Date:	Date:	Date:	Date:
(21)	r.	No longer uses bottle or breast				
(24)	s.	Distinguishes between edible and nonedible substances				
	17.	**Grooming**				
(15)	a.	Cooperates in hand-washing				
(18)	b.	Cooperates in toothbrushing				
(21)	c.	Washes own hands				
(24)	d.	Wipes nose if given a handkerchief (or cooperates if cannot get hands to nose)				
	18.	**Dressing**				
(12)	a.	Cooperates in dressing and undressing				
(15)	b.	Removes loose clothing (socks, hats, untied shoes)				
(18)	c.	Unties shoes, hats, as an act of undressing				
	d.	Unzips own clothing as appropriate				
(21)	e.	Puts on hat				
(24)	f.	Puts on loose shoes or slippers				
	19.	**Reaching and Grasping**				
	a.	Moves arms actively when sees or hears object				
(3)	b.	Bats at object at chest level				
	c.	Grasps object placed in his or her hand (not reflexive grasp)				
	d.	Reaches out and grasps objects near body				
	e.	Displays extended reach and grasp				
(6)	f.	Rakes and scoops small objects (fingers against palm)				
	g.	Releases 1 object to take another				
	h.	Grasps, using thumb against index and middle finger				
	i.	Uses inferior pincer grasp (thumb against side of index finger)				
	j.	Uses index finger to poke				
(9)	k.	Uses neat pincer grasp (thumb against tip of index finger)				
	20.	**Object Manipulation**				
	a.	Looks at hand (or toy) to one side				

Age (Months)	Curriculum Sequences	Date:	Date:	Date:	Date:
	b. Looks at or manipulates toy placed in hands at midline				
	c. Brings toy and hand into visual field and looks at them when toy is placed in hand (may move head or hand), or moves toy to mouth or midline (if a visually impaired child)				
(3)	d. Watches hands at midline—actively moves and watches result				
	e. Plays with own feet or toes				
(6)	f. Glances from 1 toy to the other when toy is placed in each hand, or plays alternately with the toys				
	g. Reaches out for toys and picks them up when both toys and hands are in visual field (modify for visually impaired children)				
	h. Reaches out for toys and gets them when toys, but not child's hands, are in child's visual field (modify for visually impaired children)				
(9)	i. Looks toward object and visually directs reach or adjusts reach to get noisy object (if has no functional vision)				
	20. Object Manipulation (continued) **I. Form manipulation**				
(15)	a. Places large round form in form board				
(18)	b. Places square form in form board				
	c. Places round and square forms in correct holes when they are presented simultaneously				
(21)	d. Places triangular form in hole				
	e. Places round, square, and triangular forms in form board when they are presented simultaneously				
	f. Completes simple puzzles				
(24)	g. Places correct forms in form ball				
	II. Block patterns				
(12)	a. Imitates building a 2-block tower				
	b. Imitates building a 3-block tower				
(15)	c. Imitates building a 6-block tower				
(18)	d. Imitates building a "chair" with blocks				
(21)	e. Imitates building 2 or more patterns of blocks				
	III. Drawing				
	a. Holds large writing utensil and marks with it				
(15)	b. Scribbles spontaneously				

Age (Months)	Curriculum Sequences	Date:	Date:	Date:	Date:
(18)	c. Makes single vertical stroke in imitation				
(21)	d. Shifts from scribble to stroke and back again in imitation				
	e. Imitates vertical and horizontal strokes				
(24)	f. Imitates circular strokes				
	IV. Placing pegs				
	a. Removes small round pegs from holes				
	b. Puts 1 large round peg in hole				
(15)	c. Puts 2 or more large round pegs in holes				
	d. Puts 1 small round peg in hole				
(18)	e. Puts 5 to 6 small pegs in holes (completes task)				
(21)	f. Puts square peg in hole				
(24)	g. Puts square pegs in holes (completes task)				
	V. Putting in and taking out				
	a. Removes objects from container by reaching into container				
(12)	b. Puts 1 or 2 objects in container				
	c. Puts many (6+) objects into container (completes task)				
(15)	d. Puts small objects through small hole in container				
(18)	e. Puts many (6+) small objects through small hole (completes task)				
	21. Bilateral Hand Activity				
	a. Bats at objects at chest level				
(3)	b. Raises both hands when object is presented— hands partially open				
	c. Brings hands together at midline				
	d. Places both hands on toy at midline				
(6)	e. Transfers object from hand to hand				
(9)	f. Claps hands				
(12)	g. Plays with toys in midline; one hand holds toy and the other manipulates				
	h. Pulls pop beads or balls apart at midline				
(15)	i. Holds dowel in one hand and places ring over it				
	j. Puts pencil through hole in piece of cardboard				
(18)	k. Removes loose wrappers				

Age (Months)		Curriculum Sequences	Date:	Date:	Date:	Date:
	l.	Unscrews small lids				
(21)	m.	Puts loose pop beads together				
(24)	n.	Strings 3 large beads				
	22.	**Gross Motor Activities: Prone (On Stomach)**				
	a.	Lifts head, freeing nose; arms and legs flexed				
(3)	b.	Lifts head to 45° angle, with arms and legs semi-flexed				
	c.	Extends arms, legs, head, and trunk in prone position				
	d.	Bears weight on elbows in prone position				
	e.	Rolls from stomach to back				
	f.	Reaches while supported on one elbow				
	g.	Supports self on hands with arms extended and head at 90°				
(6)	h.	Pivots in prone position				
	i.	Pulls forward on stomach				
	j.	Pulls self to hands and knees				
	k.	Rocks forward and backward in all-fours position				
(9)	l.	Plays with toys in an asymmetrical half-sitting, half–side-lying position				
	m.	Moves forward (creeps) on hands and knees				
(12)	n.	Raises one hand high while on hands and knees				
	o.	Crawls up stairs				
(15)	p.	Crawls down stairs, backward				
	23.	**Gross Motor Activities: Supine (On Back)**				
	a.	Turns head from side to side in response to visual and/or auditory stimuli while in supine position				
	b.	Bends and straightens arms and legs				
	c.	Brings hands to mouth				
(3)	d.	Maintains head in midline position while on back				
	e.	Reaches out with arm				
	f.	Feet in air for play				
(6)	g.	Rolls from back to stomach				

Age (Months)		Curriculum Sequences	Date:	Date:	Date:	Date:
	24.	**Gross Motor Activities: Upright**				
(3)	a.	Head steady when held				
(6)	b.	Holds trunk steady when held				
(9)	c.	Moves to sitting position from stomach or all-fours position				
	d.	Sits alone				
	e.	Pulls self to standing position				
	f.	Steps sideways holding a support				
	g.	Stoops to pick up toy while holding on to a support				
	h.	Removes hands from support and stands independently				
(12)	i.	Takes independent steps				
(15)	j.	Moves from hands and knees, to hands and feet, to standing				
	24.	**Gross Motor Activities: Upright (continued)** **I. Stairs**				
	a.	Walks up stairs with railing				
(18)	b.	Walks down stairs with railing				
(21)	c.	Walks up stairs without railing, placing both feet on 1 step at a time				
(24)	d.	Walks down stairs without railing, placing both feet on 1 step at a time				
		II. Balance				
(18)	a.	Stands on one foot while hands are held				
(21)	b.	Walks with one foot on the walking board and one foot on the floor				
	c.	Stands on one foot without help				
(24)	d.	Walks on line independently, following the general direction				
		III. Jumping				
(21)	a.	Jumps off floor with both feet				
(24)	b.	Jumps off step with both feet				
		IV. Posture and locomotion				
	a.	Walks sideways				
(18)	b.	Walks backward				

59

Age (Months)		Curriculum Sequences	Date:	Date:	Date:	Date:
	c.	Squats in play				
(21)	d.	Runs stiffly				
(24)	e.	Runs well				

Developmental Progress Chart

Name: _____

Dates: _____

Legend:
- ▨ No norms available.
- ■ Items beyond this point are necessary only for certain populations (see Assessment Log).

	Sequence	0 – 3 mo.	3 – 6 mo.	6 – 9 mo.	9 – 12 mo.	12 – 15 mo.	15 – 18 mo.	18 – 21 mo.	21 – 24 mo.
Cognition	1. Tactile Integration and Manipulation	a	b c	d e f	g	h		k	
	2. Auditory Localization and Object Permanence	a b c	d e	f g				j	
	3. Visual Pursuit and Object Permanence	a b c d e	f	g	h			i k	l
	4. Object Permanence (Visual-Motor)	a b c		d e f g	h	i j		l m	n
	5. Spatial Concepts	a b	c d	e	g	i	j k	l	
	6. Functional Use of Objects and Symbolic Play	a b	c d e	f g	h	i	j	k	l
	7. Control over Physical Environment	a	b c	d	e	f	g	h	i
	8. "Readiness" Concepts						a b	c d	e f g
Communication/ Language	9. Responses to Communication from Others	a b	c d e f g	h i	i j k	l m	n o	q r s	t u v
	10. Gestural Imitation	a	b	c d e	f	g h	i	j	
	11. Gestural Communication	a b	c d e	g h i	j	k	l	m n	o
	12. Vocal Imitation	a b c d	e f g h	e f	g	h i	j	k	l
	13. Vocal Communication	a b c	d e f g h	i j	k	l m n	o p	q r s	t u v
S.S./A.ª	14. Social Skills	a b c	d	e f g	h i	j k	l m n o	p q	r s
	15. Self-Direction	a	b	c d e f	g h		e	e	f
Self-Help	16. Feeding	a b	c d e f g	h i j k l	a b	m	n o	p q	r s
	17. Grooming	a	b	c			a b	c	d
	18. Dressing	a b c d	e f g	g h i		a b	c	d e	f g
Fine Motor	19. Reaching and Grasping	a b	c d e f	g h i j k	I, II, III, IV	a	b	c d	e f g
	20. Object Manipulation	a b c d	e f	g h i	V, a b	c d	d	d e	e f
	21. Bilateral Hand Activity	a b c d	c d e f g h	i j k l	g	h i	I, j k	II, l m	III, n
Gross Motor	22. Gross Motor Activities: Stomach	a b	c d e	f	m n	o	IV, a	b	c d
	23. Gross Motor Activities: Back	a b c d	c d e f g				a	a b	c d
	24. Gross Motor Activities Upright	a	b	c	d e f g h i	j	a b	c d	e

ª S.S./A. = Social Skills/Adaptation.

Curriculum
Sequences

1.

Tactile Integration and Manipulation

ALTHOUGH IT HAS LONG been recognized that tactile stimulation is important to infant development, items related to tactile exploration are rarely included in infant curricula. This is probably because most curricula have been based on the developmental milestones included in standardized tests and the fact that milestones pertinent to the acceptance of tactile stimulation have been hard to identify. The items included in the first part of this sequence come primarily from the Callier-Azusa Scale (Stillman, 1977), prepared for deaf-blind youngsters. Field-test experience suggests that these items are the least ordinal of any in the curriculum. Therefore, it is important to check all 0- to 12-month items in every child to determine appropriate intervention. It is also crucial to remember that many handicapped children demonstrate very atypical responses to tactile stimulation. Some are "defensive," withdrawing from or showing distress at any light touch. Others are underresponsive, apparently unaware of any stimulus until it reaches a painful level. Many become fascinated, in a stereotypic way, with particular stimuli. Such problems should be called to the attention of an occupational or physical therapist.

REFERENCE

Stillman, R. (Ed.). (1977). *The Callier-Azusa Scale.* Dallas: Callier Center for Communication Disorders, University of Texas.

1. Tactile Integration and Manipulation

a. Responds differently to warm/cold, rough/smooth
b. Permits soft, smooth textures to be rubbed on hands, feet, or body; or moves own body over such textures
c. Reacts to tactile stimulation with movement
d. Permits hands, feet, or body to be moved over rough-textured surfaces; or moves them over these surfaces spontaneously
e. Explores objects with fingers
f. Plays in water
g. Finds object hidden in textured material
h. Plays with soft-textured materials
i. Spreads soft materials with fingers
j. Spreads firmer materials with hands
k. Pokes or plays with clay

AREA: **1. Tactile Integration and Manipulation**
BEHAVIOR: 1a. Responds differently to warm/cold, rough/smooth

Position of Child: Any position that decreases abnormal posturing and maximizes responses
Materials: Objects with a wide variety of textures, some of which are metal and can be warmed or
cooled rapidly (e.g., a piece of indoor-outdoor carpet, spoon, fabric scraps sewn on a foam cube)

Teaching procedures	Steps for learning/evaluation
When bathing or dressing the child, and the child is either naked or has just been diapered, gently rub different objects over child's skin for brief periods. Try the palms of hands, face, abdomen, soles of feet, arms, legs, and so forth, waiting for a few seconds after each stimulation to observe the child's response. Vary stimuli. If child makes any response to indicate he or she has felt the stimulus item, continue touching or rubbing with it until child stops responding. Then try a high contrast stimulus to the same area (e.g., after using a rough piece of carpet or washcloth, try a piece of velvet or a metal spoon). Continue these activities as a part of dressing and play. If the youngster is physically handicapped, be sure to include stimulation of the palms of the hands as sensitivity may be reduced in this area (relaxation exercises may be necessary to get the hand open for stimulation).	***Record*** + if the child: 1. Makes any response (change in activity, visual searching, vocalization, withdrawal, and so forth) to a stimulus (it may be helpful to record which stimuli bring forth + and − responses and which stimuli produce withdrawal or other negative responses); and 2. Makes any different response to the second stimulus presented. ***Criterion:*** Child responds differently to the two stimuli presented; 3 of 3 trials in 2 consecutive sessions.

Note: The items in the Tactile Integration and Manipulation sequence are presented here roughly in the order of their emergence in normal children. The order may vary considerably in handicapped children. Several of the items may be worked on at one time, integrating them into daily care routines for the child.

AREA: **1. Tactile Integration and Manipulation**
BEHAVIOR: 1b. Permits soft, smooth textures to be rubbed on hands, feet, or body;
or moves own body over such textures

Position of Child: Any position that facilitates responding
Materials: A variety of soft, smooth toys and objects (stuffed animals, powder puffs, etc.)

Teaching procedures	Steps for learning/evaluation
Stimulate the child as in item 1a, but focus on soft, smooth objects and rub back and forth for about 15–20 seconds. If child withdraws from light touch or gentle rubbing with these objects, try stimulating with a firmer touch. If child tolerates the firmer touch, stimulate in that manner several times a day for at least 1 week. Then try a slightly lighter touch. Continue until child tolerates and/or enjoys gentle rubbing on hands, arms, abdomen, legs, *and* face.	***Record*** + if the child: 1. Does not react negatively to stimulation by a soft, smooth toy. ***Criterion:*** Child permits soft, smooth textures to be rubbed on hands, feet, or body; 3 trials in 3 consecutive sessions.

AREA: **1. Tactile Integration and Manipulation**
BEHAVIOR: 1c. Reacts to tactile stimulation with movement

Position of Child: Any position that facilitates a response
Materials: A variety of toys made from different-textured materials (e.g., furry, coarse, smooth)

Teaching procedures	Steps for learning/evaluation
Rub a textured object lightly over face, hands, arms, or legs in a place where clear responses have been elicited in the past. Observe the child for any movement. Stimulate again and move the stimulus item away from and back toward the child, talking about what you are doing (e.g., "What was that? Let's see if we can find it"). With *motorically impaired* children, precede tactile stimulation with a period of preparation: 1. With *spastic* children, do relaxation activities. 2. With *hypotonic* children or those very slow to respond, try some "rough" play, perhaps bouncing or tickling, prior to stimulation; once child is moving on his own, pause and resume the item.	*Record* + if the child: 1. Moves within 5 seconds after being stimulated by a textured object. *Criterion:* Child moves part of his or her body within 5 seconds following the initiation of tactile stimulation; 3 consecutive trials on 3 different days.

AREA: **1. Tactile Integration and Manipulation**
BEHAVIOR: 1d. Permits hands, feet, or body to be moved over rough-textured surfaces; or moves them over these surfaces spontaneously

Position of Child: Any position that facilitates a response
Materials: Various rough-textured toys or materials; things that have not been used on previous items

Teaching procedures	Steps for learning/evaluation
Present an object to the child, rubbing your hands over it and talking about it, using words like "scratchy," "bumpy," and so forth, as appropriate. Place the object within easy reach of the child and observe. If child does not spontaneously explore the object by feeling it in some way, gently approach the child and rub it over a part of his or her body that you have observed to be sensitive to touch. Make a game of it! "Here is the bumpy one"; "Here comes the scratchy one!"; and so on.	*Record* + if the child: 1. Spontaneously feels the object; *or does not* pull away or otherwise react negatively to stimulation but *does* indicate attention to the stimulation. *Criterion:* Child permits rough-textured surfaces to be moved over parts of his or her body; 3 trials in each of 3 consecutive sessions.

Note: If the child cannot or does not feel rough-textured objects spontaneously, but does permit stimulation with them, it is particularly important to continue providing stimulation every day. Emphasize the fingers and palms of the hands, where sensitivity may be decreased.

AREA:　**1. Tactile Integration and Manipulation**
BEHAVIOR:　1e. Explores objects with fingers

Position of Child:　Any position that facilitates movement in upper extremities (side-lying, over a roll, seated, etc.)
Materials:　Objects with holes or indentations in them and that have different textures

Teaching procedures	Steps for learning/evaluation
Show an object to the child while feeling it and poking your fingers into it. Give the toy to the child (put it in child's lap, place it in child's hands, or wherever it will make it easier for child to explore it with his or her fingers). Observe child's actions. If child does not explore with his or her fingers, rub them over the objects. Tap on child's wrist or elbow if necessary to loosen fingers. Help child poke fingers into the holes. Talk about what you are doing. Try different objects and see if any spontaneous exploration occurs. Make it fun for the child!	*Record* + if the child: 1.　Runs his or her fingers over an object to explore it spontaneously. *Criterion:*　Child spontaneously explores 3 different objects when they are presented to him or her in a play situation; 3 consecutive days.

AREA:　**1. Tactile Integration and Manipulation**
BEHAVIOR:　1f. Plays in water

Position of Child:　Any position that facilitates movement; may be on a roll with hands in water in a tub
Materials:　Water in a large basin

Teaching procedures	Steps for learning/evaluation
Place the child's hands or body in water. Help child splash the water, push it back and forth, and play in it. Observe child's behavior. Play games with child, allowing child to splash you. Do not frighten child by splashing his or her face. Drip water from your hands onto child's nose or cheeks.	*Record* + if the child: 1.　Splashes or moves spontaneously in water or after being splashed. *Criterion:*　Child plays or splashes in water; 3 separate occasions.

Note:　This is an item for daily use regardless of whether or not the child becomes actively involved. Have fun with it!

AREA: **1. Tactile Integration and Manipulation**
BEHAVIOR: 1g. Finds object hidden in textured material

Position of Child: Any position that facilitates use of the upper extremities
Materials: A tub full of a mixture of beans, rice, macaroni, and so forth, and a favorite toy

Teaching procedures	Steps for learning/evaluation
Place the child's hands in the tub and help him or her to feel the materials. Place a smooth toy in tub and push it into the bean (or rice or macaroni) until practically covered. Then pull toy out (or let child pull it out); then put it back in and hide it completely. Say, ''Where did the _____ go? Can you get it?'' If child makes no attempt to uncover the toy: Take the child's hands and push the beans aside until the toy is uncovered. Pull it out and let the child play with it. Talk about what you are doing. Hide it again. If there is still no searching behavior, repeat the game, just covering toy partially; *and* Play the game of covering the child's own hand(s) with the beans, rice, or macaroni, so the child must pull his or her hands out to uncover them.	***Record*** + if the child: 1. Plays in the materials (squeezes, drops, rakes, etc.); and 2. Puts his or her hands in the tub, pushes beans (and the like) out of the way until the toy is uncovered. ***Criterion:*** Child finds an object hidden in a tub of textured material; 3 of 3 trials in 2 consecutive sessions.

Notes: Many *motor-impaired* children enjoy this activity but are unable to move enough to ever uncover objects. Help them to continue playing in the material and try changing the contents of the tub fairly often to change the stimulation offered by it.
   Reasonable care should be taken to prevent children from putting items from the tub into their mouths. They could cause choking.

AREA: **1. Tactile Integration and Manipulation**
BEHAVIOR: 1h. Plays with soft-textured materials

Position of Child: Any position that facilitates movement of upper extremities
Materials: Finger paint, cooked cornstarch mixture (the consistency of pudding), canned imitation cream, and so forth

Teaching procedures	Steps for learning/evaluation
Many children demonstrate enjoyment of soft-textured materials by feeling their food, squishing soap through their hands, and so on. If this is observed spontaneously, the item does not need to be worked on. If it is not:	***Record*** + if the child: 1. Touches the material briefly; and 2. Explores or plays with the material for 2 to 3 minutes.

(continued)

Teaching procedures	Steps for learning/evaluation
Put a glob of materials in front of the child and help child put his or her fingers into it and explore it. If child withdraws or cries, do not force child to keep his or her hands in contact with the material, but show the child what you can do with it. Then leave child for a few minutes to explore and play independently. Take material away if child continues to object, and try again a few days later. Add a few drops of food coloring to light-colored materials and demonstrate color mixing.	***Criterion:*** Child plays with soft-textured material for 3 to 5 minutes on 3 separate days (see note below).

Note: This item should be continued periodically throughout the first 3 years of life or longer, since it helps children manipulate with their fingers and provides tactile input. At times you may wish to increase the tactile input by adding sand, oatmeal, or some other "gritty" substance.

AREA: **1. Tactile Integration and Manipulation**
BEHAVIOR: 1i. Spreads soft materials with fingers

Position of Child: Any position that maximizes the child's ability to manipulate materials with his or her hands (preferably sitting/standing at a table; prone-stander)
Materials: Paper (try using variety of shapes, colors, and textures), finger paints, paper towels and water for clean-up

Teaching procedures	Steps for learning/evaluation
Show the paints to the child if he or she has vision. Otherwise, describe the paints ("slippery," "wet," "cool," and different colors). Allow child to touch the paints, getting some on his or her fingers/hands. If child shows no interest in touching the paint, gently prompt child to do so. Take child's hand in yours and guide child to touch the paint. Show child how to spread the paint on paper. If child does not respond to your modeling by "painting" also, prompt child again by taking his or her hand and making a simple design on the paper with the paint on the child's fingers. Initially, put plastic bags over the hands of extremely tactilely defensive children. Vary the textures of paints with flour, water, sand, and so on. Try painting with pudding instead of finger paint. Paint with foam made by mixing dishwashing detergent with water and paint and then whipping with an egg beater.	***Record*** + if the child: 1. Touches paint; and 2. Spreads soft materials with fingers. ***Criterion:*** Child spreads materials on paper and maintains interaction with the materials for at least 15 seconds; 3 trials within 5 days.

Note: Any of these activities can be used with small groups of children to facilitate sharing and communication.

AREA: **1. Tactile Integration and Manipulation**
BEHAVIOR: 1j. Spreads firmer materials with hands

Position of Child: Any position that maximizes the child's ability to manipulate materials with his
or her hands
Materials: Paste or thick glue, thinned-down clay, paper towels and water for cleanup, paper or
other material on which to spread substances

Teaching procedures	Steps for learning/evaluation
Show the materials to the child if he or she has vision. Otherwise describe the paints ("slippery," "wet," "cool," and different colors).	*Record* + if the child:
	1. Spreads soft materials on paper; and
	2. Spreads firmer materials with hands.
Allow child to touch the different materials, getting some on his or her fingers/hands.	*Criterion:* Child spreads firmer materials on paper and maintains interaction with the materials for at least 30 seconds; 3 trials within 5 days.
If child shows no interest in touching, gently prompt child to do so. Take child's hand in yours and guide child while touching the materials.	
Show child how to spread the materials on paper. If child does not respond to your modeling by also "painting," prompt child again by taking his or her hand and making a simple design on the paper with one of the materials on the child's fingers.	
Have child spread peanut butter on wafers with his fingers.	
Have child spread a water-base glue on the paper and sprinkle fine materials over the glue, such as glitter, bark, small noodles to create a preservable piece of artwork.	
Vary the textures of the glue with flour, sand, salt, sugar, ground-up bark, and so forth.	

Note: This is a good group activity.

AREA: **1. Tactile Integration and Manipulation**
BEHAVIOR: 1k. Pokes or plays with clay

Position of Child: Any position that maximizes the child's ability to manipulate materials with his
or her hands (preferably sitting/standing or prone position with weight on elbows)
Materials: Salt dough, starch dough, play-dough, or clay

Teaching procedures	Steps for learning/evaluation
Hand the child a piece of clay or dough.	*Record* + if the child:
Take a piece yourself and show child that you can roll it, pat it flat, stretch it, and the like.	1. Moves hands about clay or dough; and
	2. Pokes or plays with clay or dough.

(continued)

Teaching procedures	Steps for learning/evaluation
Reinforce child for imitating you and/or for playing with the clay in any manner. If child merely holds the clay, physically assist child to poke, pat, and stretch it. Reinforce all attempts to do something purposeful with the clay. *Variations:* Vary colors of the clay by mixing in tempera paints. Vary textures of clay by adding sand, flour, water, oil, soap, and so on. Try making imprints in the dough with fingers, hand, foot, or small objects (footprints/handprints can be saved and later painted). For a child who imitates well, try modeling several activities with the clay such as patting flat, rolling into ball, making a snake.	***Criterion:*** Child pokes at or plays with clay or dough independently for at least 30 seconds; 3 consecutive trials within 5 days.

2.

Auditory Localization and Object Permanence

T HIS SEQUENCE BEGINS with items related to a child's ability to identify the direction from which sounds come and concludes with the use of these localization skills to demonstrate the concept of object permanence. Items *h, i,* and *j* are designed specifically for visually impaired children who cannot proceed through sequence 4 (Object Permanence); these items should be omitted for other children.

Visually impaired children have been noted to be very slow to develop the concept of object permanence, perhaps because they are denied the common appearance-disappearance-reappearance experiences (e.g., peek-a-boo games) of visually intact children and because they cannot demonstrate object permanence in the standard fashion (removing a cloth from an item after having seen it covered). Thus, the last two items (*i* and *j*) of the sequence are designed both to teach object permanence and to provide a means of demonstrating acquisition of the concept.

2. Auditory Localization and Object Permanence

a. Quiets when noise is presented

b. Visually searches for sound

c. Turns head and searches or reaches for ear-level sound while lying down

d. Turns head or reaches toward source of sound while sitting; sound at ear or shoulder level

e. Turns head toward sound and looks or reaches directly at noisemaker when noise presented at ear or shoulder level

f. (1) Looks directly at noisemaker when sound presented to the side and at waist level

(2) *Alternate for visually impaired children* Reaches in the right direction when sound presented below ear level

g. (1) Turns head and looks back and forth to 2 sounds

(2) *Alternate for visually impaired children* Reaches to either side for noisy object

Omit the following for children physically able to do sequence 4.

h. *For visually impaired children* Reaches for object after it no longer makes noise

i. *For visually impaired children* Reaches for object that no longer makes noise, at midline and on both sides, above and below shoulder level

j. *For visually impaired children* Reaches correctly for object that has made noise in several places

AREA: **2. Auditory Localization and Object Permanence**
BEHAVIOR: 2a. Quiets when noise is presented

Position of Child: Any position, though lying on back or side may make observations easier
Materials: Noisy, shiny toys; variety of noisemakers

Teaching procedures	Steps for learning/evaluation
Make sounds with a noisemaker about 6 inches from the child's ear at ear level, presenting the sound for 3–5 seconds. Begin with toys that make relatively soft and pleasant sounds.	**Record** + if the child:
	1. Makes a slight response to a noise presented; and
Observe child for any indication of decreased activity in response to the sound presented.	2. Quiets when a noise is presented.
	Criterion: Child quiets when a noise is presented; 3 of 3 trials on 3 different days.
Present the same noisemaker to the other ear and observe.	
Change noisemakers and try again. If child does not respond, gradually increase the loudness of the sounds presented.	
This response cannot be "taught," although you can experiment with noises in the everyday environment to see what appears to promote a response from the child. For example, have a very quiet room with no talking prior to presenting a noise, or place the child in different positions, varying the distance from the child's ear, and so on.	
When child quiets, bring noisemaker in view (or touch it to child) and make the noise again.	

Note: Some children habituate (stop responding) to sounds rather quickly, so it is important to change noisemakers frequently and to try this item for only 5–6 trials at one time.

AREA: **2. Auditory Localization and Object Permanence**
BEHAVIOR: 2b. Visually searches for sound

Position of Child: Any position, though lying on back or side may make observations easier
Materials: Noisy, shiny toys; variety of noisemakers with interesting appearance

Teaching procedures	Steps for learning/evaluation
Make sounds with a noisemaker about 6 inches from the child's ear at ear level, presenting the sound for 3–5 seconds. Begin with toys that make relatively soft and pleasant sounds.	**Record** + if the child:
	1. Searches for a sound after having object brought to midline to gain attention; and
	2. Visually searches for a sound without efforts to increase visual attention.

(continued)

Teaching procedures	Steps for learning/evaluation
Observe child's eyes. If child does not look back and forth for the noise, attract the child's attention to the object by bringing it to the midline, make the noise, and then move it back and forth, trying to get visual attention to it. Then remove, wait for a few seconds, and present to the side again. Wiggle the toy again to make the sound and create a visual effect when the child does search for it.	*Criterion:* Child visually searches for a sound; 3 of 3 trials on 3 different days.

Note: Many *visually impaired* children will respond with searching movements even if they cannot see the object. Look for this response as an indication of attention. If a *visually impaired* child does not visually search, look for other indications of attention (e.g., moving head from side to side or increased motor activity).

AREA: **2. Auditory Localization and Object Permanence**
BEHAVIOR: 2c. Turns head and searches or reaches for ear-level sound while lying down

Position of Child: On back if possible, or in a side-lying position
Materials: Noisy toys; those that have gotten best responses in previous items

Teaching procedures	Steps for learning/evaluation
Make sounds with a noisemaker about 6 inches from the child's ear at ear level and observe child's response. Randomly try one ear then the other, changing toys frequently and giving only 6–8 trials at a time. If child does not turn head to find the toy, gain visual attention at midline; then move the toy to one side slowly while making noise. Remove the toy, wait for a few seconds, then present it again at the side. If this procedure does not work after 5 trials, present the sound at the side and gently turn child's head in the direction of the sound. As child's head is turned, make the sound again and move the object in such a way as to produce an interesting visual effect. For the *visually impaired* child, touch the child's face with the toy as you make a noise with it. Move toy and make the sound on one side, guiding the child's hand to the toy. Remember to keep making the noise until you get or prompt a response.	*Record* + if the child: 1. Turns head in direction of a sound (and visually searches) when lying down, having had assistance to make the response on the previous trial; *or* searches with hand on correct side after having had hand guided to object on previous trial; and 2. Turns head or reaches in direction of sound without assistance on the previous trial. *Criterion:* Child turns head in the direction of sound and visually searches or reaches, when lying down; 4 of 5 trials on 3 different days.

Note: It may be unclear whether or not a child is visually impaired. Always work for the visual response first. If you cannot get any indication of looking at the noisemaker, use the modification for *visually impaired* children.

AREA: **2. Auditory Localization and Object Permanence**
BEHAVIOR: 2d. Turns head or reaches toward source of sound while sitting; sound at
ear or shoulder level

Position of Child: Seated with sufficient support to maximize head control (e.g., leaning on adult,
in an infant seat, or using some other appropriate, adapted equipment
Materials: Variety of noisy toys

Teaching procedures	Steps for learning/evaluation
Make sounds with a noisemaker about 6 inches from the child's ear at ear level and observe child's response. Randomly try one ear then the other, changing toys frequently and giving only 6–8 trials at a time. If child does not turn head to find the toy, gain visual attention at midline; then move the toy to one side slowly while making noise. Remove the toy, wait for a few seconds, then present it again at the side. If this procedure does not work after 5 trials, present the sound at the side and gently turn child's head in the direction of the sound. As child's head is turned, make the sound again and move the object in such a way as to produce an interesting visual effect. For the *visually impaired* child, try to have the noisemaker at ear level and at the side (the easiest position for localization), but also enough forward of the body to facilitate reaching. Experiment to find the best position.	***Record*** + if the child: 1. Turns head to source of sound when sitting, following a trial in which assistance was given; and 2. Turns head or reaches toward sound without assistance on previous trial. ***Criterion:*** Child turns head or reaches toward the source of a sound, when sitting; 4 of 5 trials on 3 different days.

Note: Reaching for a sound is much slower to develop than reaching for something that can be seen. Totally blind children will be slow to develop this response.

AREA: **2. Auditory Localization and Object Permanence**
BEHAVIOR: 2e. Turns head toward sound and looks or reaches directly at noisemaker
when noise presented at ear or shoulder level

Position of Child: Any position, though seated with sufficient support or prone over a bolster (or the
like) may work best; adult must be able to see child's eyes
Materials: Variety of noisy toys

Teaching procedures	Steps for learning/evaluation
Make sounds with a noisemaker about 6 inches from the child's ear at ear level and observe child's response. Randomly try one ear then the other, changing toys frequently and giving only 6–8 trials at a time.	***Record*** + if the child: 1. Turns head towards sound and fixes eyes on noisemaker. ***Criterion:*** Child turns head toward the sound and fixes eyes on noisemaker; 4 of 5 trials on 3 different days.

(continued)

Teaching procedures	Steps for learning/evaluation
When child turns head toward the sound, note whether child looks directly at the noisemaker. If child does not look at noisemaker, wiggle it to attract child's attention. As soon as child looks at it, place it in child's hand, touch it to him or her, pat the child, or otherwise "reward" the child's having looked at it. Omit this item for seriously *visually impaired* children. Continue working on reaching toward sounds.	

AREA: **2. Auditory Localization and Object Permanence**
BEHAVIOR: 2f(1). Looks directly at noisemaker when sound presented to the side and at waist level

Position of Child: Any position that allows head movement; adult must be able to see the child's eyes
Materials: Variety of noisy toys

Teaching procedures	Steps for learning/evaluation
Make sounds with a noisemaker on one side of the child about 8 inches from body at waist level. Repeat on the other side, then randomly present the sound on each side on successive trials. Many children will turn their heads to the correct side but will not look down to find the noisemaker. If this occurs, make the noise again while the head is turned. If child still does not look down, bring the toy up to eye level and make noise with it as child visually tracks it down to waist level. Attract child's attention to you back at midline; then make the noise again at waist level and observe child's response. Whenever child does look at the toy, be sure to move it, give it to the child, or otherwise let the child know it was good that he or she found the noise-maker. See item 2f(2) for *visually impaired* youngsters.	***Record*** + if the child: 1. Turns head toward sound and looks at noisemaker when sound is below ear level, after having visually tracked noisemaker to waist on previous trial; and 2. Turns head and looks to side and then down at noisemaker without help on previous trial; and 3. Looks directly at noisemaker when sound presented to the side at waist level. ***Criterion:*** Child turns head toward sound and looks toward noisemaker when sound presented below ear level; 4 of 5 trials on 3 different days.

AREA: **2. Auditory Localization and Object Permanence**
BEHAVIOR: 2f(2). *Alternate for visually impaired children*   Reaches in the right direction when sound presented below ear level

Position of Child: Any position that allows freedom of movement of head and arms
Materials: Variety of noisy toys

Teaching procedures	Steps for learning/evaluation
Make sounds with a noisemaker on one side of the child about 8 inches from body at waist level. Repeat on the other side, then randomly present the sound on each side on successive trials. If child reaches in the right direction, move the toy to child's body until it touches child at the level where it was presented. Place child's hands over it, encouraging child to feel it. If child does not reach, guide his or her hand to the toy while it is making noise. Place the toy in child's hands and let child explore it.	***Record*** + if the child: 1. Reaches to the correct side when sound presented to one side at waist level after assistance on the previous trial; and 2. Reaches in right direction when sound presented to one side at waist level, without assistance on previous trial. ***Criterion:*** Child turns head toward the sound or reaches in the correct direction when sound presented below ear level; 4 of 5 trials on 3 different days.

AREA: **2. Auditory Localization and Object Permanence**
BEHAVIOR: 2g(1). Turns head and looks back and forth to 2 sounds

Position of Child: Any position that maximizes head control and reaching
Materials: Noisy, shiny toys; variety of noisemakers

Teaching procedures	Steps for learning/evaluation
Hold a different toy in each hand 10–11 inches from the child's midline, at ear level but 6–8 inches in front of face. Make a noise with one of the toys for 2–3 seconds. Pause about a second, then make a noise with the other toy. Repeat twice, making 3 presentations with each sound. Repeat this same procedure with 2 different toys. If child does not look at the toy that is making the noise, move the toy to midline to get visual attention and then take it slowly back to the side. Then make noise with the second toy. Bring it to midline and back if necessary to get attention. Wait and be quiet for 5 seconds or more, then do it again. After child has looked back and forth at the 2 toys, place the toys in the child's hands and let the child manipulate or touch them.	***Record*** + if the child: 1. Looks back and forth between 2 sounds after assistance through visual teaching; and 2. Looks back and forth toward 2 different sounds without assistance ***Criterion:*** Child looks back and forth to 2 sounds; 4 of 5 trials on 3 different days.

AREA: **2. Auditory Localization and Object Permanence**
BEHAVIOR: 2g(2). *Alternate for visually impaired children*   Reaches to either side for
noisy object

Position of Child: Any position that maximizes use of upper extremities
Materials: Noisy toys with interesting textures or shapes

Teaching procedures	Steps for learning/evaluation
Make a noise with a toy in easy reaching distance anywhere between shoulder and hip level. When child reaches for toy and gets it, let child play briefly with it. Then present a noise on the other side. Alternate sides and positions of objects to promote good localization of the objects. Continue making the noise as the child gropes to find it. Do not physically assist child unless child loses interest or gets too frustrated to continue reaching.	***Record*** + if the child: 1. Reaches and grasps noisy objects on either side. ***Criterion:*** Child reaches correctly when toys are presented randomly to each side; 3 of 3 trials.

AREA: **2. Auditory Localization and Object Permanence**
BEHAVIOR: 2h. *For visually impaired children*   Reaches for object after it no longer
makes noise

Position of Child: Any position that maximizes head control and reaching
Materials: Noisy toys

Teaching procedures	Steps for learning/evaluation
Make a noise briefly (to one side at waist level) and wait for the child to reach. If child does not, make the sound a little longer, then stop and again wait. Continue increasing the duration of the sound until child does reach, but always stop the sound before child actually touches the object. Make the sound again only if necessary to maintain child's effort to find the object. If the child cannot reach, seek help from the physical or occupational therapist in identifying a response that indicates the child knows the toy is there, even though it can no longer be heard.	***Record*** + if the child: 1. Continues to reach for object on either side when it stops making noise (noise is sustained until reaching is initiated); and 2. Reaches for object on either side after it no longer makes noise (noise sufficiently brief that reaching begins after noise stops). ***Criterion:*** Child reaches for object on either side after it no longer makes noise; 3 of 4 trials on 3 separate days.

AREA: **2. Auditory Localization and Object Permanence**
BEHAVIOR: 2i. *For visually impaired children* Reaches for object that no longer makes noise, at midline and on both sides, above and below shoulder level

Position of Child: Any position that maximizes head control and reaching
Materials: Noisy toys

Teaching procedures	Steps for learning/evaluation
Make a noise briefly with a toy and encourage the child to find it. If child does not, make the sound a little longer, then stop and wait again. Increase the duration of sound as necesary to promote reaching. Vary the place the toy makes noise—from above shoulder level to hip level, from far left through midline to far right. Talk to the child as he or she searches, to give the child feedback on how well he or she is doing. Make slight noise to aid in a continued search if necessary. Always give the toy to the child to play with when the child touches it; or make a game of letting the child touch it, praising the child, and moving it to another location, whichever approach is best suited to the child.	*Record* + if the child: 1. Reaches for object after it no longer makes noise. (Record placement of object.) *Criterion:* Child reaches for objects above and below shoulder level, to right, left, and at midline; 2 of 3 trials each location on 3 separate days.

AREA: **2. Auditory Localization and Object Permanence**
BEHAVIOR: 2j. *For visually impaired children* Reaches correctly for object that has made noise in several places

Position of Child: Any position that maximizes head control and reaching
Materials: Noisy toys

Teaching procedures	Steps for learning/evaluation
Make a brief noise with a toy in one location; move the toy; and make the noise again. Observe where the child reaches. If the child reaches toward where the toy first made noise, make the noise in the last location again and wait for the child to find the toy. Talk about what happened ("I fooled you; it's over here. Can you find it?"). Gradually work up to moving the toy rapidly through 4 places, making the noise momentarily in each. Reward the child's attempts with praise and letting the child have the toy to play with. Make this game fun!	*Record* + if the child: 1. Reaches for toy in the right direction when it has made noise in 2 places; and 2. Reaches for toy in the right direction when it has made noise in 3 or 4 places. *Criterion:* Child reaches for toy in the right direction when it has made noise in 3 or 4 places; 4 of 5 trials on 3 separate days.

3.

Visual Pursuit and Object Permanence

AN INFANT'S ABILITY to explore the world visually is critical to the development of many concepts in the first 2 years of life. The beginning items in this sequence should be worked on with children under 2 months of age, even if they have been diagnosed as blind, since such a diagnosis is frequently incorrect in this age period.

The first part of this sequence (items *a–g*) focuses on developing visual tracking skills and on instilling the understanding that objects continue to exist even if they disappear for a few seconds (i.e., the beginnings of object permanence). The latter part of the sequence (items *h–l*) is specifically designed for children whose handicaps prevent them from reaching, grasping, and removing covers from objects to indicate that they know the objects exist even if they are out of sight for long periods of time (a stronger indication of the concept of object permanence). Thus, items *h* through *l* should be omitted for children able to do sequence 4 (Object Permanence).

3. Visual Pursuit and Object Permanence

a. Visually fixates for at least 3 seconds
b. Visually tracks object from side to side
c. Visually tracks object from forehead to chest
d. Visually tracks object moving in a circle
e. Gaze lingers where object disappears
f. Continues to look at caregiver when caregiver's face is covered with a cloth
g. Looks at cover under which object has disappeared

Omit the following for children physically able to do sequence 4.

h. Looks to the correct place when object is hidden in 1 of 2 places
i. Looks to the correct place when object is hidden in 1 of 3 places
j. Looks at correct place for toy after seeing it covered in 3 places successively
k. Looks successively at 2 different covers until toy is found that was hidden from the child's view (invisible displacement)
l. Looks systematically at 3 different covers until toy is uncovered that was hidden from the child's view

AREA: **3. Visual Pursuit and Object Permanence**
BEHAVIOR: 3a. Visually fixates for at least 3 seconds

Position of Child: Lying on back, perhaps with head supported in midline
Materials: A variety of interesting objects (e.g., silver ball, red pom-pom, red flashlight, small checkerboard, or bull's-eye drawn on a card)

Teaching procedures	Steps for learning/evaluation
Hold object 6–10 inches from the child's eyes, wiggling it gently to attract child's attention. Repeat with a different object.	**Record** + if the child: 1. Looks at the object momentarily; and 2. Looks at the object for 3 seconds or more. **Criterion:** Child looks at a toy for 3 seconds or longer; 3 of 5 trials involving different objects on 2 separate days.

Note: It is very difficult to get some handicapped infants to look at anything. They often respond first to something very shiny like a Christmas ball. Once a child responds to one object, it is alright to begin working on tracking (item *b*), but it is important to keep working on this item until the child looks at several kinds of objects.

AREA: **3. Visual Pursuit and Object Permanence**
BEHAVIOR: 3b. Visually tracks object from side to side

Position of Child: Sitting or lying on back
Materials: A variety of toys for which the child has shown preference

Teaching procedures	Steps for learning/evaluation
Present an object at midline about 12 inches from the baby's face. When the child looks at it, move it slowly to one side and then to the other (5–8 inches to either side). Use additional objects in the same manner. Hold child's attention and have child track from side to side for 2 to 3 minutes. If child does not track at all, try: Varying the distance of the object from the infant's eyes; Using noisy objects; Varying the illumination of the room and the brightness of the object.	**Record** + if the child: 1. Moves eyes a few inches to right or left but not smoothly across midline; and 2. Moves eyes to edge of the visual field (6–8 inches) and back to center but not across the midline; and 3. Moves eyes from side to side to follow an object across midline. **Criterion:** Child visually tracks at least 3 different objects from one side of visual field to the other, crossing the midline smoothly; 3 consecutive trials in 2 consecutive sessions.

Note: Watch for preferred toys or objects and change toys and objects frequently.

AREA: **3. Visual Pursuit and Object Permanence**
BEHAVIOR: 3c. Visually tracks object from forehead to chest

Position of Child: Sitting or lying on back
Materials: Bright, shiny objects, especially those that the child has shown preference for previously

Teaching procedures	Steps for learning/evaluation
Present a bright object directly in front of the child about 18 inches from his or her eyes, or closer if you know the child cannot see at that distance. When the child looks at the object, move it slowly to the level of the child's chest and then back to the height of his forehead. Use a variety of objects, following this procedure for about 3 to 5 minutes. If child does not track the object with his or her eyes at all, try one of the following until child begins to do so: Vary the distance of the object from the child's eyes and the speed with which it is moved. Wiggle the toy to try to get and maintain the infant's visual attention to it. Use noisy objects. Vary the illumination of the room and the brightness of the object.	*Record* + if the child: 1. Tracks a short distance (2–3 inches); and 2. Tracks from chest to forehead. *Criterion:* Child visually tracks at least 3 different objects at midline from chest level to forehead level and back again; 3 consecutive trials in 2 consecutive sessions.

AREA: **3. Visual Pursuit and Object Permanence**
BEHAVIOR: 3d. Visually tracks object moving in a circle

Position of Child: Sitting or lying on back
Materials: A variety of bright, shiny objects that the child has shown preference for on previous sequence items

Teaching procedures	Steps for learning/evaluation
Present an object at midline and attract child's attention by jiggling or moving it. Move the object slowly to one side and then move it in a circle a little larger than the child's face. Use a variety of objects, continuing for 3 to 5 trials with each of several different objects for 2 to 3 minutes. If child does not track the object for the full circle, do one or more of the following until the complete track is achieved:	*Record* + if the child: 1. Tracks at least half of a full circle; and 2. Tracks the full circle. *Criterion:* Child tracks at least 3 different objects through a full circle; 3 consecutive trials on 3 different days.

(continued)

Teaching procedures	Steps for learning/evaluation
Vary the speed with which you make the circle (generally make it slower). Wiggle the item gently as it moves. Use a noisy toy, but make noise with it only at 3 or 4 points in the circle, making noise at the points where the child looks away. Vary the room illumination and object brightness.	

AREA: **3. Visual Pursuit and Object Permanence**
BEHAVIOR: 3e. Gaze lingers where object disappears

Position of Child: Any position that facilitates head support and good visual tracking. For some children, side-lying may be the best position. If so, have them on a table or other support where an object can fall from view.
Materials: A variety of bright, shiny objects that the child has shown preference for previously

Teaching procedures	Steps for learning/evaluation
Present an object at midline and move it slowly to the left and then to the right. Let the object drop from sight at the child's right. As it drops, talk about it (e.g., "Where's the ball? Where did it go?"). Wait 5 seconds and make the object reappear at the same place ("Here it is!"). When the child looks at the object or at the place it disappeared, bring it closer for the child to inspect. Help the child touch it, make a noise with it, or do something else pleasing with it. Repeat the procedure, but drop the toy on child's opposite side. Vary the side where the object disappears randomly as you continue this activity. Make the teaching sequence as much fun as possible. You may, on some trials, want to substitute yourself for the object, making this a kind of peek-a-boo game.	***Record*** + if the child: 1. Gazes for 3 seconds or more at the point the object or person disappeared. ***Criterion:*** Child's gazes lingers for 3 to 5 seconds in the direction where an object (or person) has disappeared from sight; 3 of 4 trials in 2 different sessions.

AREA: **3. Visual Pursuit and Object Permanence**
BEHAVIOR: 3f. Continues to look at caregiver when caregiver's face is covered
with a cloth

Position of Child: Any position in which the infant can observe you
Material: Cloth or a light scarf

Teaching procedures	Steps for learning/evaluation
Place a cloth over your head, saying something like, "Where's_____?" Wait 5 seconds and remove the cloth quickly. Note whether or not the child is still looking at you (or have someone else observe child's behavior and record how long the child looks, *or* have a small hole in the cloth through which you can see the child and note how long he or she looks). If child does not maintain his or her gaze toward you, do one of the following: Continue talking to the child for the full time your face is covered, to see if this maintains attention; gradually reduce the amount of talking you do. Cover your head for only 1 or 2 seconds (a brief enough time to maintain child's gaze). Gradually increase the time your head is covered; always come out from under the cloth smiling, talking, or laughing, to reinforce the child for looking.	***Record*** + if the child: 1. Maintains gaze toward you for 5 or more seconds. ***Criterion:*** Child maintains gaze toward caregiver for at least 5 seconds when caregiver's face is covered; 3 of 5 trials in 2 consecutive sessions.

AREA: **3. Visual Pursuit and Object Permanence**
BEHAVIOR: 3g. Looks at cover under which object has disappeared

Position of Child: Any position that facilitates looking
Materials: A variety of toys the child enjoys and a variety of covers (e.g., handkerchiefs, cup, can, box)

Teaching procedures	Steps for learning/evaluation
Place an object in front of the child. Name it and talk about it. Cover it completely, call the child's name, or do something to get the child to look away from the cover momentarily; then ask, "Where is the _____?" As soon as child looks at the cover, say, "That's right, it is under the_____." Lift the cover and show it to the child, talk about it more, help child play with it, and so forth. Repeat the procedure with the same toy and a different cover. If child does not look at the cover, say, "Let's find the_____. I'll bet it's here under this_____ (lift cover). Here it is!" Then repeat the procedure. For some trials you may cover something edible and allow the child to eat it after he or she uncovers it.	***Record*** + if the child: 1. Continues looking for 5 seconds at the cover under which an object has been hidden. ***Criterion:*** Child continues looking for 5 seconds at the cover under which an object has been hidden; 3 of 4 trials in 3 consecutive sessions.

AREA: 3. Visual Pursuit and Object Permanence
BEHAVIOR: 3h. Looks to the correct place when object is hidden in 1 of 2 places

Position of Child: Any position that facilitates head support and sustained looking
Materials: Several of the child's favorite toys; cloths, boxes, or other objects that can be used to cover the toys

Teaching procedures	Steps for learning/evaluation
Place 2 crumpled cloths or 2 containers in front of the child. Take a toy and let the child hold it. Rub it against the child or otherwise get child to focus attention on it. Place the toy under one of the covers as you talk about what you are doing (be sure child watches what you do). Call child by name and try to get him or her to look at you; then say, "Where is the _____?" If child looks at the right cover, take it off and give the toy to him or her, rub the child with it, or do whatever is pleasing to the child. Repeat several times, randomly changing the side under which the toy is hidden. *Do not just alternate sides.* If child does not look at the right cover, say, "Uh-oh, that's not where it is," lift the other cover, and show the child. Lower the cover slowly and ask again where it is. Make sure child is watching!	***Record*** + if the child: 1. Looks to the correct cover under which object has been hidden *after* a correction by the teacher; and 2. Looks to the correct cover without a correction. ***Criterion:*** Child looks to correct cover 4 of 5 trials on 3 separate days.

Note: It is important to teach the child to look at you or at something else at the midline momentarily before looking for the toy. Only in this way can you be sure the child is looking for the toy and not merely tracking the movements of your hand. This may be facilitated by carefully returning your hands to the midline after you have placed the cover over the toy.

AREA: 3. Visual Pursuit and Object Permanence
BEHAVIOR: 3i. Looks to the correct place when object is hidden in 1 of 3 places

Position of Child: Any position that facilitates head support and a sustained gaze
Materials: Several favorite toys and a variety of "covers"

Teaching procedures	Steps for learning/evaluation
Place 3 crumpled cloths or 3 containers in front of the child. Take a toy and let the child hold it. Rub it against the child or otherwise get child to focus attention on it. Place the toy under one of the covers as you talk about what you are doing (be sure child watches what you do).	***Record*** + if the child: 1. Looks to the correct cover under which object has been hidden *after* a correction by the teacher; and 2. Looks to the correct cover without a correction by the teacher.

(continued)

Teaching procedures	Steps for learning/evaluation
Call child by name and try to get him or her to look at you; then say, "Where is the _____?" If child looks at the right cover, take it off and give the toy to him or her, rub the child with it, or do whatever is pleasing to the child. Repeat several times, randomly changing where the toy is hidden. If child does not look at the right cover, say, "Uh-oh, that's not where it is," lift the correct cover, and show the child. Lower the cover slowly and ask again where it is. Make sure the child is watching! Place the 3 covers far enough apart so that you can tell when the child is looking at each one. This may involve placing the covers on a shelf or table near the child's eye level so that you can easily see his eyes.	***Criterion:*** Child looks to correct cover 4 of 5 times in 2 separate sessions.

Note: It is important to teach the child to look at you or at something else at the midline momentarily before looking for the toy. Only in this way can you be sure the child is looking for the toy and not merely tracking the movements of your hand. This may be facilitated by carefully returning your hands to the midline after you have placed the cover over the toy.

AREA: 3. Visual Pursuit and Object Permanence
BEHAVIOR: 3j. Looks at correct place for toy after seeing it covered in 3 places successively

Position of Child: Any position that facilitates head support and a sustained gaze
Materials: Favorite toys and a variety of covers

Teaching procedures	Steps for learning/evaluation
Place 3 covers in front of child in a position to allow good judgment of where he is looking. Show child the toy, then slowly place it under one cover. Take it out, let child see it, and place it under the next cover in sequence. Then let child see it as you take it out and put it under the last cover. Leave it there and show the child that your hand is empty. Get child to look at you and then ask where the toy is. If child looks toward the right cover, uncover the toy and give it to the child, rub him or her with it, or let child enjoy it in some way. On the second trial place the object under the covers in the opposite direction, then mix up the order. On subsequent trials, randomly vary the order.	***Record*** + if the child: 1. Looks at correct place when a toy is placed successively under 3 covers. ***Criterion:*** Child looks at the correct place to find a toy after it has been successively placed under 3 covers; 4 of 5 trials on 3 separate days.

(continued)

Teaching procedures	Steps for learning/evaluation
If child does not look correctly, lift the cover where child looked and say, "Oops, it's not there. Look again." Always let child see toy at the end of the trial.	
If necessary, exaggerate your actions as you hide and uncover the toy under the cloths, moving the toy up close to the child after each uncovering.	
Be sure to play with the child, showing surprise and reinforcing child for finding the object.	

AREA: **3. Visual Pursuit and Object Permanence**
BEHAVIOR: 3k. Looks successively at 2 different covers until toy is found that was hidden from the child's view (invisible displacement)

Position of Child: Any position that facilitates head control and sustained gaze
Materials: Favorite toys; a variety of covers (scarfs, boxes, etc.)

Teaching procedures	Steps for learning/evaluation
Place 1 cover in front of the child. Show child a small object. Close your hand around it so that he or she cannot see the toy. Put your hand under the cover and leave the toy. Bring out your hand, closed so that it still looks like the toy is in it. Then open your hand and say, "Uh-oh, it's gone! Where is the _____?" Uncover toy as soon as child looks toward the cover. If child does not look, attract his or her attention to the cover, remove it, and talk about finding the toy.	***Record*** + if the child: 1. Looks at the cover when asked where the toy is (1 cover present); and 2. Looks at covers in succession until the toy is found (2 covers); and 3. Looks toward covered item after it has been covered while out of view of the child.
As soon as child is looking for the toy under 1 cover, introduce 2 covers, far enough apart to allow easy judgment of when he or she is looking from one to the other. Put the toy in your hand. Place your hand under one of the covers momentarily, then move it under the second cover. Leave the toy under the second cover.	***Criterion:*** Child looks at covers in succession until a toy is found that was hidden out of view of the child; 4 of 5 trials in 2 separate sessions.
Show your empty hand or the empty box to the child and say, "Uh-oh, it's gone, where is the _____?"	
Lift the cover the child looks at. If the cover is not the one with the item under it, say, "That isn't where it is. Where could it be?" Remove the correct cover when he looks at it.	
Repeat the item. Vary hiding the toy under the right or left covers.	

Note: It is important to vary the covers or containers used on different days. Also, play other hiding games during the course of the day to increase the generalization of this skill and the precision of "eye pointing."

AREA: **3. Visual Pursuit and Object Permanence**
BEHAVIOR: 3l. Looks systematically at 3 different covers until toy is uncovered that
was hidden from the child's view

Position of Child: Any position that facilitates head control and sustained gaze
Materials: Favorite toys; a variety of covers

Teaching procedures	Steps for learning/evaluation
Place 3 covers in front of the child, far enough apart to allow good judgment of where he or she is looking. Place a small toy in your hand or in a box. Close your hand or turn the box so child cannot see the toy. Move it under one cover, out and under the next, then out and under the third, leaving the toy under one of the covers. *Do not* allow toy to be seen between covers. Show child your empty hand or the empty box and say, "It's gone, where's the _____?" Wherever child looks, lift the cover. If it is not there, say, "Oops, not there. Now where should I look?" Continue until the toy is found, then let child have, hold, or feel the toy. Repeat, leaving toy in a different place (not always the last place you had your hand). Each time the toy is found, reward with the toy and lots of excitement! Do not always work from right to left or left to right. Vary the order of going under the covers, but always go under all three. If child stops looking after one incorrect response, encourage child by saying "Look at this one. Let's try it."	***Record*** + if the child: 1. Looks at the covers successively until the toy is uncovered; and 2. Looks systematically at the covers until the toy is uncovered (e.g., looks at the covers in order from left to right, from right to left, in the order the hand went under the covers, or in the reverse of the order the hand went under the covers). ***Criterion:*** Child uses a systematic search pattern in looking at the covers to find a toy that was hidden from his or her view; 4 of 5 trials on 2 separate days.

4.

Object Permanence (Visual-Motor)

T HE CONCEPT OF OBJECT permanence, that is, the recognition that an object continues to exist although it can no longer be seen, touched, or heard, was considered by Jean Piaget (1952) to be critical for the development of language and abstract thought. This sequence of the curriculum includes procedures useful for teaching this concept to children who do not have serious visual impairments and who have the ability to use their hands and arms sufficiently well to reach, grasp, pull, and release. Prerequisites for the sequence include items *a* through *e* in sequence 3 (Visual Pursuit and Object Permanence) *and* items *a* through *g* in sequence 19 (Reaching and Grasping).

REFERENCE

Piaget, J. (1952). *The origins of intelligence in children*. New York: International Universities Press.

4.   Object Permanence (Visual-Motor)

a. Pulls cloth from face
b. Pulls cloth from caregiver's face
c. Uncovers partially hidden toy
d. Removes cover from fully hidden toy
e. Finds toy hidden under a cover when 2 covers are present
f. Finds toy when it is hidden under 2 covers, alternately
g. Removes cover when object is hidden under 1 of 3 covers
h. Finds toy hidden under 3 superimposed covers
i. Finds toy after seeing it covered in 3 places successively
j. Finds object after searching under 2 covers (invisible displacement)
k. Finds object after systematic search under 3 covers (invisible displacement)

AREA: **4. Object Permanence**
BEHAVIOR: 4a. Pulls cloth from face

Position of Child: Infant can be supine or sitting, so long as one hand is free to reach and grasp
Materials: A soft cloth, diaper, towel, or scarf

Teaching procedures	Steps for learning/evaluation
When you have the child looking at you, play a peek-a-boo game by putting a cloth over his or her face. Say something like, ''Where's baby?'' Pause to allow child the opportunity to remove the cloth on his or her own. Continue the game through several trials, smiling as child removes the cloth. If child does not pull off the cloth, you remove it, saying, ''There you are!'' Attend to the child's movements that suggest he or she is attempting to remove the cloth. Assist movements in removing the cloth, decreasing your help as child is able to do more of it.	*Record* + if the child: 1. Reaches for cloth or shakes head to free it; and 2. Removes cloth successfully and completely. *Criterion:* Child completely removes a cloth placed over his or her face in a peek-a-boo game; 3 consecutive trials on 3 different days.

Note: Some children may show fear of the cloth. You may have to gradually introduce the cloth by initially placing it on only part of the face or body or by using a ''see-through'' cloth.

AREA: **4. Object Permanence**
BEHAVIOR: 4b. Pulls cloth from caregiver's face

Position of Child: Infant can be supine or sitting, so long as at least one hand is free to reach and
          grasp
Materials: A soft cloth, diaper, towel, or brightly colored scarves

Teaching procedures	Steps for learning/evaluation
Item 20g in Object Manipulation is a prerequisite skill for this behavior. Talk to and smile at the child. When you have his or her attention, place cloth over your face saying, ''Where's _____ [Mommy, caregiver's name, etc.]?'' Pause to allow child to remove the cloth. Say, ''Here I am!'' Repeat. If child does not pull the cloth off, remove it yourself and smile at the child as your face reappears. Then put it over your face again. Attend to movements that indicate child's attempt to remove the cloth. Assist him or her, decreasing your help as the child is able to do more of it.	*Record* + if the child: 1. Reaches for cloth; and 2. Removes cloth successfully and completely. *Criterion:* Child completely removes a cloth placed over adult's face in a peek-a-boo game; 3 consecutive trials on 3 different days.

Note: If the child seems afraid when the caregiver/trainer covers herself or himself with cloth, help child adapt to the game by hiding behind sheer scarves, toys, chairs, and so on, in a gamelike manner.

AREA: **4. Object Permanence**
BEHAVIOR: 4c. Uncovers partially hidden toy

Position of Child: A sitting position with hands free to manipulate object
Materials: A variety of toys or objects, including ones for which child has shown preference (e.g.,
   car keys, small rubber doll, brightly colored beads, small metal car); also a variety of covers
   (e.g., cloths, cushions, scarves, etc.)

Teaching procedures	Steps for learning/evaluation
Show an object to the child. Cover more than half of the object with a cloth. If child removes the cloth, allow him or her to have the toy. If child seems to show no interest in the toy after it is hidden, say, "Where's the _____ [car, cookie, etc.]? Oh, there it is!" as you cover and uncover it several times. Then partially cover again and wait for a response. If child does not remove the cloth, but makes movements that indicate an attempt, assist him or her, gradually decreasing your help as child is better able to do the task. Try using varied objects the child likes (e.g., musical or noisemaking objects, or food under the cloth).	***Record*** + if the child: 1. Removes cover and gets toy after demonstration; and 2. Removes cover and gets toy spontaneously (or grabs visible part of toy and pulls it from under the cover). ***Criterion:*** Child removes a cloth and gets a toy; 3 of 5 trials on 3 different days.

Note: Encourage searching for objects in play throughout the day. For example, as you put the child to bed, cover all but one leg of
a favorite teddy bear and say, "Now, what did I do with Teddy? Where's your bear?"

AREA: **4. Object Permanence**
BEHAVIOR: 4d. Removes cover from fully hidden toy

Position of Child: A sitting position with hands free
Materials: A variety of toys or objects, including ones for which the child has shown preference
   (e.g., car keys, small rubber doll, brightly colored beads, small metal car); also a variety of
   covers (e.g., cloths, cushions, scarves, etc.)

Teaching procedures	Steps for learning/evaluation
Present an object to the child. Allow child to watch while you "hide" it under a cloth. Encourage child to find it, saying, "Where are the keys?" If child is successful, you can also present objects to him or her, placing them under an upside-down shoe box or pot. Allow him to watch the procedure and recover the object. Another variation is to place the object in a shoe box or pot and cover with the lid.	***Record*** + if the child: 1. Removes cloth and gets object. ***Criterion:*** Child will remove the cover from a completely hidden toy and play with the toy; 3 consecutive trials on 2 different days.

(continued)

Teaching procedures	Steps for learning/evaluation
If child does not remove the cover, you remove it; then direct child's attention to the object and "hide" it again. If you find child does not look for toys, he or she may look for food. Be sure to hide something you know he or she wants. Praise child for getting the object, not just for pulling the cloth.	

Note: Sometimes children will learn to pull cloths off the table in order to get praise from an adult, rather than to get the toy beneath. Observe the child's behavior carefully. Try to hide objects that are sufficiently interesting, so that finding them will be rewarding.

AREA: **4. Object Permanence**

BEHAVIOR: 4e. Finds toy hidden under a cover when 2 covers are present

Position of Child: Any position that facilitates reaching and grasping
Materials: A variety of different covers (scarves, pan lids, box tops, etc.) and a variety of interesting toys

Teaching procedures	Steps for learning/evaluation
Hide a toy under one cover. When child uncovers it, introduce a second cover a few inches away from the first. Take the toy and hide it under the second cover while the child watches. If child looks under the cover where he or she previously found the toy, say, "Oops, where is it?" Encourage child to remove the other cloth. If child does not, you do it to show the child where it is. Repeat the procedure, letting him find the toy under one cover and then introducing a second cover. Vary the side to which the second cover is introduced. (If using scarves or cloths, be sure to bunch them up so that the shape of the toy is not visible.)	***Record*** + if the child: 1. Gets toy from under the second cover only after searching first under the in-correct cloth; and 2. Gets toy from under the correct cover immediately. ***Criterion:*** Child gets a toy hidden under a second cover on the first trial; 3 of 3 trials on 2 separate days.

AREA: **4. Object Permanence**

BEHAVIOR: 4f. Finds toy when it is hidden under 2 covers, alternately

Position of Child: Any position in which one hand is free to reach and grasp
Materials: A variety of covers and interesting toys

Teaching procedures	Steps for learning/evaluation
Place 2 covers in front of the child and let him or her watch as you put the toy under one of them. Allow child to recover the item. Say, "Where did the keys go? There they are!"	***Record*** + if the child: 1. Finds toy hidden under 1 of 2 covers.

(continued)

Teaching procedures	Steps for learning/evaluation
Then hide the toy under the other cover. Continue to alternate, letting child play with the toy between trials. Introduce new toys to maintain interest.	*Criterion:* Child finds toy alternately hidden under 1 of 2 covers; 3 consecutive trials on 2 separate days.

Note: Hiding and finding objects can be great fun for a child. Help child enjoy the play aspect of these tasks.

AREA: **4. Object Permanence**
BEHAVIOR: 4g. Removes cover when object is hidden under 1 of 3 covers

Position of Child: Any position in which one hand is free to reach and grasp objects
Materials: A variety of toys and covers

Teaching procedures	Steps for learning/evaluation
Place 3 covers on the table or floor. Put the toy under one of these and allow the child to look for it. On subsequent trials vary the placement of the toy. If child looks in the wrong place, encourage child to continue looking. It is common for children to look in the place they looked on the previous trial before they learn to look directly in the correct place.	*Record* + if the child: 1. Finds toy after 1 or 2 errors; and 2. Finds toy without error. *Criterion:* Child finds toy under 1 of 3 covers without errors; 4 of 5 trials on 2 separate days.

AREA: **4. Object Permanence**
BEHAVIOR: 4h. Finds toy hidden under 3 superimposed covers

Position of Child: Any position in which at least one hand is free to reach and grasp
Materials: A variety of covers and interesting toys

Teaching procedures	Steps for learning/evaluation
Present a toy. When the child looks at it, place it on the table. Cover it with 3 covers added one at a time. Allow the child to remove the covers until the object is found. It may be helpful to hold each cover lightly and unobtrusively to prevent child from removing all three at once. Try additional objects with the same procedure several times. If child does not retrieve the toy, try: Repeating the procedure slowly, explaining that you are hiding the toy and that the child is to find it; Demonstrating the removal of 1 cover at a time saying, "Is it under here? No . . . Is it here?" and so forth; Physically assisting child as needed to remove the 3 covers.	*Record* + if the child: 1. Removes 1 or 2 covers but not the 3rd; and 2. Finds toy immediately. *Criterion:* Child removes 3 superimposed covers to get toy; 3 of 4 trials on 2 separate days.

AREA: 4. Object Permanence
BEHAVIOR: 4i. Finds toy after seeing it covered in 3 places successively

Position of Child: Any position with at least one hand free to reach and grasp object
Materials: A variety of different covers and interesting toys

Teaching procedures	Steps for learning/evaluation
Place 3 covers in front of the child. Introduce a favorite toy or interesting object. Allow the child to watch as you put the object under the cover on the child's left. Bring the toy out from under the cover, letting the child see it. Then put it under the second cover. Repeat, leaving the toy under the third cover. Allow the child to search for the toy. If the child does not look for the toy, demonstrate looking under each screen, saying, "Where did those keys go? There they are!"	**Record** + if the child: 1. Finds toy after 1 or 2 errors; and 2. Finds toy without error. **Criterion:** Child finds toy without error after seeing it covered in 3 places successively; 3 of 3 trials on 2 separate days.

AREA: 4. Object Permanence
BEHAVIOR: 4j. Finds object after searching under 2 covers (invisible displacement)

Position of Child: Any position that facilitates movement of the hands and arms and visual attention
Materials: A variety of toys or objects, including ones the child has shown a preference for.
Examples: small rubber doll, brightly colored beads, small metal car, plus a variety of covers (cloths, cushions, scarves, lids, etc.)

Teaching procedures	Steps for learning/evaluation
Place 1 cover on the table. Show the child a small object. When child looks at it, close your hand over it. Without the object being visible, slide your hand under the cloth and release object. Present your empty hand to the child, saying, "Where did it go?" Permit child to search under the screen for the object and uncover it. If child is successful, place a second cover on the table in view of and in reach of child. Again show the object to the child, then close your hand on it. Place your hand under first cover and slowly move it out and under the second cover. The child should see your hand between the first and second covers but not be able to tell whether the toy is still in it. Release the toy under the second cover and allow the child to search.	**Record** + if the child: 1. Finds toy when only 1 cover is present; and 2. Finds toy when 2 covers are present. **Criterion:** Child finds toy hidden under 1 of 2 covers; 3 trials in 2 different sessions.

(continued)

Teaching procedures	Steps for learning/evaluation
Repeat, but leave the object under the first cover, putting your hand under the second as a "trick." If child gives up after looking under one incorrect cover, encourage him to continue. Find the toy yourself, if necessary.	

Note: Use attractive objects and opaque covers. Emphasize the game aspect of the task.

AREA: **4. Object Permanence**

BEHAVIOR: 4k. Finds object after systematic search under 3 covers
(invisible displacement)

Position of Child: Any position that facilitates movement of hands and arms and visual attention
Materials: A variety of interesting small toys and a variety of covers

Teaching procedures	Steps for learning/evaluation
Place 3 covers on the table. Show the child a small toy. Close your hand over the toy and move your hand under the first cover. Pull out your hand (with the toy still inside but invisible to the child) and put it under the second cover. Repeat, and put it under the third cover. Leave the toy there. Bring out your hand and show the child it is empty. Ask where the toy is. Continue encouraging child to look, showing excitement when the child finds the toy. Repeat the procedure, leaving the toy under a different cover each time and varying the order in which you put your hand under the covers. Always move your hand under all 3 covers so that the child has no way of knowing where the toy was left.	*Record* + if the child: 1. Finds toy by searching randomly under the 3 covers; and 2. Finds toy by using a systematic pattern of search (e.g., works from one end to the other, searches in the order the hand was seen to go under the covers, or searches in the reverse order the hand was seen to go under the covers). *Criterion:* Child finds object after systematic search under 3 covers; 4 of 5 times on 2 separate days.

5.

Spatial Concepts

Two important cognitive tasks for infants to learn are: 1) where they are relative to the space around them, and 2) where objects in space are relative to one another. This sequence is directed toward the development of these concepts. Most of the items have a fairly strong motor component. Research evidence suggests that spatial concepts are most readily developed by the experience of actively moving through space; neither passive movement through space nor simply observing movement of objects and people through space are very effective in promoting a good sense of distance, spatial orientation, and spatial relationships.

For severely motorically impaired children, the items in this sequence will become increasingly inappropriate after item *d*. Curriculum users are encouraged to modify items to fit a child's motor capabilities to the extent possible, but also to be creative in designing alternative items that actively engage the child in the exploration of space, even if he or she cannot reach or locomote through it. Headsticks, scooter boards, and other devices that involve self-initiated and monitored movement but limited motor capabilities may be particularly useful to incorporate into alternative items.

5. Spatial Concepts

a. Shifts attention (visual fixation or body orientation) from 1 object to another
b. Looks for or reaches toward objects in sight that touch the body (omit for visually impaired children)
c. Looks for or reaches toward objects out of sight that touch the body
d. Looks for or reaches for objects that fall from view while making a noise
e. Looks for or reaches for objects that fall quietly from view
f. Looks or moves in the right direction for objects that fall and roll or bounce to new location
g. Searches for objects moved out of visual field or (for visually impaired children) away from midline

h. Retrieves toys from a container when they have been dropped through a hole in the top
i. Pulls string to get object from behind barrier
j. Reaches object from behind barrier
k. Moves self around barrier to get object
l. Retrieves objects from usual locations in another room
m. Puts objects away in correct places
n. Uses "tools" to deal with spatial problems (extends reach with a stick, extends height with a stool, etc.) (same as item 7i)

AREA: **5. Spatial Concepts**
BEHAVIOR: 5a. Shifts attention (visual fixation or body orientation)
from 1 object to another

Position of Child: Held on caregiver's lap, in infant seat, or any position that will facilitate
head-turning
Materials: A variety of small (3- to 5-inch) toys that are brightly colored and have different textures
(checkerboard patterns, foil balls, bells, rattles)

Teaching procedures	Steps for learning/evaluation
Present a toy to the child, holding it about 10 to 15 inches from his or her face, at eye level, and 6 to 8 inches to the left or right of midline. When child's attention is fixed on the object, present a second object at the same distance on the opposite side. Alternately shake or wiggle the 2 objects for 20 seconds. Observe whether the child shifts attention from one object to another (indicated by looking back and forth or moving head from side to side). On every trial in which the child fails to shift attention between the 2 objects, do one or more of the following until the response is achieved: Alternately move the items into the midline and closer to the child to attract his or her attention, and then move items back to original position. Position the second item next to the first item and then move it to its original position. Alternately present an item on either side, removing one as you present the other.	*Record* + if the child: 1. Looks at object or reaches for it within 10 seconds after it initially touches him or her. *Criterion:* Child looks at or reaches for objects within easy sight; 4 of 5 trials on 3 separate days.

Notes: Change the toys frequently so as to hold the child's attention. Make notes regarding which toys the child seems to prefer. Use these as preferred stimulus items for future teaching sessions. For *visually impaired* children, use toys that make pleasant but different noises. Emphasize the sounds made by the toy and reinforce the child for orienting toward them (turning the head or reaching).

AREA: **5. Spatial Concepts**

BEHAVIOR: 5b. Looks for or reaches toward objects in sight that touch the body
(omit for visually impaired children)

Position of Child: Any position that facilitates use of arms and hands

Materials: A variety of barriers common to environment (e.g., partially opened door, upholstered armchair, cardboard box); also, a variety of toys with strings attached (e.g., stuffed animal with long tail, toy with noise component such as pull-along xylophones)

Teaching procedures	Steps for learning/evaluation
Observe where child is looking and touch his or her body with one of the objects well within his or her line of vision. Note whether child looks at the toy. Talk about the toy, wiggle it, and place it in child's hand (or allow child to take it if he or she reaches for it). Touch child's body in another area outside of his or her direct line of vision but where child could easily see (on hand or leg, for example). Observe to see if child looks. Talk about the toy, wiggle it, and place it in his or her hand (or allow child to take toy if he or she reaches for it). On every trial in which the child fails to look or reach for the object, do one or more of the following until the response is achieved: Choose a different object and touch the child. Gently rub child's skin with the object or apply slightly more pressure as you touch him or her. Attract child's attention to the object at eye level. Then move it slowly to the place where it touched the child, trying to keep child's gaze on the object. Touch child again with it and talk about it as you rub object against him or her. Then place object in child's hand (or guide his or her hand to it). Physically guide the child's hand to the object. For the *visually impaired* or *physically handicapped* child, it is important to both guide the child's hand to the toy and talk about where the toy is, to promote a sense of body awareness and the body's relationship to space.	***Record*** + if the child: 1. Looks at object or reaches for it within 10 seconds after it initially touches him or her. ***Criterion:*** Child looks for or reaches for objects within easy sight; 4 of 5 trials on 3 separate days.

Note: Be sure child has tactile sensitivity in areas being stimulated.

AREA: **5. Spatial Concepts**
BEHAVIOR: 5c. Looks for or reaches toward objects out of sight that touch the body

Position of Child: Any position that facilitates looking
Materials: Objects with a variety of textures, shapes, and colors (e.g., bells, rattles, balls)

Teaching procedures	Steps for learning/evaluation
Touch object on the bare skin of the infant, outside his or her visual field (on the back of child's leg or arm, or on the side of his or her abdomen). Observe whether child looks for and/or reaches for the object. Vary objects and the places where the child is touched with them (e.g., legs, arms, trunk), again keeping the object from being seen by the child before it touches his or her body. On trials in which child fails to look at or reach for the object after being touched, bring the item into the child's view, get his or her attention to the object, and then touch area again. Physically guide child's hand to the toy if necessary. There is no difference between items 5b and 5c for severely *visually impaired* children. Credit both for criterion performance on 5b and move on to 5d.	*Record* + if the child: 1. Looks for or reaches toward object out of sight that touches body. *Criterion:* Child looks for or reaches toward object out of sight that touches body; 4 of 5 trials on 3 separate days.

AREA: **5. Spatial Concepts**
BEHAVIOR: 5d. Looks for or reaches for objects that fall from view while making a noise

Position of Child: Any position that facilitates looking
Materials: Objects that are visually interesting (bright colors, varied patterns) and that make noise (bells, rattles)

Teaching procedures	Steps for learning/evaluation
Hold an object at eye level, making sure child's attention is focused upon it. Drop item from view, making sure it makes a noise loud enough to be heard by the child and that it does not touch the child as it falls. Observe whether or not child searches visually or reaches for object in the direction of the sound made by the object as it fell. If child does not look or reach, hold the object at eye level; make a noise with it to attract child's attention; move it slowly downward to floor (or other	*Record* + if the child: 1. Looks or reaches toward object that falls noisily from view. *Criterion:* Child looks for or reaches for object that falls from view while making noise; 4 of 5 trials on 3 separate days.

(continued)

Teaching procedures	Steps for learning/evaluation
surface below waist level) and make the noise again. Physically assist child in reaching for the object, if necessary. After 2 or 3 trials, try dropping the object again and physically assist child to reach in the right direction if necessary.	
For *visually impaired* children, focus on the reaching response and always drop objects to one side, since sound localization is much more difficult at midline.	
Rely on looking responses in *physically handicapped* children.	

AREA: 5. Spatial Concepts

BEHAVIOR: 5e. Looks for or reaches for objects that fall quietly from view

Position of Child: Any position that facilitates looking

Materials: Objects that have bright visual qualities (e.g., Nerf ball, stuffed toy) and that make no noise when dropped. Vary the objects used and note those objects that are interesting enough to gain child's attention.

Teaching procedures	Steps for learning/evaluation
Hold an object at eye level, making sure the child's attention is on the object.	***Record*** + if the child:
Drop the object from the child's view.	1. Looks for or reaches for object when it drops quietly from sight.
Watch carefully to see if child attends to and follows the dropped object with a visual search for it. Also look for movement of the eyes with or without head movement, which may also indicate searching acitivity on the part of the child.	***Criterion:*** Child looks for or reaches for object that falls quietly from view; 4 of 5 trials on 3 separate days.
Vary the objects used and the positions from which objects are dropped (away from midline but easily within view of the child).	
If child does not look for or reach for the fallen object, hold object at midline eye level; slowly move object vertically out of sight of child. Move object slowly enough to allow child to follow object. Vary starting positions and objects used. Physically guide child to reach in the right direction.	
For *visually impaired* children: Give child a toy that does not make a noise when dropped. When child drops it, say, "Uh-oh, you dropped it. Can you find it?" Physically guide child's hand toward toy and help child pat the surface to find it. Talk about it as you do it.	
For the *physically handicapped* child who cannot reach, rely on visual responses and talk throughout about what is happening.	

AREA: **5. Spatial Concepts**

BEHAVIOR: 5f. Looks or moves in the right direction for objects that fall and roll or
bounce to new location

Position of Child: Any position that facilitates looking
Materials: Objects that combine visual and auditory stimulation and that, when dropped within the
visual field of the child, will bounce and/or roll from the child (e.g., squeaky toys, balls with
bells inside)

Teaching procedures	Steps for learning/evaluation
Hold the object at eye level, making sure that the child is visually attending to it. Drop the object within the child's view and in an area that allows it to bounce/roll while remaining in view of the child. If child does not look around to find the object, call his or her attention to where it is and say something about its having rolled or bounced. Try again with a different object, perhaps one that is larger and/or makes a noise as it rolls or bounces. For the *visually impaired* child, work on expanding the surface he or she "pats" when searching for an object that he or she drops. Talk about what is happening. Show excitement when child finds object.	*Record* + if the child: 1. Looks or moves in right direction for object that falls and then rolls/bounces away. *Criterion:* Child looks or moves in the right direction for object that falls and rolls or bounces; 4 of 5 trials on 3 separate days.

Note: Think about language concepts (e.g., "Uh-oh, where did it go?"; "Look over here"; "It fell down") as you do this item.

AREA: **5. Spatial Concepts**

BEHAVIOR: 5g. Searches for objects moved out of visual field or (for visually impaired
children) away from midline

Position of Child: Any position that facilitates visual searching and movement
Materials: Objects that are colorful and noisy (e.g., windup toys, friction cars), as well as objects
that do not make noise

Teaching procedures	Steps for learning/evaluation
Get the child's attention on an object at midline and at eye level. Move object slowly out of the visual field of the child (behind the child, behind you, or behind some other barrier). Vary the objects used as well as the speed and direction of movement of objects as they are moved from the child's visual field.	*Record* + if the child: 1. Searches for object after it has been moved away, returned, and is moved away again; and 2. Searches for object after it has been moved away. *Criterion:* Child searches for object moved out of visual field; 4 of 5 trials on 3 separate days.

(continued)

Teaching procedures	Steps for learning/evaluation
Watch for indications that the child knows where to look for the object (he or she tries to look or reach behind you or himself or herself, moves in the right direction, etc.).	
If child does not search in the right direction, make noise with the object behind the barrier, bring it back in view, and then move it away again. Change objects to maintain interest.	
For the *visually impaired* child, it may be necessary to just move an object from one side to the other, at first with the child's hand on it, then waiting for the child to reach at various positions. Continue to make noise with the object as the child searches for it.	

Notes: A *physically handicapped* child may "search" for objects out of the visual field with eye movements. In this case, look for fixation at the point where the object disappeared, perhaps alternating with fixations on the teacher. Children occasionally will protest or show distress at the loss of the object. Keep the activity gamelike and help youngsters to enjoy themselves.

AREA: **5. Spatial Concepts**
BEHAVIOR: 5h. Retrieves toys from a container when they have been dropped through a hole in the top

Position of Child: Any position that maximizes visual attention and fine motor activity
Materials: Toys with openings to drop objects in and an opening at bottom to retrieve them (e.g., Fisher-Price Mail Box, or several boxes with holes in the tops and toys to fit through the holes)

Teaching procedures	Steps for learning/evaluation
Drop 1 or more toys through the opening at the top of the container, saying, "Oops, where did it go?" Wait to see if the child lifts up the box to get the toy or opens the door of the mailbox toy to get the forms.	***Record*** + if the child: 1. Lifts box or opens door to retrieve toy immediately after demonstration; and 2. Lifts box or opens door to retrieve toy on any trial without demonstration.
If child does not seem to recognize that the toy can be retrieved from the bottom, show the child that it can and repeat. Physically assist the child in lifting the box or opening the door if necessary.	***Criterion:*** Child retrieves toys from a container when they have been dropped through a hole in the top; 4 of 5 trials on 3 separate days.
For the *visually impaired* child, the toys and containers may need to be large or brightly colored to facilitate learning. The blind child should be guided to feel the box; perhaps place one of the child's hands in the bottom as the child drops a toy through the top to feel it fall. An alternate activity would be to teach the child to open a variety of containers to find objects inside.	
The severely *physically handicapped* child may need to learn by observing and hearing the caregiver talk about the events.	

AREA: **5. Spatial Concepts**
BEHAVIOR: 5i. Pulls string to get object from behind barrier

Position of Child: Any position that facilitates use of arms and hands
Materials: A variety of barriers common to environment (e.g., partially opened door, upholstered
   armchair, cardboard box); also, a variety of toys with strings attached (e.g., stuffed animal with
   long tail, toy with noise component such as pull-along xylophones)

Teaching procedures	Steps for learning/evaluation
Show toy to child, being sure he or she is attending to and interested in toy. Place toy slightly out of child's reach and demonstrate pulling the string to obtain the toy. Hand the end of the string to the child and wait for child to pull toy to himself or herself. While child is watching, place toy behind a barrier with the string still visible. If child does not spontaneously pull the string, demonstarte pulling it in order to obtain the toy. Say something such as, "Let's pull the string to get the _____." Physically assist child to pull string if necessary. Replace toy behind the barrier and observe. Help the *visually impaired* child feel the barrier; talk about it; use more physical assistance. For the *physically handicapped* child who cannot reach, grasp, or pull, it will be necessary to demonstrate what happens as you pull the string. Talk throughout about what you are doing, using spatial words such as "up," "down," "behind," and so forth.	***Record*** + if the child: 1. Pulls string to get object within view; and 2. Pulls string to get an object from behind a barrier. ***Criterion:*** Child gets object from behind barrier by pulling a string; 4 of 5 trials on 3 separate days.

AREA: **5. Spatial Concepts**
BEHAVIOR: 5j. Reaches object from behind barrier

Position of Child: Any position that facilitates use of arms and hands
Materials: Any object that the child is particularly fond of, plus a variety of barriers available in the
   environment (e.g., partially opened door, upholstered chair)

Teaching procedures	Steps for learning/evaluation
Show child the object that he or she likes and make sure child is paying attention to it. While child is watching, hide the object behind a barrier close enough to the child so that he or she can reach behind it.	***Record*** + if the child: 1. Reaches object from behind barrier. ***Criterion:*** Child reaches object from behind barrier; 4 of 5 trials on 3 separate days.

(continued)

Teaching procedures	Steps for learning/evaluation
Demonstrate reaching behind the barrier in order to retrieve the object.	
Make a game (hide and seek or peek-a-boo) using the object, repeating steps several times while saying things like: "Here's _____"; "Oops, there goes _____"; "Where's _____?"; "I found _____"; Here _____ is"; and "Can you find _____?"	
Help the child participate in the game and retrieve the object.	
Help the *visually impaired* child feel the barrier; talk about it; use more physical assistance.	
For the child who is too *physically handicapped* to move, you may have to teach spatial concepts by talking about your movements or moving the child to see what has happened.	

AREA: **5. Spatial Concepts**
BEHAVIOR: 5k. Moves self around barrier to get object

Position of Child: Any position that allows child to locomote to the best of his or her ability
Materials: Any object that the child is particularly fond of, plus a variety of barriers available in the environment (e.g., partially opened door, upholstered chair)

Teaching procedures	Steps for learning/evaluation
While the child is watching, place a toy behind a barrier that the child must go around to get to the toy. If the child does not try to go around the barrier, make the toy reappear and then disappear again, playing peek-a-boo; ask the child to go get it.	***Record*** + if the child: 1. Moves self around barrier to get an object or communicates a desire to get around barrier (if too physically handicapped to move alone).
Help the *visually impaired* child feel barriers to his or her locomotion in the environment. Physically assist the child in going around barriers to get things. Talk about what he or she is doing.	***Criterion:*** Child moves around barrier to get an object; 4 of 5 trials on 3 separate days
If necessary, carry the *physically handicapped* child around the barrier, talk to him or her about it and try to assess child's understanding through his or her response to questions or his or her affective responses.	

AREA: **5. Spatial Concepts**
BEHAVIOR: 5l. Retrieves objects from usual locations in another room

Position of Child: Any position that facilitates locomotion
Materials: Shelves or other method of organizing child's toys or household items so that they are
accessible to the child

Teaching procedures	Steps for learning/evaluation
Keep the child's toys and other items in specific locations in home or classroom whenever they are not in use. Have the child observe you putting things away and removing them from this location when they are brought out to be played with or used. Talk to the child frequently about the location of where items are kept. (Example: ''The ball is on the bottom shelf.'') While the toys or other familiar items are in the same room as the child, ask him or her to retrieve a particular item. When the child is able to do this, begin asking the child to retrieve toys when he or she is not in the same room. Whenever the child does not attempt to retrieve the toy, physically assist him or her in getting it. With *blind children,* it is even more important to be sure that there is a special place for everything. ''Labels'' with different textures may assist the child in remembering which objects belong in which compartment.	***Record*** + if the child: 1. Retrieves objects from usual locations in the same room; and 2. Retrieves objects from usual location in another room. ***Criterion:*** Child retrieves objects from specific, regularly kept locations; 4 of 5 trials on 3 separate days.

Note: Have the child ''help'' you put objects away when he or she is through playing with them.

AREA: **5. Spatial Concepts**
BEHAVIOR: 5m. Puts objects away in correct places

Position of Child: Any position that facilitates activity
Materials: Normal household objects and toys

Teaching procedures	Steps for learning/evaluation
Keep many familiar objects in specific places and encourage the child to help you put them away. As you put things away, talk about where they go (''up here,'' ''on that bottom shelf,'' ''in the drawer,'' etc.).	***Record*** + if the child: 1. Correctly puts away an object with assistance (pointing to correct spot, physical guidance, etc.); and 2. Correctly puts away an object without assistance.

(continued)

Teaching procedures	Steps for learning/evaluation
Try handing the child a toy and asking him or her to put it away. If child puts it in the wrong place, help him or her move it to the correct place by pointing, physically assisting the child, and so forth, with the least help necessary to accomplish the task. For a child too *physically handicapped* to place items, you put the item away but ask if each is in the right place. Deliberately misplace an item now and then—look for amusement or other indications the child knows it is wrong—then correct it. Give the child credit for the item if it is clear he or she knows where the items belong.	*Criterion:* Child puts objects away in correct places; 4 of 5 subjects on 3 separate days.

AREA: **5. Spatial Concepts**

BEHAVIOR: 5n. Uses "tools" to deal with spatial problems (extends reach with a stick, extends height with a stool, etc.) (same as item 7i)

Position of Child: Any position that facilitates optimal use of body
Materials: Various toys, sticks, stool, household items

Teaching procedures	Steps for learning/evaluation
When spatial problems occur naturally or when you create one, observe the child's responses. For example, if a favorite toy is under the couch or a ball rolls there, what does the child do if he or she cannot reach it? If child attempts to extend his or her reach with a stick, a toy, or some other object, assist the child only enough to ensure success. If the child simply gives up or fusses for you to do something, help child solve the problem with as little help as possible (e.g., hand her the stick, saying, "Would this help?"). If that does not work, show how to use the stick but pull the toy out only part way and let the child finish. Set up the situation again when the stick is not available but another long object is. You may also try climbing on a chair; standing to get something on the top of a table; pushing a stool to the wall in order to stand on it to reach the light switch.	*Record* + if the child: 1. Uses tool to solve a spatial problem after help from caregiver; and 2. Uses tool to solve a spatial problem spontaneously. *Criterion:* Child uses tool to solve a spatial problem spontaneously; 1 trial on 5 separate days.

Note: Use your imagination to create interesting problems that are solvable, given the child's motor capabilities. Make it fun to solve problems. *Blind* children will be very slow to master this item and will require a great deal of physical assistance.

6.

Functional Use of Objects and Symbolic Play

LEARNING TO USE OBJECTS in an adaptive and socially appropriate way lays the groundwork for some aspects of problem solving, role taking, and other forms of imaginative play. One of the earliest means a child has of defining or understanding objects and, therefore, of developing concepts about categories or classes of objects is through the functions they serve. Normal children spend a great deal of time manipulating objects in order to understand their properties and potential uses, and it is experiences with objects and observations of other people's interactions with objects that promotes discrimination.

The items in this sequence are designed to help the handicapped child develop appropriate ways to interact with objects and play constructively within the constraints imposed by his or her handicapping conditions. Although suggestions are included for modifying the items to meet the needs of visually impaired and motorically handicapped children, further modifications will undoubtedly be necessary for children with severe and/or multiple handicaps. For example, for some very severely physically handicapped children, the only mode of teaching available for an extended time period may be to simply demonstrate appropriate object usage repeatedly over a period of time and to then check for learning by abruptly shifting to inappropriate usage and watching for signs of amusement, surprise, or dismay. Data should always be obtained regarding the use of modified items as well as of those included in the curriculum.

6. Functional Use of Objects and Symbolic Play

a. Moves hand to mouth
b. Explores objects with mouth
c. Plays with (e.g., shakes or bangs) toys placed in hand
d. Commonly performs 4 or more activities with objects

e. Explores toys and responds to their differences
f. Demonstrates appropriate activities with toys having obviously different properties

g. Combines 2 objects in a functional manner
h. Imitates activities related to the function of objects
i. Plays spontaneously with variety of objects, demonstrating their functions

j. Imitates adult behavior with props
k. Spontaneously engages in adult activities with props
l. "Talks" to dolls or animals or makes them interact with one another

AREA: **6. Functional Use of Objects and Symbolic Play**
BEHAVIOR: 6a. Moves hand to mouth

Position of Child: Any position that facilitates movement in upper extremities. Side-lying may be particularly effective for some physically handicapped children. Relaxation exercises prior to and during this item will be helpful for spastic children.
Materials: Something sticky that the child enjoys eating (e.g., honey, jelly, syrup)

Teaching procedures	Steps for learning/evaluation
Watch for hand to mouth movement. The movement may already be occurring spontaneously. If it does not occur or is infrequent (3–4 times a day), put a small amount of something sweet or "good tasting" on the back of the child's hand (on knuckle above index finger or wherever it will be easiest for the child to suck it off). Grasp the child's elbow and use it to move child's hand to his or her mouth. Hold it there until child has a chance to taste the substance on it. Talk about how good it is. Release elbow, put more "sweet" on the child's hand, and observe. If child does not take hand to mouth, repeat the above procedure several times, giving as little assistance as necessary.	*Record* + if the child: 1. Takes hand to mouth and sucks after being physically assisted and having sweet substance on hand; and 2. Gets hand to mouth within 10 seconds after sweet substance is put on it, without physical assistance; and 3. Moves hand to mouth spontaneously, and there is nothing sweet on the hand. *Criterion:* Child moves hand to mouth spontaneously; 10 times a day on 3 separate days.

Note: Primary caregivers will need to make observations on this behavior. As soon as hand-to-mouth behavior is established, toys should be introduced and other activities encouraged. Hand-to-mouth activity is an important part of body awareness, but can become a powerful self-stimulating behavior if not modified with more advanced behaviors.
    Caution: Some children develop a "bite reflex" and will clamp down on anything touching their teeth. Do *not* work on this item if the child shows this reflex. Do get help from a speech pathologist or physical therapist.

AREA: **6. Functional Use of Objects and Symbolic Play**
BEHAVIOR: 6b. Explores objects with mouth

Position of Child: Any position that allows maximum use of hands and back; a bolster or corner chair may be desirable for physically handicapped children
Materials: A variety of small objects that are appropriate for holding and mouthing (i.e., teething toys and rattles); texture, temperature, and taste may be varied to increase the probability of mouthing

Teaching procedures	Steps for learning/evaluation
Mouthing is usually the first way babies explore the properties of objects. It is also useful in helping the child develop oral-motor skills. Place objects in the child's hands and observe.	*Record* + if the child: 1. Spontaneously carries an object to mouth after it is placed in his or her hand or grasped voluntarily; and

(continued)

Teaching procedures	Steps for learning/evaluation
Does child drop the toy and simply put his or her hand in mouth? If so, substitute other toys to see if some are easier for child to grasp than others. Or, physically assist by keeping your hand over the child's hand and helping guide the toy to his or her mouth.	2. Explores a toy with his or her mouth. *Criterion:* Child explores 3 or more objects with his or her mouth on 3 separate days.
Does child explore the toy in some way other than mouthing (e.g., looking at it as he or she moves it, shaking it)? This may mean child is beyond mouthing. Go on to the next item in sequence.	
Does child seem to try to get objects to his or her mouth but then draws back suddenly when they get near his or her face. Or does child drop the object and extend arm as he or she turns his or her head to look at the object? Either of these behaviors could mean abnormal reflexes are interfering with the behavior. Try working with the child in a side-lying position and ask for help from a physical therapist.	

Note: If a child is incapable of hand-to-mouth movement, try holding an object near child's mouth or touch child's lips with the object and observe. Credit + if child mouths under these circumstances. Provide many opportunities for this experience.

AREA: **6. Functional Use of Objects and Symbolic Play**
BEHAVIOR: 6c. Plays with (e.g., shakes or bangs) toys placed in hand

Position of Child: Any position that allows maximum use of arms and hands
Materials: A variety of small objects that can be held in the hand of an infant and that produce
         sounds when shaken or dropped—or an interesting visual spectacle

Teaching procedures	Steps for learning/evaluation
Hold toy out to the child and shake it. If child does not take it spontaneously, place it in child's hands. If child does not attempt to shake the toy, place your hand over the child's hand and help the child shake the toy. Then release the child's hand. If child still does not attempt to shake the object, assist by jiggling the arm at the elbow. Repeat with other toys. Also try banging an object on a table or other surface to make a noise. Give the object to the child. If child does not bang the object, physically assist the child in doing it. Try again.	*Record* + if the child: 1. Shakes or bangs object after given physical assistance; and 2. Spontaneously shakes or bangs object. *Criterion:* Child shakes or bangs at least 3 different objects on 5 separate days.

Note: Even the most *physically handicapped* child may enjoy and benefit from this activity, although the child's actual participation may be limited. Use relaxation techniques for a very "tight" child before beginning the activity. Hold your hand over the child's and help him or her to shake the toy. Score + if child begins to do a part of the movement on his or her own. Continue doing the activity occasionally even after criterion is reached; it may be hard for the child to initiate the activity, but he or she learns from doing it.

AREA: **6. Functional Use of Objects and Symbolic Play**
BEHAVIOR: 6d. Commonly performs 4 or more activities with objects

Position of Child: Any position that allows maximum use of arms and hands
Materials: A variety of small toys that reinforce particular behaviors (e.g., squeaky toys that respond to patting; rattles that respond to shaking or waving; toys with interesting textures; paper)

Teaching procedures	Steps for learning/evaluation
Present a variety of toys, one at a time, to the child and observe what he or she does with each. If a child has only 1 or 2 activities that he or she does with objects (for example, mouthing or shaking), demonstrate another activity and physically assist child in doing it (for example, waving, hitting a surface with a toy, patting or hitting a toy with his or her hand). Repeat with other toys and other activities.	***Record*** + if the child: 1. Demonstrates 2 activities with objects in a 5-minute recording period; and 2. Does 4 different activities in a 30-minute play session (e.g., hits, waves, shakes, looks at, pats, throws, mouths, crumples [as paper], pushes, squeezes) after demonstrations of these activities; and 3. Does 4 different activities spontaneously in a 30-minute play session. ***Criterion:*** Child spontaneously engages in 4 or more different activities with objects in a 30-minute play session on 5 separate days.

Note: Because of the limited response capabilities of many *physically handicapped* children, you can proceed to the next item even though fewer than 4 activities are engaged in commonly. It is important to continue trying to find even slightly different things the child can do in order to promote development of whatever motor skills he or she has and in order to prevent stereotypic behavior from developing.

AREA: **6. Functional Use of Objects and Symbolic Play**
BEHAVIOR: 6e. Explores toys and responds to their differences

Position of Child: Any position that facilitates use of arms and hands
Materials: 3 to 5 "sets" of toys. Each set should have 3 similar toys and 1 that is different (e.g., 3 squeaky toys and a rattle, or 3 blocks and a ball).

Teaching procedures	Steps for learning/evaluation
Present the child with 1 set of toys and observe his or her play for 2 to 3 minutes. Watch for changes in activities—for example, from shaking to squeezing, increased interest (spending a longer time examining the "odd" toy), or other indications of responding to the differences.	***Record*** + if the child: 1. Responds differently to the 1 different object in the set (e.g., spends more time inspecting it, changes activity when picks it up, etc.).

(continued)

Teaching procedures	Steps for learning/evaluation
If the child does not seem to respond to the differences: Demonstrate the properties of the objects to the child by doing different things with them. Physically guide the child to do the things demonstrated if necessary, but be sure to talk about it as you do it. Present a new set of toys and observe again.	**Criterion:** Child responds differently to different toys; 5 successful trials on 3 separate days.

Note: Some *physically handicapped* children will be able to manipulate very little. For these children it is extremely important for you to spend time talking about and demonstrating the different things toys do. Rub the toys against the child's hands to help him or her get the "feel" of the toys, whether or not he or she can manipulate them.

AREA: **6. Functional Use of Objects and Symbolic Play**
BEHAVIOR: 6f. Demonstrates appropriate activities with toys having obviously different properties

Position of Child: Any position that allows maximum use of arms and hands
Materials: A variety of toys with different requirements for producing a response (e.g., squeaky toys to be patted or squeezed; balls to be rolled; various shapes and textures to be felt; mirror to be looked in)

Teaching procedures	Steps for learning/evaluation
Present 1 toy at a time (allow 30 seconds to 2 minutes with each, depending on the child's interest) and record behavior the child shows with each toy. Try to present toys in a sequence to maximize differences (e.g., follow a squeaky toy with a hard, shiny bell). If the child does not change activities as a result of changes in toys, demonstrate an appropriate use of each toy before handing it to the child. Then physically assist child in doing that activity.	**Record** + if the child: 1. Engages in an appropriate activity with a toy although he or she may also try some nonspecific or "inappropriate" activities too (e.g., child may mouth and shake a squeaky toy before squeaking it). **Criterion:** Child engages in appropriate activities with 3 different toys on 3 separate days.

AREA: **6. Functional Use of Objects and Symbolic Play**
BEHAVIOR: 6g. Combines 2 objects in a functional manner

Position of Child: Any position that maximizes ability to use arms and hands. The child may be placed in an infant seat, corner chair, and so forth, as is necessary, or may be held on the caregiver's lap.
Materials: Examples of functionally related objects: doll with hair and comb or brush; xylophone and stick; drum and stick; spoon and bowl

Teaching procedures	Steps for learning/evaluation
Present the child with a box of toys and observe child's spontaneous behavior with them. If child does not combine 2 objects appropriately (such as hitting xylophone or drum with stick), initiate the activity by holding 1 of the 2 items and touching it to the item the child is holding. For example, touch the doll's hair to the comb the child is holding and watch for his or her response. If the child still does not combine the objects functionally, demonstrate for the child: pick up an object from the box, look for the thing that goes with it, combine the objects in play, return them to the box, and repeat it with another set of objects. It may be necessary to reduce the number of objects to just 3, 2 of which relate to each other functionally and 1 of which is unrelated.	*Record* + if the child: 1. Combines objects after demonstration; and 2. Spontaneously combines the 2 related objects in a functional manner. *Criterion:* Child spontaneously combines 3 different sets of 2 objects within a 1-week period.

Note: If the child is unable to use both hands, the teacher may function as a second hand, holding one object for the child to act upon with the second object.

AREA: **6. Functional Use of Objects and Symbolic Play**
BEHAVIOR: 6h. Imitates activities related to the function of objects

Position of Child: Any position that facilitates use of the arms and hands
Materials: Comb, brush, ball, whistle, mirror

Teaching procedures	Steps for learning/evaluation
Show the child an object, being sure he or she is attending to it. Demonstrate to the child how the object is used (e.g., brush your hair with hairbrush). Give child the object and watch what he or she does. If necessary, physically assist child to use the object in the way you demonstrated. Tell the child how the object should be used. Sit with the child in front of a mirror and model the use of the object for him or her, physically assisting the child in imitation if necessary.	*Record* + if the child: 1. Imitates activities related to the function of an object. *Criterion:* Child imitates activities related to the function of 3 different objects on 3 separate days.

Note: Where possible, demonstrate activities so that when performing an action the child can see what he or she is doing.

AREA: **6. Functional Use of Objects and Symbolic Play**
BEHAVIOR: 6i. Plays spontaneously with variety of objects, demonstrating their functions

Position of Child: Any position that facilitates use of arms and hands
Materials: Hairbrush, ball, squeaky toy, cup, spoon, doll, and so forth

Teaching procedures	Steps for learning/evaluation
Give the child a box of objects and observe what he or she does with each one while playing with it. If the child does not use the object functionally, say, "Show me what you do with the _____." If the child does not spontaneously use items functionally, go back to modeling the correct use of objects and encouraging the child to imitate. For the *visually impaired* child, be sure to select objects that are familiar to the child and easily distinguishable by touch. For the *physically handicapped* child, try to find objects whose functions can be demonstrated within the constraints of the child's motor deficits. If little motor behavior is possible, try telling the child, "The _____ is for _____," as you demonstrate usage. Then, once in a while use the object incorrectly and ask the child, "Is this what we do with the _____?" or simply look for signs of amusement or other indications of understanding.	***Record*** + if the child: 1. Plays spontaneously with an object, demonstrating its functions. ***Criterion:*** Child plays spontaneously with a variety of objects (4 or more), demonstrating their functions; 4 of 5 trials for 3 days.

AREA: **6. Functional Use of Objects and Symbolic Play**
BEHAVIOR: 6j. Imitates adult behavior with props

Position of Child: Any position that promotes freedom of movement
Materials: Child-sized broom, mop, Mom's or Dad's hat, mirror, dust mop, playhouse, dolls, animals, play telephone, and so forth

Teaching procedures	Steps for learning/evaluation
Observe the child's spontaneous play. Watch to see if child treats dolls or animals as people (putting them to bed, dressing them, etc.) or sees them in imitation of household chores or other activities. If such activities rarely or never occur, select an object and show the child what might be done with it. Talk about what you are doing, and make it fun! Encourage imitation. If imitation does not occur, physically assist child to imitate, talking about what you are doing.	***Record*** + if the child: 1. Imitates adult behavior with props. ***Criterion:*** Child imitates adult behavior with props; 4 different activities on 3 separate days.

(continued)

Teaching procedures	Steps for learning/evaluation
Allow the child to choose and use objects he or she enjoys. Have a mirror handy so the child can see what he or she is doing. For the *visually impaired* child, it is critical to talk constantly about what you are doing with various objects and physically assist him or her in using the objects as you do. *Blind* children are frequently very delayed in caregiving activities with dolls. Concentrate on activities easier to understand without vision (e.g., using a cloth to wipe up spills).	

AREA: **6. Functional Use of Objects and Symbolic Play**
BEHAVIOR: 6k. Spontaneously engages in adult activities with props

Position of Child: Any position that promotes freedom of movement
Materials: Dust cloth, small broom, dress-up clothes, playhouse, dolls, toy animals, toy telephone, and so forth

Teaching procedures	Steps for learning/evaluation
Observe the child's spontaneous play. Watch for the child taking an adult role (e.g., putting dolls to bed, wiping up spills, talking on a play telephone, etc.). If child does this only with 1 or 2 things, expand the repertoire through specifically modeling activities and encouraging imitation (physically assisting as necessary). Talk throughout about what you are doing to focus child's attention on it. For the *physically handicapped* child, the adult may have to do most of the playing while talking about the activities and giving the child lots of physical assistance. For the *visually impaired* child, it is important to select activities that can be experienced well through tactile stimulation. *Blind* children are very slow to develop imitative and pretend behaviors.	*Record* + if the child: 1. Engages spontaneously in an adult activity with a prop. *Criterion:* Child spontaneously engages in adult activities with 5 different props on 3 separate days.

AREA: **6. Functional Use of Objects and Symbolic Play**
BEHAVIOR: 61. "Talks" to dolls or animals or makes them interact with one another

Position of Child: Any position that facilitates movement
Materials: A variety of toys that stimulate imaginative play (e.g., dolls, cars, trucks, toy animals, puppets)

Teaching procedures	Steps for learning/evaluation
Play "pretend" with the child. Hug and kiss a baby doll or toy animal, take them for a ride in a car or truck, talk for them, and so forth. Encourage the child to participate (e.g., "Is the bear hungry?"). Watch for the child's spontaneous use of fantasy play in which he or she talks to animals or dolls, or has the animals or dolls interact with one another. For the *physically handicapped* child, it may be necessary for the adult to do most of the playing for the child. It is important to talk about what is happening and to ask questions of the child (e.g., "Does the baby need a kiss?") before continuing with the play. Look for pretend activities suitable to the child's motor and language capabilities.	*Record* + if the child: 1. Participates with adult in imaginative play; and 2. Spontaneously engages in imaginative play. *Criterion:* Child spontaneously engages in imaginative play on 5 separate days.

7.

Control over Physical Environment

A PERSON'S ABILITY to exert some control over his or her surrounding environment is critical both for developing a sense of competence and maintaining motivation for learning. Yet, this control is often extremely difficult for a severely handicapped child to achieve. This sequence serves three purposes. First, it should help enhance the child's ability to influence his or her environment in a predictable way. Second, it can promote the child's awareness of how he or she influences the environment. Third, it helps the caregiver define and shape skills in severely handicapped children that might be used to operate a communication board or other prosthetic devices, should these become necessary.

Some children will be too handicapped to accomplish many of the items in the sequence. For those children it is critical to continue to search for any behaviors that are or can be shaped to become voluntary. These behaviors can then be used either to activate toys or other items (with electronic switches if necessary) or to signal an adult of a desired interaction. The pleasure usually demonstrated by the child the first time the child recognizes he or she is making something happen justifies whatever effort has been necessary to get to that point.

7. Control over Physical Environment

a. Repeats activity that produces an interesting result
b. Persists in effort to obtain something
c. Uses simple "tool" to obtain an object or effect
d. Overcomes obstacles to get toys
e. Plays with variety of toys to produce effects

f. Uses adults to solve problems (work on items 7f and 7g simultaneously)
g. Imitates adult action to solve problem
h. Solves simple problems without adult assistance
i. Uses "tools" to solve problems (same as item 5n)

AREA: **7. Control over Physical Environment**
BEHAVIOR: 7a. Repeats activity that produces an interesting result

Position of Child: Any position that allows maximum use of limbs
Materials: A variety of "responsive" toys (e.g., roly poly chimes, crib mobiles, bells, squeaky toys [very soft rubber])

Teaching procedures	Steps for learning/evaluation
Provide the child a variety of toys that "respond" to activity on the part of the child (e.g., squeak when squeezed; chime when pushed; ring when shaken). If the child does not seem to repeat activities that produce noises or sights, tie a bell to the child's wrist or ankle with brightly colored ribbon for 15-minute periods 3 times a day. Observe carefully. Record the number of times the wrist or ankle moves in the 3 minutes prior to attaching the bell. Compare this with the number of times limb is moved in the 3 minutes after the bell has been attached. If the youngster does not move his or her "belled" limb spontaneously in the first minute, physically assist movement several times. Observe another 5 minutes and physically assist again if necessary. Attach the bell to another limb after 4 trials. Another approach is to attach a string to the child's wrist or ankle and to a mobile or other toy in his crib. Leave it attached for 10–15 minutes or until the child is tired and fussy. Take data on movement as with the "belled" limb. For *motorically handicapped children,* seek out toys that require minimal motor responses. Attaching things to the child may be the best means of helping him or her to interact with them. Look for a variety of different things with different effects that can be attached. If the child cannot move any of his or her limbs well enough to ring bells or cause other effects, identify a behavior you can readily discriminate (e.g., a particular facial expression or a small movement of the hand), then you make something happen (a bell ring or a stuffed animal wiggle) each time the child does that behavior. Record whether the behavior increases in the presence of the rewarding toy.	***Record*** + if the child: 1. Repeats activity after having been physically guided through it a few times; and 2. Changes rate of a response when it produces an interesting result. ***Criterion:*** Child repeats an activity several times (changes rate of response) when it produces an interesting result; 3 separate days.

AREA: **7. Control over Physical Environment**
BEHAVIOR: 7b. Persists in effort to obtain something

Position of Child: Any position that facilitates movement
Materials: Any interesting toys

Teaching procedures	Steps for learning/evaluation
If a child is physically capable of reaching, place a favorite toy just beyond his or her reach and observe child's reactions. If he or she cries or immediately loses interest, bounce the toy or do something else to make it attractive and place it a little closer. Make it possible for child to get the toy, but only with a little extra effort. Gradually increase the amount of effort necessary or the length of time the effort must take. Sometimes dangling a toy from a string so that it moves when the child tries to get it will help promote persistence. Be sure to arrange the situation so that persistence pays off. For the *orthopaedically* or *visually handicapped* child, identify something the child does do to obtain a desired outcome. Then try to arrange the environment so that he or she must persist in order to obtain that outcome.	*Record* + if the child: 1. Briefly persists in an effort to obtain something (5–10 seconds or 2–3 unsuccessful attempts prior to obtaining the object or creating the desired effect); and 2. Persists in an effort to obtain something for 11–30 seconds or 4–6 unsuccessful attempts prior to obtaining the object or creating the desired effect. *Criterion:* Child persists in an effort to obtain something; 3 of 5 trials on 3 separate days.

AREA: **7. Control over Physical Environment**
BEHAVIOR: 7c. Uses simple "tool" to obtain an object or effect

Position of Child: Any position that facilitates movement
Materials: Desired toys

Teaching procedures	Steps for learning/evaluation
Select pull toys or attach strings to favorite toys. If the child has adequate visual and motor skills, put a toy out of reach but with the string in front of the child. If child does not pull the toy to himself or herself with the string, demonstrate how to do it. Or place a toy on top of a cloth (diaper or blanket) and show how you can get the toy by pulling the cloth toward you. For the *visually impaired child,* help the child feel the toy and the string as you talk about them. Place the toy at a distance and the string in the child's hand. Talk about getting the toy. If child does not pull the string, put your hand over the child's and show child how to do it. Start with a very short string and work up to a longer one.	*Record* + if the child: 1. Uses "tool" after demonstration; and 2. Spontaneously uses "tool" to obtain a desired object or effect. *Criterion:* Child spontaneously uses tool to obtain a desired object or effect; 3 of 5 trials on 2 separate occasions.

(continued)

Teaching procedures	Steps for learning/evaluation
For the *motorically impaired* child, devise a comparable activity by assessing what motor acts the child can perform and determining what simple tool use could be encouraged. It may be that the child's only usable tool is the adult working with him or her. If so, continue to play "games" with the child in which you do something the child enjoys each time he or she does a particular behavior you have identified as the child's part of the game.	

AREA: **7. Control over Physical Environment**
BEHAVIOR: 7d. Overcomes obstacles to get toys

Position of Child: Any position that facilitates movement
Materials: Any favorite toys

Teaching procedures	Steps for learning/evaluation
Considering the physical capabilities of the child, arrange a situation in which the child can see or hear a toy he or she wants but in which the child must overcome some simple obstacle to get it. For example, place the toy in a transparent plastic container or behind a sheet of Plexiglas so that the child must dump the container, remove a loose-fitting lid, or push a barrier aside to get the toy. If child does not spontaneously overcome the obstacle, demonstrate how it can be done and/or physically guide the child through the process. Reduce the help given as rapidly as possible. Once a child masters one kind of obstacle, try others. Make it a game!	*Record* + if the child: 1. Overcomes an obstacle to get a toy after demonstration; and 2. Spontaneously overcomes an obstacle to get a toy. (Record the kind of obstacle.) *Criterion:* Child overcomes 3 different obstacles to get toys on 3 separate days.
Children with very *limited motor skills* may do something as simple as touch your hand (moving, perhaps no more than one-half inch) to cause you to give a toy to him or her (or to make the toy move or make a sound). Be creative in devising tasks for this population!	

AREA: **7. Control over Physical Environment**
BEHAVIOR: 7e. Plays with variety of toys to produce effects

Position of Child: Any position that facilitates movement
Materials: "Busy box" or other responsive toys

Teaching procedures	Steps for learning/evaluation
Observe the child's play with a "busy box" or with several toys. Does child manipulate them in such a way as to produce sight or sound effects? If not, demonstrate and physically guide child through manipulating the toys appropriately. Get excited about the effects! Work toward as much variety of movement as the child's handling will allow. For example, have toys that respond to pushing, pulling, sliding, poking, hitting, and so on. The more *motorically handicapped* a child is the more it may be necessary to rely on electronic or battery-operated toys that require only minimal response. If the child can only engage reliably in one motor behavior (e.g., pushing), try to maintain variety by attaching that switch to different toys at different times. Avoid creating boredom with just one toy.	*Record* + if the child: 1. Plays with toy to produce an interesting effect. (Record which toys.) *Criterion:* Child plays with 5–6 toys (or with 5–6 different parts of the "busy box") to produce interesting effects once, on at least 3 separate days.

AREA: **7. Control over Physical Environment**
BEHAVIOR: 7f. Uses adults to solve problems (work on items 7f and 7g simultaneously)

Position of Child: Any position that facilitates movement
Materials: Windup toys, shape boxes, toy cash register, jack-in-the-box, and so forth (i.e., toys that create an interesting sight and/or sound for a period of time and then stop)

Teaching procedures	Steps for learning/evaluation
Select a toy requiring a motor response that is new and/or moderately difficult for the child. Show the child how to get the desired effect from the toy. For example, wind up a toy car and let it run down. Observe the child's reaction when the effect stops. If he or she loses interest, try a new toy or try the first toy again, acting more excited about what happens. If the child picks up the toy and tries but cannot work it, or if he or she cries, hold out your hand and say "Do you want some help?" Be sure the child watches how you make the toy work (or if child is *visually impaired,* that the child attends while you physically guide him or her through what is to be done with the toy).	*Record* + if the child: 1. Gives toy to the caregiver for help after being requested to do so; and 2. Spontaneously gives toy to the caregiver for help or asks for help. *Criterion:* Child uses the adult to solve problems; 3 times per session on 3 separate sessions.

(continued)

Teaching procedures	Steps for learning/evaluation
Watch for the child to bring the toy to you for help either before or after attempting to make it work on his or her own.	

AREA:　**7. Control over Physical Environment**
BEHAVIOR:　7g. Imitates adult action to solve problems

Position of Child:　Any position that facilitates movement
Materials:　Windup toys, shape or puzzle boxes, toy cash register, jack-in-the-box, and so forth

Teaching procedures	Steps for learning/evaluation
Select a toy requiring a new motor response and/or a moderately difficult one for the child. Make the toy work (e.g., wind up a car and let it run down). Observe the child's responses when the effect stops. If the child asks for your help, tell him or her to watch you carefully while you make the toy go again (or, if the child is *visually impaired,* have the child feel what you are doing). When the toy stops again and the child asks for help, suggest that he or she try to do it. If the child does not try, show him or her again, but physically assist part of the action. Repeat trials, always demonstrating first and keeping the amount of physical assistance you provide to a minimum. Try this with a variety of toys, being careful to select toys requiring responses within the child's capabilities (electronic toys with simple interfaces may be necessary for *severely motorically impaired* children).	***Record*** + if the child: 1. Makes some attempt to imitate adult actions to make a toy work; and 2. Imitates adult actions sufficiently well to make the toy work. (Record which toys and actions are used.) ***Criterion:***　Child imitates adult actions to solve problems (i.e., to make a toy work); 2 different actions on 3 separate days.

AREA:　**7. Control over Physical Environment**
BEHAVIOR:　7h. Solves simple problems without adult assistance

Position of Child:　Any position that facilitates movement
Materials:　A variety of containers with objects inside, as well as responsive toys; general household or classroom environment

Teaching procedures	Steps for learning/evaluation
Select materials carefully to fit a child's sensory and motor capabilities. Play with the child for awhile, showing him or her how some of the things	***Record*** + if the child: 1. Makes an attempt to solve a problem on his or her own before requesting help

(continued)

Teaching procedures	Steps for learning/evaluation
work but without focusing too much attention on your actions. Then let the child play on his or her own as you observe, responding naturally to his or her attempts to involve you in play. Encourage child to figure things out on his or her own when child asks for help, but give as much help as necessary to keep child from becoming too frustrated. Watch for child's efforts to solve simple problems on his or her own (e.g., opening drawers to remove objects, removing various kinds of lids to get objects out of containers, turning on a switch to make a battery-operated toy work, etc.).	(unwraps, removes covers, opens drawers, makes a toy work, etc.); and 2. Solves simple problems on his or her own. (Record which kind of activity the child does.) ***Criterion:*** Child solves 3 different problems on his or her own, on each of 3 separate days.

AREA: **7. Control over Physical Environment**
BEHAVIOR: 7i. Uses "tools" to solve problems (same as item 5n)

Position of Child: Any position that facilitates movement in a normal household or classroom environment
Materials: Toys and objects that can be used as "tools" (e.g., small broom, coat hanger)

Teaching procedures	Steps for learning/evaluation
In day-to-day interactions with the child, demonstrate how to solve problems with "tools." For example, if a ball rolls under the couch, use a broom to get it out; when something is too high to reach, push a chair over and climb on it. Always talk to the child about what you are doing and make sure he or she attends to you. When the child runs into similar situations, do not immediately solve the problem for the child. Ask what the child thinks he or she could do; call attention to a tool, or otherwise make a suggestion without actually directing the child to do a particular thing. If that is not effective, demonstrate what could be done and physically guide the child through the activity. Re-create the problem (e.g., put the ball back under the couch and see if, as a result of the demonstration, the child can help solve the problem).	***Record*** + if the child: 1. Uses a tool to solve a problem immediately after a demonstration (record problem and tool); and 2. Uses a tool to solve a problem after a suggestion (record problem and tool); and 3. Spontaneously uses a tool to solve a problem (record problem and tool). ***Criterion:*** Child spontaneously uses tools to solve problems; 3 different problems over a week's time.

8.

"Readiness" Concepts

THE ITEMS IN THIS sequence are included to promote the acquisition of some of the basic skills and concepts that are important in normal nursery school and prekindergarten settings. It is difficult to determine precise prerequisites for beginning the sequence, except for the fact that children must have some reliable means of indicating a choice—for example, pointing, picking up, moving, or looking at. In general, it will probably not be productive to work on these concepts until a child has mastered the skills represented in items *a* through *l* of sequence 9 (Responses to Communication from Others) (i.e., skills around the 12- to 14-month developmental level).

8. "Readiness" Concepts

a. Matches simple geometric shapes
b. Matches objects to pictures
c. Matches colors
d. Matches "big" and "little"
e. Identifies circle and square when they are named
f. Understands "same"
g. Understands "big"

AREA: **8. "Readiness" Concepts**
BEHAVIOR: 8a. Matches simple geometric shapes

Position of Child: Any position that facilitates ability to identify objects (e.g., pointing, touching, focusing on shape with eyes)
Materials: Objects with simple geometric shapes (e.g., variety of jar lids, small square items)

Teaching procedures	Steps for learning/evaluation
Present the child with several shapes (circle, square, and triangle are among the easiest). Then show child a shape identical to one included in the group. Ask the child to show you the one that is the same.	***Record*** + if the child: 1. Matches a simple geometric shape with 1 distractor shape; and 2. Matches a simple geometric shape with 2 distractor shapes; and
If the child seems to have difficulty with the concept of "same," ask for the one that is "just like this one," while pointing to or touching the shape.	3. Matches a simple geometric shape from among 3 or more distractor shapes; and 4. Matches 3 or more simple shapes.
As the child identifies the correct shape, positively reinforce by saying, "Yes, that is just the same." If the child selects an incorrect match, say, "No, that is not the same. This one is the same" (pointing and then holding the two shapes side by side). Repeat the above procedure with the same shape.	***Criterion:*** Child correctly matches 3 simple geometric shapes; 3 of 4 trials on 3 different days.
When 1 shape is identified correctly from 3 choices, ask for a second shape. Continue until all can be matched.	
If the child has difficulty selecting the correct shape from 3 or more choices, give only 2 choices and repeat the trial. As soon as the child correctly identifies 1 shape 3 times among 2 choices, increase the number of shapes to 3 or 4.	
Physically assist if necessary.	

AREA: **8. "Readiness" Concepts**
BEHAVIOR: 8b. Matches objects to pictures

Position of Child: Any position that facilitates ability to identify objects (e.g., pointing, touching, focusing eyes, etc.)
Materials: Clear, lifelike pictures of objects, as well as the objects they represent (e.g., spoon, ball, brush, etc.)

Teaching procedures	Steps for learning/evaluation
Present the child with a familiar toy (e.g., a ball). Name the toy. Then show the child two pictures, one of the ball and another of a very different toy (e.g., a	***Record*** + if the child: 1. Correctly matches object to its picture with no distractors; and

(continued)

Teaching procedures	Steps for learning/evaluation
stuffed animal). Ask the child to put the ball on the picture of the ball (or point to the picture). If the child does it correctly, proceed by placing 3 or 4 pictures out and ask him or her to place the appropriate toys on them (or point to them as the toys are presented, one by one). If the child cannot match the object to 1 of 2 pictures, have the child do it with only 1 picture present. Physically assist the child to touch the picture if necessary. Gradually increase the number of objects the child has to choose from and the complexity of the objects, choosing those that are less familiar to the child. Also try using less lifelike pictures of the objects, (e.g., line drawings, black and white and/or smaller pictures, etc.). Praise the child for correct responses and correct those that are incorrect.	2. Correctly matches object to its picture with 1 dissimilar picture distractor; and 3. Correctly matches object to its picture when 3 or more objects are presented; and 4. Correctly matches 4 or more objects to pictures. *Criterion:* Child correctly matches 4 or more objects to pictures; 3 of 4 trials on 3 different days.

AREA: 8. "Readiness" Concepts
BEHAVIOR: 8c. Matches colors

Position of Child: Any position that facilitates ability to identify color (e.g., pointing, touching, focusing eyes, etc.)
Materials: Choose objects that are simple and have color as the primary attribute (e.g., pieces of colored paper that are the same shape, colored blocks)

Teaching procedures	Steps for learning/evaluation
Present the child with a red block. Talk about the color, then present a red and yellow block. Ask the child to show you the one that is the same, or ask for the one that is just like "this one," while pointing to the first red block. If the child identifies the correct color, say, "Yes, this is the same." If the child selects an incorrect match, say, "No, that is not the same. This one is the same," and repeat the procedure. As soon as the child matches red correctly from red and yellow, use the same procedure to match red from among yellow, red, and blue. Gradually add colors. As soon as the child correctly matches red when given several choices, use the same procedure with yellow, then the other colors.	*Record* + if the child: 1. Matches 1 color correctly with one distractor color; and 2. Matches 1 color correctly from among 2 distractors; and 3. Matches 1 color from among 3 or more distractors; and 4. Matches basic colors (red, blue, green, orange, yellow, purple, black, and white). *Criterion:* Child correctly matches all basic colors; 3 of 3 trials on 3 different days.

Note: The child does not need to understand color names at this point. Often matching occurs considerably earlier than naming. Starting with red and yellow or blue and yellow is helpful, since three colors will be seen as different even if the child is color-blind. If the child only matches yellow consistently, check the family history for color blindness.

AREA: **8. "Readiness" Concepts**
BEHAVIOR: 8d. Matches "big" and "little"

Position of Child: Any position that facilitates ability to identify objects (e.g., pointing, touching, focusing eyes)
Materials: Identical, simple objects that come in 2 sizes (e.g., blocks, balls, lids, etc.)

Teaching procedures	Steps for learning/evaluation
Choose 2 objects of the same shape and color but clearly discrepant in size (e.g., a 6-inch circle and a 2-inch circle). Place them in front of the child, identifying them as "big" and "little." Then give child another big circle and ask him or her to put it on the big one. If child does it correctly, give child a little one and ask him or her to put it on the little one. When child learns to match "big" and "little" with one set of objects, change to other objects and gradually reduce the size discrepancy. Then introduce different colors as a distractor but continue to match objects on the basis of size. Physically assist if necessary. Always praise a correct response and correct those responses that are incorrect.	*Record* + if the child: 1. Matches 1 set of big and little objects that are identical except for size; size differences large; and 2. Matches several big and little objects that are the same except for size; size differences large; and 3. Matches big and little objects that vary in size difference; and 4. Matches big and little objects that vary in size differences and have color differences. *Criterion:* Child correctly matches big and little objects; 3 of 3 trials on 3 separate days.

AREA: **8. "Readiness" Concepts**
BEHAVIOR: 8e. Identifies circle and square when they are named

Position of Child: Any position that facilitates ability to identify objects (e.g., pointing, touching, focusing eyes)
Materials: Several sizes of objects that are circles and squares

Teaching procedures	Steps for learning/evaluation
Present the child with an object that is a circle (a jar lid, a paper cutout, a block). Say, "This is a circle; touch (see, feel, pick up) the circle." Remove the circle; then present the child with 1 square and 1 circle. Ask the child to show you the circle. If the child correctly identifies the circle, praise him or her, change the position of the two objects, and repeat the trial. If child picks the wrong object, or hesitates very long, show child the correct object, then discuss its shape (e.g., "No, this is the circle. Feel how it's round and smooth"). Repeat the procedure with the square. Next randomly ask for the circle and the square. Then introduce some other shapes as distractors but ask only for the circle and the square.	*Record* + if the child: 1. Identifies a circle from a square; and 2. Identifies a square from a circle; and 3. Identifies square and circle when 2 or more other shapes are present. *Criterion:* Child correctly identifies a circle and a square when 2 or more other shapes are present; 3 of 3 trials on 3 separate days.

AREA: 8. "Readiness" Concepts
BEHAVIOR: 8f. Understands "same"

Position of Child: Any position that facilitates ability to identify objects (e.g., pointing, touching, focusing eyes)

Materials: Variety of objects, each with a matched pair (e.g., 2 balls, 2 cars, 2 blocks, etc.)

Teaching procedures	Steps for learning/evaluation
Present the child with an object, then show him or her 2 objects, 1 of which is the same as the first one given.	*Record* + if the child:
	1. Demonstrates understanding of "same" by matching 2 similar objects with 1 distractor; and
Ask the child to show you the "same" object as the one he or she has. If the child correctly identifies the object, praise him or her and repeat the exercise, using new objects.	2. Demonstrates understanding of "same" by selecting 2 similar objects with 2 or more distractors.
If the child guesses incorrectly, show him or her the correct object and use different verbal cues to explain "same" (e.g., "See, this one is just like that one"). Physically assist the child to make the correct response if necessary.	*Criterion:* Child correctly demonstrates "same" with a variety of objects; 3 of 3 trials on 3 separate days.
Repeat using several objects, up to 5. Make the task more difficult by making discriminations more difficult. (For example, start using things very different, like a car, a stuffed bear, and a spoon. Later use a spoon, a knife, and a fork; or a block, a ball, and a rattle; or a shoe, a sock, and a glove. Also try pictures.)	

AREA: 8. "Readiness" Concepts
BEHAVIOR: 8g. Understands "big"

Position of Child: Any position that facilitates ability to identify objects (e.g., pointing, touching, or focusing eyes)

Materials: Variety of objects of different sizes with several exceptionally big

Teaching procedures	Steps for learning/evaluation
Present the child with 2 objects, one of which is much bigger than the other. Ask the child to show you the big one.	*Record* + if the child:
	1. Demonstrates the understanding of "big" by selecting the bigger object of 2 when the size difference is great; and
If the child responds correctly, praise the child and repeat, using objects where the size difference is not so great.	2. Demonstrates the understanding of "big" by selecting the biggest object from among 3 or more objects.
Then present 3 or more objects of varying sizes and ask for the "big" one or the "biggest" one (interchange the terms).	*Criterion:* Child correctly chooses the biggest of several objects; 3 of 3 trials on 3 separate days.
If the child is incorrect, show him or her the biggest; ask child to show you which is the biggest; if necessary, guide his or her hand to the biggest one.	

9.

Responses to Communication from Others

MOST CURRICULA WOULD INCLUDE the items featured in this sequence under the heading "receptive language." Our purpose in changing the name was simply to provide consistency among the five sequences relating to communication skills.

It is impossible to overstress the importance of communication skills for handicapped children. Often, handicapping conditions preclude the child's holding up his or her end of the "conversation." A hearing impairment, a visual impairment, oral motor problems, or learning difficulties may cause delayed or atypical responses to the efforts of adults to stimulate language. A frequent result is that the child gradually "teaches" the adult to stop talking. One need only compare the verbal output of a caregiver to a normal 2-year-old to that of a caregiver to an older child with severe cerebral palsy, even when cognitive functioning is normal. A child's responses do shape the responses of adults normally interacting with the child.

This sequence attempts to make the caregiver more aware of the child's responses, and thus more able to stimulate appropriately. However, it is important to remember to talk even when responses from a child are absent or hard to understand.

It is also vital to recognize that many handicapped children will rely on some alternate form of communication some time during their development. In this sequence, it is suggested that gestures and manual signing accompany speech for many children. Be sure to consult with your communications disorders specialist for advice on the extent to which manual signing is appropriate for any given child.

9. Responses to Communication from Others

a. Quiets to voice
b. Smiles to person talking and gesturing
c. Turns to name being called
d. Responds to intonation or attitudes expressed by intonation
e. Stops activity when name is called
f. Vocalizes when talked to
g. Does previously learned task on verbal or gestural cue
h. Responds with correct gesture to "up" and "bye-bye"
i. Responds to "No"

j.   Points to or looks at 3 objects or people named or signed

k.   Responds to "Give me" (word and/or gesture) (same as item 14k)

l.   Follows simple commands (signed and/or spoken)

m.   Points to or looks at most common objects when they are named and/or signed

n.   Indicates "Yes" or "No" appropriately in response to questions (signed or spoken)

o.   Points to or otherwise indicates 2 body parts when they are named or signed

p.   Retrieves visible object on verbal or signed request

q.   Points to at least 4 animals in pictures when they are named or signed

r.   Points to or otherwise indicates 15 or more pictures of common objects

s.   Responds to simple questions correctly

t.   Understands 2 or more "category" words (e.g., "animals")

u.   Points to or otherwise indicates 5 body parts

v.   Correctly follows 3 different 2-part commands involving 1 object

w.   Follows 3 different 3-part commands

AREA: **9. Responses to Communication from Others**
BEHAVIOR: 9a. Quiets to voice

Position of Child: Lying or seated in a comfortable position
Materials: None needed

Teaching procedures	Steps for learning/evaluation
Observe child in a noninteracting state. If child becomes fussy, move to the child, touch him or her, and speak quietly to the child. You might pick child up, but remember to continue speaking to him or her in a comforting fashion. Following several trials of the above, attempt to talk to the child before you move into the child's view or make tactile contact with him or her. Observe to see if he or she quiets at the sound of your voice. If so, move into the child's view and continue talking and touching him or her. If child does not quiet, return to the initial activities above for several more trials.	***Record*** + if the child: 1. Quiets to tactile, visual, and auditory stimulation; and 2. Quiets to voice alone. ***Criterion:*** Child quiets at the sound of a pleasant, friendly voice when fussing mildly, or showing mild discomfort; once a day on 3 separate days.

AREA: **9. Responses to Communication from Others**
BEHAVIOR: 9b. Smiles to person talking and gesturing

Position of Child: Seated or lying facing you
Materials: None needed

Teaching procedures	Steps for learning/evaluation
Most of a child's earliest smiles (1–2 months) are in response to inner states (e.g., feeling full or comfortable). Thereafter, the child begins to smile at certain tactile stimuli (being kissed, patted, tickled, rubbed, etc.) and at sounds. It is important to respond to all of these early smiles by talking, gesturing, and otherwise interacting with the child. In this way the smiles become truly interpersonal and a part of the child's communication system. For this item specifically, talk to the child in an animated rhythmic fashion, using hand gestures appropriate to what you are saying. If child smiles as you speak/gesture, touch him or her, return child's smile, and continue to speak. If child does not smile, try to elicit a smile through various kinds of tactile stimuli (tickling, patting, etc.) as you continue to talk to the child. In children whose *vision* and/or *hearing* is questionable, it is particularly important to include numerous tactile stimuli in interpersonal interactions.	***Record*** + if the child: 1. Smiles in response to your talking/gesturing to him or her. ***Criterion:*** Child smiles in response to an adult's talking/gesturing to him or her 3 times a day on 3 separate days.

AREA: **9. Responses to Communication from Others**
BEHAVIOR: 9c. Turns to name being called

Position of Child: Occupied in an activity—not attending to trainer/parent
Materials: None

Teaching procedures	Steps for learning/evaluation
In a quiet room, standing several feet from the child, call his or her name softly and observe child's reaction. Vary your position and place in the room as well as the pitch and intensity of your voice as you call to the child. If child turns toward you, talk to him or her, pick up the child, or play with the child in some way. Then, try calling the child's name in a situation where there are other noises (the television is on, other people are talking, etc.). Again, if child turns, respond by picking him or her up or attending to the child in some other way. For a *hearing-impaired* child, stand within the child's visual field and sign a "name sign" as you call his or her name. Credit this item if child looks at you in response to his or her name or in response to another gesture you have designated as "pay attention."	***Record*** + if the child: 1. Turns toward you when his or her name is called in a quiet room; and 2. Turns toward you when his or her name is called in a noisy room. ***Criterion:*** Child turns toward the person calling his or her name in a normally noisy room; 3 of 3 trials on 3 separate days.

AREA: **9. Responses to Communication from Others**
BEHAVIOR: 9d. Responds to intonation or attitudes expressed by intonation

Position of Child: Any position; child in various states (i.e., upset, angry, calm, active)
Materials: None required

Teaching procedures	Steps for learning/evaluation
This is not a skill to be trained; rather, it requires that the caregiver be *consistent* in speaking to the child in terms of combining intonation patterns with other events in the environment. For example, when the child is upset the caregiver should talk in soothing tones as he or she pats, rocks, hugs the child, and so forth. When the child does something funny the caregiver laughs and talks in an animated fashion; when the child begins to do something unacceptable (puts something dangerous in mouth, tips something over), caregiver says "No" in a firm voice and immediately stops what is going on.	***Record*** + if the child: 1. Responds appropriately to attitude expressed by intonation. ***Criterion:*** Child shows appropriate responses to intonation (changes in volume/voice quality) by caregiver; observed by someone other than the caregiver; 2 times on 2 separate days.

(continued)

Teaching procedures	Steps for learning/evaluation
Observe to see if the child responds appropriately (ceases activity, calms, etc.) to the intonation of the caregiver's voice *prior* to physical intervention (i.e., prior to patting, soothing, or making child stop an unacceptable activity). Exaggerate intonation for the *hearing-impaired* child. Also, be sure to accompany statements with clear gestures or signs. Credit the child with this item if he or she demonstrates an understanding of the meaning of any gesture.	

AREA: **9. Responses to Communication from Others**
BEHAVIOR: 9e. Stops activity when name is called

Position of Child: Any position
Materials: None required

Teaching procedures	Steps for learning/evaluation
When the child is busy playing, call his or her name. Observe to see if upon hearing his or her name, child stops the activity engaged in and turns toward the source of his or her name. If child stops and turns toward you, talk to him or her, pick child up, or otherwise let child know you are pleased. If child does not respond, call his or her name a little louder, wait for a few seconds, and then with a gentle touch guide child to turn his or her face toward you. Say something to the child, pick him or her up, or otherwise reward child's looking at you. For a *hearing-impaired* child, be sure to be in child's visual field as you call; simultaneously make his or her name sign.	***Record*** + if the child: 1. Responds by stopping activity when name is called and turning toward the source of his or her name. ***Criterion:*** Child stops activity when name is called 3 of 5 trials on 3 separate days.

AREA: **9. Responses to Communication from Others**
BEHAVIOR: 9f. Vocalizes when talked to

Position of Child: Lying or sitting facing the trainer or parent
Materials: None

Teaching procedures	Steps for learning/evaluation
As you interact with the infant, talk with varying pitch and rhythm. If child vocalizes, listen and attempt to imitate his or her vocalizations.	***Record*** + if the child: 1. Responds to being talked to by vocalizing.

(continued)

Teaching procedures	Steps for learning/evaluation
Be sure to insert short pauses in your talking to show the youngster that you are waiting for him or her to respond. The more animated your conversation, the more apt the child will be to vocalize in response. Certain situations tend to stimulate more vocalization than others. Watch for these and capitalize on them. Most children vocalize more at mealtime than at any other time. Be sure to allow time for this rather than just hurrying the child through. Some children vocalize the most during movement activities—during physical therapy or their self-initiated motor activities. Attend to these vocalizations, talk back to the youngster, and make it as social a time as possible. It is especially important to attend to the vocalizations of children who are *hard of hearing*. Gesture or sign as you talk back to them. Also encourage them to feel your throat as you talk and their own as they make sounds.	***Criterion:*** When youngster is attentive, he or she can be engaged in "verbal interaction"; 3 of 5 trials on 3 consecutive days.

Note: Prior to learning to vocalize when talked to, it is normal for an infant who vocalizes spontaneously to stop when an adult talks to him or her. It is important to continue talking to the child when he or she talks, even if the child is already at this stage of development. It is simply part of the normal process of learning to "take turns" in a conversation.

AREA: **9. Responses to Communication from Others**
BEHAVIOR: 9g. Does previously learned task on verbal or gestural cue

Position of Child: Seated facing trainer/parent
Materials: None required

Teaching procedures	Steps for learning/evaluation
Select any behavior a child has learned to do when playing with you (e.g., kissing, hugging, clapping, etc.). Try to initiate that activity with just a verbal cue. For example, say "Pat-a-cake" before you do anything and see if the child claps. If he or she does, go on and play the game. If the child does not, again say "Pat-a-cake" and you start clapping or physically guide him or her to start clapping. Then play the game. The next time, start again with just the verbal cue. If the child is not yet participating in any activities that lend themselves to being initiated by a verbal cue, begin playing games with the child that can be used in this way. For example, kiss the baby and then	***Record*** + if the child: 1. Does task on verbal cue or gestural command. ***Criterion:*** Child responds to verbal or gestural cue by demonstrating the associated behavior; 3 of 5 trials on 3 separate days.

(continued)

Teaching procedures	Steps for learning/evaluation
say "Give me a kiss," putting your face close to the child; help the child put his or her mouth to your face and then hug him or her. Other things to try are "How big is Johnny? So big" (raising child's hands above his or her head); "Blow bubbles" (as you demonstrate); "Knock, Knock" (as you hit something on the table). For *hearing-impaired* children, "sign" and talk as you play games. Credit the child for responding to a gestural cue.	

AREA: **9. Responses to Communication from Others**
BEHAVIOR: 9h. Responds with correct gesture to "up" and "bye-bye"

Position of Child: Any position where face-to-face contact is maintained
Materials: None required

Teaching procedures	Steps for learning/evaluation
Consistently match your verbalization of "up" and "bye-bye" with the appropriate gestures (e.g., reaching for child or waving). In appropriate situations (e.g., when it is time to get the child out of bed or someone is leaving), say "Do you want to get up?" or "Wave bye-bye." Physically assist the child to hold his or her hands up or to wave as appropriate. Gradually reduce the amount of assistance you give the child until he or she does it unassisted. For the child who is *hard of hearing*, make sure your gestures are consistent and precise.	***Record*** + if the child: 1. Responds with the correct gesture to verbalizations "up" or "bye-bye," in response to verbal cue and gesture with minimal assistance (record responses to "up" and "bye-bye" separately); and 2. Responds with the correct gesture to verbalizations "up" or "bye-bye," in response to verbal cue and gesture with no assistance. ***Criterion:*** Child responds with the correct gestures to "up" and "bye-bye" with no assistance, in response to verbal cue and gesture 3 times to each word on 3 separate days.

AREA: **9. Responses to Communication from Others**
BEHAVIOR: 9i. Responds to "No"

Position of Child: Any position
Materials: None required

Teaching procedures	Steps for learning/evaluation
When the child engages in inappropriate activity that should be stopped, say "No" firmly. If the child does not stop the activity, look for a logical way to make him or her refrain (i.e., gently hold child's hands on the table top or in his or her lap to stop banging, for example, while saying "No" to the child, and then try to engage him or her in an appropriate activity). Always respond to even momentary cessation of activity with praise and presentation of a distractor activity. This will help the child learn to substitute appropriate for inappropriate activities, as well as the meaning of "No." For the child who is *hard of hearing* or generally unresponsive to commands, always accompany "No" with a gesture that means "No" or "Stop."	**Record** + if the child: 1. Ceases activity upon hearing the command "No" or seeing the gesture meaning "No" or "Stop." **Criterion:** Child ceases activity upon hearing the command or seeing the gesture meaning "No" or "Stop," each time it is used during a day; 3 separate days. (The child may return to the inappropriate activity if a substitute is not provided.)

AREA: **9. Responses to Communication from Others**
BEHAVIOR: 9j. Points to or looks at 3 objects or people named or signed

Position of Child: In the natural environment or facing trainer with tray between trainer and baby.
Materials: Objects known to baby

Teaching procedures	Steps for learning/evaluation
This item may be done naturally in the child's environment by asking the child "Where is _____?" ("your bottle," "Daddy," "the teddy bear") when these are readily in view, easily reached, or easily retrieved (if the child is locomoting). If this approach is inconvenient or the child is in an unfamiliar setting, you can work on it with the baby seated facing you. Place two familiar objects 10 inches apart on a tray in front of the child. Say and/or sign the name of one of the objects, saying, "Where is the _____?"; "Give me the _____"; "You can get the _____"; or something similar. If child picks up, points to, or otherwise indicates an under-	**Record** + if the child: 1. Looks at or points to object named. (Record which objects or people.) **Criterion:** Child looks at or points to 3 objects or people named or signed. Each one on 3 of 5 trials on 3 separate days.

(continued)

Teaching procedures	Steps for learning/evaluation
standing, praise child and let the child play with the object. Then take it from the child and present two other objects. If the child makes no attempt to point to or look at the object named, you point to the object or pick it up, repeat the name, and again ask the child where it is. If child still does not point to or look at the object, physically guide his or her hand to the object (or tap the table near the object to get the child to look at it). Continue this procedure, allowing increasing amounts of time between when you say or sign the object's name and when you assist the child's response.	

AREA: **9. Responses to Communication from Others**

BEHAVIOR: 9k. Responds to "Give me" (word and/or gesture) (same as item 14k)

Position of Child: Facing caregiver, in a play situation
Materials: Small toy for child to play with

Teaching procedures	Steps for learning/evaluation
With child involved in playing with a small toy, say or sign "Give me the _____," holding out your hand. If child does not give you the toy, gently take it from the child, say (and sign) "Thank you," and immediately give the toy back to the child. Make a game of giving and returning a variety of toys. Avoid asking for favorite toys until the child clearly understands that you will give them back. *Do not* take a toy if the child unduly protests.	**Record** + if the child: 1. Allows toy to be taken after the request without protest; and 2. Gives toy to the person requesting it. **Criterion:** Child gives toy (or other object) to the person requesting it; 3 of 5 trials on 3 separate days.

Note: It is helpful to model "giving" for the child. Be sure he or she observes you giving to other people when they make a request and vice versa. Also, when the child reaches for something you have, say (and sign) "You want me to give the _____ to you. Here it is."

AREA: **9. Responses to Communication from Others**
BEHAVIOR: 91. Follows simple commands (signed and/or spoken)

Position of Child: Variable
Materials: Variable

Teaching procedures	Steps for learning/evaluation
Select several simple commands other than those already taught in this sequence, fitting the commands to the motor capabilities of the child and the kind of environment in which he or she lives. Some examples might be: "Come here," "Sit down," "Hands down," "Get the _____," "Open your mouth," and so on. For fairly unresponsive children, it is important to choose commands that you can physically guide the child through. Be consistent in your approach to teaching. First, say (and sign) the command; then wait long enough to allow the child time to think about responding. If child makes no move to respond, give the command again and either demonstrate what child is to do or physically guide him or her through the activity (whichever is most appropriate and effective for that child). On subsequent trials give the command only once and then demonstrate or physically guide compliance. Always praise compliance even if it comes only after your help. Gradually reduce help until child can follow a command independently. Avoid repeating a command several times before insisting on compliance (i.e., do not "nag").	***Record*** + if the child: 1. Follows simple command with some assistance (record which command); and 2. Follows simple command independently. ***Criterion:*** Child follows 2 or more simple commands (other than "Give" and "Stop"); each command followed on 3 of 5 trials on 2 separate days.

AREA: **9. Responses to Communication from Others**
BEHAVIOR: 9m. Points to or looks at most common objects when they are named and/or signed

Position of Child: Any
Materials: No special materials are required; items in the child's natural environment should be used

Teaching procedures	Steps for learning/evaluation
This item involves teaching the names of the wide variety of items one confronts in the natural environment. "Most common" objects and those of importance vary considerably for different children in different settings.	***Record*** + if the child: 1. Points to or otherwise indicates a common object when it is named (record which object); and

(continued)

Teaching procedures	Steps for learning/evaluation
In previous items the child has been taught to "point to" and "identify." This is an extension of those skills. In a game format, say "Johnny, point to the _____ " (or "Johnny, look at . . . " if the child does not have a physical pointing response). If child does not indicate the object, you touch it, pick it up, show it to the child, and then ask again. Always praise or otherwise demonstrate pleasure when the child responds appropriately.	2. Indicates 5 or more common objects; and 3. Indicates 10 or more common objects; and 4. Indicates 15 or more common objects. ***Criterion:*** Child correctly indicates 15 or more common objects (and/or people) in his environment when they are named (or signed); 2 times for each object on 2 separate days.

Note: Children should be asked to respond in whatever way possible (e.g., pointing, eye gaze, verbal, etc.). This item should be worked on throughout the day, not in a specific teaching session.

AREA: **9. Responses to Communication from Others**
BEHAVIOR: 9n. Indicates "Yes" or "No" appropriately in response to questions (signed or spoken)

Position of Child: Any
Materials: Pictures or toys that you have decided to use when asking yes/no questions

Teaching procedures	Steps for learning/evaluation
Ask simple questions requiring a yes/no answer. Examples: "Do you want some ice cream?"; "Is this my shoe?" (as you hold child's shoe up to your foot). Begin with questions you are quite sure you and the child know the answers to. Be sure to insert short pauses after the question to show the child that you are waiting for him or her to respond. If child does not respond, demonstrate the expected response (i.e., nod your head and say "Yes, you want some ice cream" or shake your head and say "No, that's not my shoe." If the child is not vocalizing well enough to make distinguishably different sounds for "Yes" and "No," physically assist child to nod and shake his or her head appropriately, or identify some other responses (particularly for physically handicapped children).	***Record*** + if the child: 1. Responds appropriately to a yes/no question. ***Criterion:*** Child responds appropriately to 4 of 5 yes/no questions on 3 separate days.

Note: Children frequently learn to indicate "No" before they indicate "Yes." They may say or gesture "No" for negation and name or sign an object as an affirmation. This is acceptable. The issue is not the correct words, but understanding negation and affirmation.

AREA: **9. Responses to Communication from Others**
BEHAVIOR: 9o. Points to or otherwise indicates 2 body parts when they are named or signed

Position of Child: Any comfortable position facing caregiver
Materials: None required

Teaching procedures	Steps for learning/evaluation
With youngster attending to you, say or sign, "Show me your _____" (hand, hair, eyes, ear, foot, nose, etc.). If the youngster points to the right body part, reinforce him or her and repeat, "Yes, this [pointing] is your _____." If the youngster does not point, grasp his or her hand and touch the named body part with it. Pause briefly and say, "Yes, this is your _____." Gradually reduce the amount of assistance provided and delay its use by a few seconds over successive trials. When working with *hearing-impaired* children, make sure they are attending to you visually.	***Record*** + if the child: 1. Points to or otherwise indicates a body part when it is named. (Record the part indicated.) ***Criterion:*** Child points to 2 body parts; 2 times each on 3 separate days.

AREA: **9. Responses to Communication from Others**
BEHAVIOR: 9p. Retrieves visible object on verbal or signed request

Position of Child: Upright, ambulatory (see note below)
Materials: Any objects that interest the child or that child generally likes to play with

Teaching procedures	Steps for learning/evaluation
While pointing toward a given object, say or sign, "Emily, get the _____ for me." If the child moves toward the object but hesitates, repeat a partial direction (e.g., "That's right, the _____"). If the child does not move to get the object, take the child's hand and move the child physically to it, putting his or her hands upon the object, then taking it from the child, saying, "Thank you." A second adult (or another child) may assist the child in getting and returning the object initially, if necessary. Gradually decrease the amount of help given the child.	***Record*** + if the child: 1. Goes after the requested object; and 2. Brings the object to you on verbal or signed request. (Record which objects.) ***Criterion:*** Child retrieves 3 different objects on 3 separate days.

(continued)

Teaching procedures	Steps for learning/evaluation
You should also reinforce the concept of getting something for another person by describing your actions when you get something for the child (''Oh, you want me to get your bottle? O.K., here it is.'').	

Note: With minor adaptations, this item can be used with children in wheelchairs or those using other prosthetic devices who have some control over their locomotor processes.

AREA: **9. Responses to Communication from Others**
BEHAVIOR: 9q. Points to at least 4 animals in pictures when they are named or signed

Position of Child: Any comfortable position that allows free use of hands and/or eyes
Materials: Book with animal pictures; animal picture cards; photographs; pictures from magazines, and so forth

Teaching procedures	Steps for learning/evaluation
Show the child a picture of one animal. Ask the child (or sign) to ''Point to the _____,'' ''Touch the _____,'' or ''Where is the _____?'' Physically assist a response if necessary. Praise appropriate responding. When child is readily pointing to the one picture, try a second picture, again presenting it by itself. Say ''Now, this is a _____. Can you touch the _____?'' Physically assist or praise as necessary. Then present the 2 pictures side by side. Ask child to point to 1 and then the other, using several trials and randomly changing the position of the pictures. Always correct errors and praise correct responses. When 2 pictures have been learned, teach a third, fourth, fifth, and so on. Do not present more than 4 pictures at one time. Omit this item for children too *visually impaired* to see the pictures. You may substitute teaching the child to associate animal noises with animal names (e.g., ''The dog says ruf-ruf. What does the dog say?''; or ''What says ruf-ruf?'').	***Record*** + if the child: 1. Points to or otherwise indicates an animal named in a picture; 1 picture present; and 2. Points to or otherwise indicates an animal named; 2 or more pictures present. (Record which animals are correctly identified.) ***Criterion:*** Child points to or otherwise identifies 4 different animals on request; each identified at least twice, with 2 or more pictures present on 3 separate days.

Note: Physically handicapped children who do not have a pointing response should be asked to ''Look at the _____.'' The direction of their visual gaze will serve as a pointing response. These children may also be able to point with a headstick, a foot, or make some other movement to indicate an answer.

AREA: 9. Responses to Communication from Others

BEHAVIOR: 9r. Points to or otherwise indicates 15 or more pictures of common objects

Position of Child: Any position that facilitates interaction
Materials: Picture cards or books with simple pictures

Teaching procedures	Steps for learning/evaluation
Place 2 pictures in front of the child or show him or her the page of a book with 2 or more objects on it. Point to and name (and sign) each of the pictures. Then ask the child, "Where is the _____?" asking for each picture in turn. Correct errors and praise appropriate responses. Continue with other pictures or other pages in the book. If the child has difficulty learning to point to pictures in this way, it may be necessary to teach only 1 picture at a time, pairing it with a picture already learned, and providing many trials. For children too *visually impaired* to use pictures, select 2 or more objects that feel very different and ask the child to "Give me the _____."	***Record*** + if the child: 1. Points to or otherwise correctly identifies a picture of an object that is named; 2 or more pictures present. (Record which pictures are correctly identified.) ***Criterion:*** Child points to or otherwise correctly identifies 15 or more pictures of common objects; each object identified twice on 3 separate days.

AREA: 9. Responses to Communication from Others
BEHAVIOR: 9s. Responds to simple questions correctly

Position of Child: Any position that facilitates interaction
Materials: Items or pictures that will be used when asking questions; use items the child already knows the labels for

Teaching procedures	Steps for learning/evaluation
Ask simple questions that can be answered with gestures, sounds, or single words. Examples: "What does the _____ say?"; "What does the _____ do?"; "Where is Mommy [Daddy]?" (Parent must not be visible). If the child does not answer, model the desired response (e.g., "The dog says bow-wow "). Repeat the questions asked and the modeled response, if necessary. If the child gives a verbal response that is not clear, but that is similar enough to the correct pronunciation to be understood, reinforce succeeding approximations of the correct pronunciation. This may be done as part of or separate from working on "responding to questions."	***Record*** + if the child: 1. Responds to a simple question correctly with a gesture or verbal response. (Record which questions.) ***Criterion:*** Child responds correctly to 4 different questions on 3 separate days.

Note: Physically handicapped children who cannot respond verbally should be asked to respond in whatever way possible (e.g., pointing response, eye gaze).

AREA: **9. Responses to Communication from Others**
BEHAVIOR: 9t. Understands 2 or more "category" words (e.g., "animals")

Position of Child: Variable
Materials: Toys or pictures that can be grouped

Teaching procedures	Steps for learning/evaluation
Mix up 2 groups (3–4 items each) of objects (e.g., small dolls and small animals). Present 2 containers. Say (and sign), "Let's put all the animals in this box" (drop 1 in) "and all the people in this box" (drop 1 in). If child makes no move to pick up a toy, hand child a toy and ask which box it goes in. If child is too *physically handicapped* to pick up and sort the toys, you pick up each one and say "Is this one an animal? Where does it go?" relying on the child's yes/no response or other methods of communication. If child is *visually impaired,* it may be more appropriate to sort by "soft and hard," "quiet and noisy," or some other meaningful categories. Always correct errors, praise accurate responses, and make it a game.	*Record* + if the child: 1. Indicates an understanding of a category word through sorting, answering questions, or other means. (Record which category word is understood.) *Criterion:* Child indicates an understanding of 2 or more category words; each observed on 3 separate days.

Note: This is a good activity to use when working on crossing the midline, grasping and releasing, or other motor activities with children whose cognitive skills are more intact than their motor skills.

AREA: **9. Responses to Communication from Others**
BEHAVIOR: 9u. Points to or otherwise indicates 5 body parts

Position of Child: Any position that facilitates interaction
Materials: None

Teaching procedures	Steps for learning/evaluation
Play games or sing songs with the child that involve touching various parts of the body. Point to them on yourself so that the child can imitate, have him or her point to them on you, and, if necessary, physically assist child in pointing to them as you name them. If the child is too physically handicapped to point but can indicate "yes" and "no," sing songs and play games when you touch the body parts on the child. Check to see which body parts are known by occasionally naming them incorrectly and observing the child's response—for example, saying, "Is this your hair?" while touching child's nose.	*Record* + if the child: 1. Points to a body part in imitation; and 2. Spontaneously points to a body part when it is named. (Record which part.) *Criterion:* Child spontaneously points correctly to 5 or 7 body parts when they are named; 3 separate days.

AREA: **9. Responses to Communication from Others**
BEHAVIOR: 9v. Correctly follows 3 different 2-part commands involving 1 object

Position of Child: Any position; only child's attention is required
Materials: Any object(s) the child is interested in

Teaching procedures	Steps for learning/evaluation
Give a verbal direction such as: "Get the _____ and give it to _____"; or "Touch red and then blue." (This can also be done easily with a headstick.) If the child does not respond or if he or she responds to only the first direction, guide the child through the rest of the response appropriately. Then reinforce his or her response and reiterate the direction, "Good, you got the ball and gave it to Beth!" Wait a few seconds longer before assisting on succeeding trials, and fade assistance as quickly as possible.	**Record** + if the child: 1. Follows a 2-part command with 1 object. (Record the command.) **Criterion:** Child correctly follows 3 different 2-part commands, each observed twice on 3 different days.

Note: A wide variety of questions involving 2 directions are appropriate for use on this item. Use your imagination; do not restrict yourself to only the examples given above. Make a game of the procedure!

AREA: **9. Responses to Communication from Others**
BEHAVIOR: 9w. Follows 3 different 3-part commands

Position of Child: Any position
Materials: Pictures or toys that you have decided to use when asking questions

Teaching procedures	Steps for learning/evaluation
Give a 3-part verbal direction such as: "Get the ball, put it in the bag, and give it to _____"; or "Sit here, take off your socks and bring them to me"; or "Take off your hat and coat and hang them up"; etc. If the child does not respond or if he or she responds to only the first (and/or second) direction, guide child through the rest of the appropriate response. Then reinforce child's response and reiterate the direction "Good, you got the ball, put it in the bag, and gave it to Mary." Wait a few seconds longer before assisting on succeeding trials, and fade assistance as quickly as possible.	**Record** + if the child: 1. Correctly follows a 3-part command. (Record the commands.) **Criterion:** The child correctly follows 3 different 3-part commands, each observed once on 3 different days.

Note: Give command and accept responses in whatever communication mode the child uses best and most effectively.

10.

Gestural Imitation

GESTURES ARE A YOUNG child's earliest means of communication, and they later come to enrich and enhance verbal communication. Children enjoy imitating and being imitated, and they are capable of learning a great deal through this process. This sequence is intended to promote the imitation of socially recognized gestures and then to facilitate the imitation of standard manual signs if that is appropriate for a particular child.

Before deciding to teach signed communication to a youngster, it is important that you consult a specialist in communication disorders. Research has suggested that learning signed communication does not retard or prevent the development of spoken language (Silverman, 1980); rather, developing an alternate method of communication often appears to enhance future speech production. Yet, there are some children for whom time would be better spent working on the imitation of sounds than on the development of gestures. A communicative disorders specialist will be your best source of advice on this matter.

REFERENCE

Silverman, F. (1980). *Communication for the speechless*. Englewood Cliffs, NJ: Prentice Hall.

10. Gestural Imitation

a. Looks at person talking and gesturing
b. Continues a movement if it is imitated by caregiver
c. Will begin a movement already in repertoire if same activity is begun by caregiver
d. Tries to imitate unfamiliar movement; child's own action is visible to himself or herself
e. Imitates unfamiliar movement that is not visible to himself or herself
f. Imitates new activities, including use of materials

Stop here if child is progressing well with spoken words.

g. Imitates 1 sign that stands for a word (e.g., "Daddy," "all gone," "more," "eat," "drink," etc.)
h. Imitates 2 signs that stand for words
i. Imitates 3 signs that stand for words
j. Imitates sequence of 2 signs that stand for words

AREA: **10. Gestural Imitation**
BEHAVIOR: 10a. Looks at person talking and gesturing

Position of Child: Sitting or lying down
Materials: No materials needed other than a vibrant person with an engaging smile!

Teaching procedures	Steps for learning/evaluation
Place the child in a position that allows full eye contact between the child and teacher/caregiver. Get child's attention while talking and gesturing to child for communicative purposes. Use clear gestures (e.g., raising hands when you say, "Do you want to get up?" or making the sign for "Daddy" when you say "Daddy"). Remember: Pace your talking and gesturing to the "style and pace" of the child. Be aware of what he or she is doing. If child does not look at you, try to get his or her attention with an object, then put the object down and see if child looks at you.	*Record* + if the child: 1. Looks at person communicating with him or her momentarily; and 2. Looks at person communicating with him or her for 30 seconds or more. *Criterion:* Child looks at the person communicating with him or her for 30 seconds or more; 4 of 5 trials on 3 separate days.

Note: This series of items is an attempt to bring meaning to the child's gestural repertoire. It is not a replacement for oral language, but, instead, an important building block that will facilitate a general communication link between the child and another person. Once a communicative link is established and meaning is attached to gestures, a more efficient means of communication can be established.

AREA: **10. Gestural Imitation**
BEHAVIOR: 10b. Continues a movement if it is imitated by caregiver

Position of Child: Sitting or lying down in a comfortable position that allows child full movement of hands as well as eye contact with another person
Materials: An observant, relaxed person to interact with the child—one who will imitate and maintain communication with the child

Teaching procedures	Steps for learning/evaluation
With the child in a comfortable position and eye contact between the child and adult established, imitate an activity that the child has initiated (e.g., waving arm, sticking out tongue, shaking a rattle, etc.). Make sure child sees your imitative movements. If youngster does not continue the activity imitated, physically guide him or her into doing it. Say, "Let's do it more" or "Try it again."	*Record* + if the child: 1. Continues a movement after it is imitated by caregiver. *Criterion:* Child continues a movement if imitated 4 of 5 times on 3 separate days.

Note: When this item is used, look carefully for additional indications of involvement on the part of the child via affective changes (smiling, laughing), vocalizations, and general body involvement.

AREA: **10. Gestural Imitation**

BEHAVIOR: 10c. Will begin a movement already in repertoire if same activity is begun by caregiver

Position of Child: Sitting or lying down; any comfortable position that allows the child full movement of hands and eye contact with another person
Materials: No materials necessary

Teaching procedures	Steps for learning/evaluation
Caregiver/teacher should be someone familiar to the child. Get the attention of the child. As you talk or play with the child, model simple motor activities you have seen the child engage in. Make sure child is observing you. Exaggerate motions. If child does not imitate you, try to physically assist child to do the activity. Smile and praise child for doing it.	***Record*** + if the child: 1. Imitates a movement already in his or her repertoire after physical assistance; and 2. Imitates a movement in his or her repertoire spontaneously. ***Criterion:*** Child spontaneously imitates a behavior already in his or her repertoire; 4 of 5 trials on 3 separate days.

Note: When the caregiver begins one of the child's familiar activities, look for subtle changes of "recognition" on the part of the child, such as a smile, laugh, or general excitement.

AREA: **10. Gestural Imitation**

BEHAVIOR: 10d. Tries to imitate unfamiliar movement; child's own action is visible to himself or herself

Position of Child: Sitting or lying down; any comfortable position that allows the child full movement of hands and eye contact with other person
Materials: Mirror

Teaching procedures	Steps for learning/evaluation
Begin the "imitation game" by getting child to imitate some familiar movement, then introduce a new movement saying, "Now do this." If child does not change his or her behavior in an attempt to imitate, again model the behavior and physically assist child to do it. If child does imitate, you respond by laughing, praising, or doing whatever is pleasing to the child. It is helpful to use manual signs or motor movements that would be natural gestures and to pair them with the words (e.g., "bye-bye," "eat," "drink," "up"). Sometimes a mirror focuses the child's attention on both your actions and his or her own.	***Record*** + if the child: 1. Partially imitates the modeled response within 15 seconds; and 2. Imitates the modeled response within 15 seconds. ***Criterion:*** Child imitates an unfamiliar movement when child's own action is visible to himself or herself; 4 of 5 trials on 3 separate days.

Note: Be sure the behavior to be imitated is a movement the child can perform *easily*. If it is physically difficult, odds are that imitation will not be learned readily. The caregiver should be relaxed and have a good time with the child. If this activity is not fun for the caregiver and child, learning will be slow and teaching will be a drag! Make a game of activities. Also use your imagination in the simple activities to be imitated.

AREA: **10. Gestural Imitation**
BEHAVIOR: 10e. Imitates unfamiliar movement that is not visible to himself or herself

Position of Child: Sitting or lying down
Materials: Mirror

Teaching procedures	Steps for learning/evaluation
Continue the "imitation game." Get reciprocal imitation going by imitating the child, then introducing familiar activities that the child has imitated in the past. Introduce a new activity that the child cannot see himself or herself do (e.g., blinking eyes, pulling ears, opening and closing mouth). If child does not imitate spontaneously, say, "With me, now you do this," repeating the activity. If child still does not imitate, either physically assist the response or introduce a mirror so the action can be seen for 1 or 2 trials; then remove the mirror. If child does imitate, you respond by laughing, praising, continuing the game, or doing whatever is pleasing to the child.	*Record* + if the child: 1. Imitates a movement not visible to himself or herself (if looking at his or her own body) after physical assistance or after watching himself or herself in a mirror; and 2. Spontaneously imitates a movement not visible to himself or herself. *Criterion:* Child spontaneously imitates a movement not visible to himself or herself as he or she is doing it; 4 of 5 trials on 3 separate days.

AREA: **10. Gestural Imitation**
BEHAVIOR: 10f. Imitates new activities, including use of materials

Position of Child: Sitting or lying down
Materials: Materials used should be ones that create an "interesting" spectacle upon being touched, tugged, tweaked, or tumbled (e.g., pinwheel, toy car, rattles, cake pans)

Teaching procedures	Steps for learning/evaluation
Upon getting the attention of the child, perform an activity with a selected toy. Once the activity has been performed, place the toy in a position that will allow the child to repeat the activity in a similar manner. Vary activities—shaking rattle, waving pinwheel, pushing/pulling a toy, squeezing squeaky toy, and so forth. If child does not imitate you, physically assist him or her in doing so.	*Record* + if the child: 1. Imitates activities with the materials that are modeled. *Criterion:* Child imitates new activities with materials; 4 of 5 trials on 3 separate days.

Note: This activity should be made "gamelike" for both the child and caregiver. Be sure to watch carefully for changes in affect (smiling, laughing) and in turn taking that indicate that the child understands the game and is enjoying it. Again, be sure to select activities to be repeated that are within the behavioral ability of the child.

AREA: **10. Gestural Imitation**

BEHAVIOR: 10g. Imitates 1 sign that stands for a word (e.g., "Daddy," "all gone," "more," "eat," "drink ")

Position of Child: Any comfortable position
Materials: None

Teaching procedures	Steps for learning/evaluation
Consistently pair 3 or 4 signs with the appropriate words and situations. (For signs commonly used with children, refer to books listed in the note below.) Watch for the child to imitate any one of the signs. If child does not, begin introducing a sign during your imitation games with the child, always pairing it with the word. If child does not imitate in that setting, physically assist him or her in making the sign. Praise, hug, or simply continue playing with child when he or she does imitate the sign—whatever pleases child most!	***Record*** + if the child: 1. Imitates a sign for a word within the context of imitation games; and 2. Imitates a sign for a word spontaneously in play or during naturally occurring events (e.g., imitates a sign for "eat" when it is modeled at mealtime). ***Criterion:*** Child imitates a sign for a word spontaneously; 3 of 5 trials on 3 separate days.

Note: Among books that are appropriate for teaching signs are:
  Bauer, A. M., et al. (n.d.). *Signs for everyday* (Books 1 and 2). Elwyn, PA: Elwyn Institute.
  Rittenhouse, R. K., & Myers, J. J. (1982). *Teaching sign language: The first vocabulary.* Normal, IL: Illinois Associates.
  Sesame Street. (1980). *Sesame Street sign language fun.* New York: Random House.

AREA: **10. Gestural Imitation**

BEHAVIOR: 10h. Imitates 2 signs that stand for words
               10i. Imitates 3 signs that stand for words

Position of Child: Any comfortable position
Materials: None

Teaching procedures	Steps for learning/evaluation
Consistently pair 3 or 4 signs with the appropriate words and situations. (For signs commonly used with children, refer to the books listed in the Appendix). After child has learned to imitate one sign, call his or her attention to another. If child does not imitate sign spontaneously, introduce it in the context of other imitation activities. If child still does not imitate, physically assist him or her to do so. Praise, hug, or do whatever is pleasing to child when he or she does imitate appropriately.	***Record*** + if the child: (h) 1. Imitates 2 signs that stand for words. (i) 2. Imitates 3 signs that stand for words. ***Criterion:*** (h) Imitates 2 signs that stand for words; 3 of 5 trials on 3 separate days. ***Criterion:*** (i) Imitates 3 signs that stand for words; 3 of 5 trials on 3 separate days.

AREA: **10. Gestural Imitation**
BEHAVIOR: 10j. Imitates sequence of 2 signs that stand for words

Position of Child: Any comfortable position
Materials: None

Teaching procedures	Steps for learning/evaluation
Begin introducing simple sequences of signs, selecting a verb sign that can fit many nouns (e.g., "Johnny eat," "Mama eat," "Daddy eat," etc.). Say the words as you sign them. This will cause you to speak more slowly, but it is important for the sign to accompany the word being spoken. Watch for the child to imitate a 2-sign sequence spontaneously. If child does not, call his or her attention to it and physically assist child in doing it. Praise or hug child or do whatever appears to please child when he or she imitates successfully.	*Record* + if the child: 1. Imitates 1 sequence of 2 signs in the context of working on imitation skills; and 2. Spontaneously imitates 1 sequence of 2 signs in a setting appropriate to those signs (e.g., "Daddy eat" at suppertime). *Criterion:* Child imitates a sequence of 2 signs that stand for words; 3 of 4 trials on 3 separate days.

11.

Gestural Communication

ONE OF THE EARLIEST ways children have to let other persons know of their wants, likes, or dislikes is through bodily movement. Very early in life, children begin sharing their feelings with us by responding differently to different people with whom they come in contact and by engaging or "turning off" adults through their actions. As these different actions become understood by caregivers and responded to in an appropriate fashion, they become a vital part of the process of communication. This sequence of activities stresses the importance of responding to these actions as communication. Working through the development of gestural communication with young children can lead to the gradual shaping of a gestural communication system to accompany speech or to the development of a substitute system for communication if speech does not develop.

If you are working with children who are very slow to develop communication skills or who are developing atypical communication patterns, it is extremely important that you seek help from a specialist in communicative disorders as you plan a language development program. Such a specialist will be able to provide you with advice regarding the development of an augmentative communication system if spoken language is likely to be substantially delayed or nonexistent.

11. Gestural Communication

a. Shows anticipation of regularly occurring events in everyday care
b. Responds to being shifted from mother or caregiver to another person
c. Anticipates frequently occurring events in "games" (nursery rhymes, etc.)
d. Repeats activity that gets interesting reaction from others
e. Gets adult to continue activity by starting body movements
f. Initiates activity by starting movement
g. Raises arms to be picked up
h. Consistently indicates desire to "get down"
i. Reaches toward something to indicate "Get it" or "Give it"
j. Uses gestures for word concepts ("all gone," "more," "eat," "drink," etc.)

Stop here if child is progressing well with spoken words.

k. Uses gestures or signs for 5 words or concepts

l. Uses signs for 7 or more words
m. Uses signs to communicate wants
n. Uses 15 signs consistently
o. Combines signs to communicate

AREA: **11. Gestural Communication**

BEHAVIOR: 11a. Shows anticipation of regularly occurring events in everyday care

Position of Child: Any position that permits a voluntary response
Materials: Those used in everyday care

Teaching procedures	Steps for learning/evaluation
Keep a daily routine that is fairly regular and predictable. Make "rituals" out of some daily routines. For example, when you get ready to feed the baby, always say a simple phrase like "Time to eat" and use a visual or tactile cue along with this phrase like showing the child the bottle, rubbing it across his or her cheek, or taking child to the rocking chair where he or she is nursed. After child begins to show anticipatory responses, change the routine of one activity and watch for indications of surprise or distress. Return to the routine, periodically breaking it and trying to make a "game" out of the irregularities by what you do or say (e.g., laugh and correct and say, "Oops, what happened?" etc.).	*Record* + if the child: 1. Shows signs of anticipation; and 2. Shows any indication of surprise or distress. (Record which of these.) *Criterion:* Child indicates anticipation 3 times a day on 3 consecutive days; *and* 3 indications of surprise in a 2-week period (this is a stronger indicator of anticipation).

Note: Watch for signs that the child is recognizing these routine events. Some signs might be visual (e.g., child looks at the refrigerator when you are getting ready to get the bottle out), others verbal or motoric (e.g., child coos and kicks when you take child to the chair where you nurse him or her).

AREA: **11. Gestural Communication**

BEHAVIOR: 11b. Responds to being shifted from mother or caregiver to another person

Position of Child: Held in mother's arms, then handed over to another person
Materials: None

Teaching procedures	Steps for learning/evaluation
Observe child when he or she is being held by his or her mother or primary caregiver. Then ask that person to shift child to another adult. Look for any changes in the child's facial expressions, vocalization, body position, or amount of activity that would seem to indicate that the child is aware of being shifted from his or her mom's arms. If the child does not show a change, try to make the shift more noticeable by: Having the mother or caregiver talk to the child face to face and having the second person do the same;	*Record* + if the child: 1. Shows any behavior indicating recognition of the shift to another person. (Record the behavior.) *Criterion:* Child indicates recognition of the shift to another person 3 times on 5 different occasions.

(continued)

Teaching procedures	Steps for learning/evaluation
Making sure the second person is a stranger to the child; and Increasing the length of time mother interacts with the baby before she gives baby to the other person, including lots of tactile and visual contact. The second person should then interact very little.	

AREA: 11. Gestural Communication

BEHAVIOR: 11c. Anticipates frequently occurring events in "games" (nursery rhymes, etc.)

Position of Child: Any position that allows voluntary response
Materials: None—this is an interpersonal experience

Teaching procedures	Steps for learning/evaluation
Place the child on your knees and bounce him or her as you recite a favorite nursery rhyme such as: "Ride a horse, Ride a horse, Ride to town, Watch out Little Girl, Don't fall down!" On the word "down," straighten your leg and let child slide down a bit. Watch for signs of excitement or anticipation that indicate child knows you will be moving your legs on the word "down." After playing this game several times on different days, begin to pause a little before saying, "Don't fall down!" to see if the child anticipates the down movement. Other nursery rhymes to be used might be: "Pat-a-cake" (emphasis on "Toss it in the oven!"); "Eye-blinker, nose-blower, mouth-eater, chin-chucker, chin-chucker-chin" (touching eyes, nose, mouth as named and tickling under the chin for "chin-chucker"); "Here comes a little bug, walking up the hill. If he doesn't get you, Mommy will!" (Walk with fingers up child's arm or leg; tickle child on "Mommy will.")	**Record** + if the child: 1. Shows any indication of anticipation— laughing, body stiffening, extending arms, and so forth. **Criterion:** Child shows 3 indications of anticipation on 2 different days.

Note: Games must be selected that will be fun for the child but that will *not* stimulate abnormal reflexes. Speed of repetition, intensity of tactile stimulation, and places on the body that are tickled or rubbed must be carefully matched to the child's temperament and physical responses also. Some children need rapid, vigorous stimulation in order to respond; others find such stimuli aversive; still othes may become too excited to respond at all. Take your cues from the child's responses.

AREA: **11. Gestural Communication**
BEHAVIOR: 11d. Repeats activity that gets interesting reaction from others

Position of Child: Any position that permits voluntary actions on the part of the child
Materials: None needed

Teaching procedures	Steps for learning/evaluation
When the child is clapping, making a face, or making any desired response, respond immediately by laughing, cheering, or imitating child's response. If child does not repeat his or her own action, say something like, ''That's wonderful. Let's do it again.'' Physically guide child through the activity. If child spontaneously repeats the activity after this, praise child for it.	*Record* + if the child: 1. Repeats an activity that is reacted to by others. *Criterion:* Child repeats 3 different activities that get interesting reactions from others within a 2-day period.

Note: If child *spontaneously* repeats the activity immediately after the prompt, respond to the child's action, but do not prompt another repetition. Work toward getting the child to repeat a *variety of responses* as a result of your noticing and reinforcing them.

AREA: **11.   Gestural Communication**
BEHAVIOR: 11e.   Gets adult to continue activity by starting body movements

Position of Child: Any position that permits voluntary movements
Materials: None needed

Teaching procedures	Steps for learning/evaluation
When playing games with the child that he or she enjoys, play for a few minutes and stop (for examples and cautions see item 11c). Wait up to 20 seconds to see if child will try to get you to continue by putting a hand out toward you, touching you, reaching toward you with his or her feet, bouncing on your knee and so forth (anything appropriate to the content of the game). Start to play again immediately if child makes such a response. If necessary, physically guide child through an appropriate action to start the game; then begin the game. Try no more than 3 times in succession in any play session.	*Record* + if the child: 1. Does part of the movements for a game in order to get the adult to continue. *Criterion:* Child makes movements to resume an activity at least twice a day on 3 separate days.

AREA: **11.   Gestural Communication**
BEHAVIOR: 11f.   Initiates activity by starting movement

Position of Child: Any position that permits a voluntary response
Materials: None

Teaching procedures	Steps for learning/evaluation
Same as for item 11e, except that you simply place the child in the position generally used to play a game. Say the words of the game or, for a *hearing-impaired* child, make a sign that goes with the game. If child does not respond to your verbal or visual cues to start the game, physically guide child to make an appropriate movement to start the game. Play a few minutes and then wait as in item 11e, to see if child will try to continue the game. If child does not, physically guide him or her again. If child does, play the game with enthusiasm and praise. Note carefully and respond to a child's attempts to initiate any kind of game, not necessarily ones you have deliberately taught. For example, you may discover that a child likes to be spun around while you hold him or her. The child's natural tendency during the spinning will be to lean out from your body. Then child may begin to lean away in order to try to get you to spin him or her. Label what child is doing ("You want to spin, huh?") and do it.	***Record*** + if the child: 1. Tries to initiate a game by starting the movements. ***Criterion:*** Child initiates games at least once a day on 3 different days.

AREA: **11.   Gestural Communication**
BEHAVIOR: 11g.   Raises arms to be picked up

Position of Child: Any position that permits child to raise arms (even minimally)
Materials: None needed

Teaching procedures	Steps for learning/evaluation
Whenever, as part of the caregiver routine, you are going to pick the child up say "up" and hold out your arms briefly. If child does not reach out toward you, touch child's hands as you say "up" and wait for child to make some movement; then pick child up. The degree of reaching out may vary greatly. Any attempt to respond appropriately should be re-inforced with "picking up."	***Record*** + if the child: 1. Holds out arms to be picked up without assistance. ***Criterion:*** Child reaches out to be picked up 3 times a day; 3 different days.

AREA: **11. Gestural Communication**
BEHAVIOR: 11h. Consistently indicates desire to "get down"

Position of Child: Held in arms or lap of caregiver
Materials: None needed

Teaching procedures	Steps for learning/evaluation
Try to attend to the child's indications of a desire to be put down. (These might be wiggling, tensing of body, or pushing away.) Say "Do you want to get *down*?" and then put child down. Sometimes it is not appropriate to put the child down even though the signal is clear that he or she wants to get down. Under these circumstances be sure to let child know that you understand his or her signal (e.g., "I know you want to get down, but you cannot right now").	***Record*** + if the child: 1. Moves in some way to suggest he or she wants to get down *and* indicates pleasure (or, at least no displeasure) at being put down. ***Criterion:*** Child has a consistent way of indicating "down"; observed at least once a day on 3 separate days.

AREA: **11. Gestural Communication**
BEHAVIOR: 11i. Reaches toward something to indicate "Get it" or "Give it"

Position of Child: Any position that permits a voluntary response
Materials: Any toy or food

Teaching procedures	Steps for learning/evaluation
When giving toys or food to the child, say "Want it?" or a similar phrase, and hold toy or food where child can see it but not reach it. Watch for some indication that the child wants the object (e.g., a reaching motion or some movement toward the object with child's head or feet if reaching is not possible). If necessary, physically guide some movement toward the object before giving it to the child. Be sure to praise any visible attempts the child makes to indicate his or her desire for something.	***Record*** + if the child: 1. Moves or reaches toward object in response to the question "Want it?" ***Criterion:*** Child reaches or moves toward any object(s) to indicate wants; 5 times a day on 3 separate days.

AREA: **11. Gestural Communication**

BEHAVIOR: 11j.   Uses gestures for word concepts ("all gone," "more," "eat," "drink," etc.)

Position of Child: Any position that permits a voluntary response
Materials: Those used in everyday care

Teaching procedures	Steps for learning/evaluation
See note below!	***Record*** + if the child:
In an appropriate situation, say the word associated with a gesture the child has initiated and wait for child to gesture (e.g., "all gone"—hand out to sides, palms up; "drink"—hand tipping to mouth as with a cup).	1. Uses one appropriate gesture upon hearing the word associated with a gesture; and
If child does not gesture:	2. Uses two appropriate gestures upon hearing the words associated with the gestures.
Model the gesture for the child to imitate. Reward child when he or she imitates.	***Criterion:*** Child makes at least 2 different gestures—3 correct responses for each; 3 consecutive days.
If child does not imitate, say the word again and physically assist the gesture.	
Do not go beyond 5 consecutive trials on 1 word in 1 setting.	

Note: Child must be imitating gestures representing words (item 11e) before he or she will use readily understood gestures for word concepts. Teach to criterion on 11e!

AREA: **11. Gestural Communication**

BEHAVIOR: 11k. Uses gestures or signs for 5 words or concepts

Position of Child: Any position that facilitates use of hands
Materials: None

Teaching procedures	Steps for learning/evaluation
Select several natural gestures or signs to incorporate into your conversations with the child. For example, when you say "Do you want to eat?" touch your fingers to your mouth. An elementary book of manual signs (see references at the end of Chapter 5) may be helpful in selecting ones to emphasize.	***Record*** + if the child:
	1. Spontaneously makes a gesture or sign in an appropriate setting (record which word is signed); and
	2. Spontaneously uses 2 different gestures in 1 day; and
After teaching the child to initiate 1 or more signs (see gestural imitation sequence), arrange situations where using the sign spontaneously would be adaptive. For example, bring child's lunch and wait a minute or so for the sign "eat." If child does not make the sign, you make it and wait for an imitation. If you do not get an imitation, physically guide child's hand through the actions and then give child his or her food.	3. Spontaneously uses 3 to 5 different gestures in 1 day.
	Criterion: Child spontaneously gestures or signs for 5 different words or word concepts; each gesture observed once a day on 3 separate days. (Included in the 5 words may be "up," "down," "bye-bye," "Give it"—covered in items *g, h, i, j*.)

Note: Many children will begin to speak after they have learned a few signs. Whenever a child begins to learn new spoken words as fast as or faster than he or she learns new signs, continued work through this sequence is unnecessary.

AREA: **11. Gestural Communication**
BEHAVIOR: 11l. Uses signs for 7 or more words

Position of Child: Any position that facilitates use of hands
Materials: Familiar toys, people, and so forth

Teaching procedures	Steps for learning/evaluation
As you verbally label people, things, or events in the child's life, make the sign to go with each label (see note below). Observe child carefully for his or her attempt to make those same signs as he or she sees the people or things. Whenever child approximates a sign, you make the sign again. As you repeat the word and give child the toy, take him or her closer to the person or whatever action would be appropriate to reinforce child's attempts to make the sign. If the child makes no attempt to use signs, follow your demonstration of the sign with physically assisting the child to form the sign, and then reinforce. Reduce physical assistance as rapidly as possible. *Visually impaired* children will need to feel your hands as you form a sign. Begin with signs that are easily distinguished from one another.	***Record*** + if the child: 1. Spontaneously uses signs for 7 or more words. (Record which words are signed.) ***Criterion:*** Child uses signs for 7 or more different words during the course of a day on 3 separate days.

Note: Consult a speech pathologist familiar with manual signs to learn the signs. Some elementary signs are also illustrated in several books—for example: Bove, L. (1980). *Sign language fun.* New York: Random House.

AREA: **11. Gestural Communication**
BEHAVIOR: 11m. Uses signs to communicate wants

Position of Child: Any position that facilitates use of hands
Materials: None

Teaching procedures	Steps for learning/evaluation
Whenever the child indicates a want or need by pointing, whining, or other nonspecific activity, label the thing he or she appears to want both with a word and the appropriate sign, saying something like, "Oh, you want a drink, [word and sign]; say 'drink' [word and sign]." If child does not then imitate the sign, physically guide his or her hands through it and give child what he wanted. Be sure to allow enough time between your asking child to make the sign and physically assisting him or her to ensure that child has time to organize a response, and do not wait so long as to produce too much frustration. Also, avoid repeating the command ("Say 'drink' "). Say it once, wait for child to do it; if child does not do it, physically assist child and then give child what he or she wants.	***Record*** + if the child: 1. Uses a sign to get a need met after the adult labels the need and asks child to "say _____" (record which need is signed); and 2. Spontaneously uses a sign to get a need met (record which need is signed); and 3. Spontaneously uses 2 different signs to get 2 different needs met. ***Criterion:*** Child spontaneously uses 2 different signs to get 2 different needs met on 3 separate days.

AREA: **11. Gestural Communication**
BEHAVIOR: 11n. Uses 15 signs consistently

Position of Child: Any position that facilitates use of hands
Materials: None

Teaching procedures	Steps for learning/evaluation
Once a child has mastered 5 or 6 signs, it is important to begin communicating with him or her through combining signs into short sentences, trying to time the signs to fit the spoken sentence. Continue to observe the child carefully for his or her attempts to make signs, and reinforce those attempts through an appropriate means (granting a request, praising child, etc.). As you introduce new signs, try to get child to imitate the signs or physically assist child to make them—whatever methods have worked well for the signs already learned.	***Record*** + if the child: 1. Uses 15 signs for words. (Record which words are signed.) ***Criterion:*** Child spontaneously uses 15 different signs; each is used 5 or more times in the course of a week.

Note: Record keeping may be simplified by writing down each different word that is signed and making marks after it each time it is used, up through the fifth time.

AREA: **11. Gestural Communication**
BEHAVIOR: 11o. Combines signs to communicate

Position of Child: Any position that facilitates use of hands
Materials: None

Teaching procedures	Steps for learning/evaluation
Communicate with the child using "total communication" (signing and talking simultaneously). In addition, "expand" on the child's communication. When child uses 1 sign, repeat the sign but add another to produce a more complete idea. For example, if he signs "cookie," you could sign "Eat cookie" or "You want cookie." Try to get child to imitate the two signs in sequence. If child does not, physically assist him or her to make them. Observe the child carefully for his or her attempts to put 2 signs together in a sentence such as "I go," "You go," "Drink now," and so forth. Always praise these attempts, repeat the sign back to the child, and respond appropriately to the content of the communication.	***Record*** + if the child: 1. Uses 2 signs in sequence after demonstration. (Record which words are signed); and 2. Spontaneously uses 2 signs in sequence. (Record which words are signed.) ***Criterion:*** Child combines 2 or more signs to communicate; at least once a day on 3 separate days.

12.

Vocal Imitation

CHILDREN LEARN TO SPEAK largely through imitating the speech of their caregivers and others with whom they come in contact. This sequence of activities has been designed to teach youngsters to imitate speech in a reasonably systematic way. However, it cannot be stressed too much that the primary way of teaching language to children is to talk to them a great deal and to play verbal games with them. This should occur off and on during all of their waking hours, not just during times designated for the teaching of language. In fact, at the toddler stage, many children will be reluctant to vocalize either spontaneously or in imitation if they perceive particular stress being placed on the quality of their sound production. Providing children the experience of having fun with vocal games may help to avoid this problem and increase the likelihood of their vocalizing more readily. If a child is not making progress in vocalizing, have the child's hearing checked. Also, help the parents monitor middle ear infections; these can interfere with language development.

12. Vocal Imitation

a. Vocalizes in response to person talking
b. Repeats sounds just made when they are imitated by caregiver
c. Shifts sounds—imitates sound in repertoire when made by caregiver
d. Imitates inflection (pitch)
e. Attempts to match new sounds
f. Imitates familiar 2-syllable words like "baba," "Dada," or "Mama"
g. Imitates 2-syllable words with syllable changes ("baby," "uh-oh," "all gone," etc.)
h. Imitates familiar words overheard in conversation
i. Imitates novel 2-syllable words
j. Imitates environmental sounds during play
k. Imitates 2-word sentences
l. Imitates 3-syllable words

AREA: 12. Vocal Imitation
BEHAVIOR: 12a. Vocalizes in response to person talking

Position of Child: Any comfortable position
Materials: None

Teaching procedures	Steps for learning/evaluation
Talk to the child.	*Record* + if the child:
Sing and make sounds during play or caregiving activities. However, remember to pause at regular intervals so as to give the child a chance to vocalize.	1. Vocalizes in any manner immediately after being "talked to."
Stop talking when you have the child's attention, then wait.	*Criterion:* Child vocalizes when parent or trainer talks to child and then pauses; 3 times in 4 trials on 2 separate days.
If child does not vocalize freely in response to your talking, try attending to any sounds he or she makes. Reinforce these sounds through your own imitation of his or her sounds and by smiling at and touching the child.	

Note: Reinforcement of the child's vocalizations is important. Smile, vocalize, and touch child in return for his or her vocalizations.

AREA: 12. Vocal Imitation
BEHAVIOR: 12b. Repeats sounds just made when they are imitated by caregiver

Position of Child: Any comfortable position
Materials: None

Teaching procedures	Steps for learning/evaluation
Attend to sounds the infant makes spontaneously.	*Record* + if the child:
Present these and other cooing sounds to the infant in play. Be sure to pause and wait for the infant's attempts at imitation.	1. Repeats a sound he or she has made after it is imitated by caregiver. Vocalization must be heard.
Repeat several times.	*Criterion:* Child repeats sounds he or she has just made after they are imitated (approximately) by an adult; 3 of 4 trials on 2 separate days.
Make this a game. You make a sound, then the child makes a sound in a turn-taking manner. Smile and laugh with the child.	

Note: Easy, early sounds to try are: "A-Goo!"; "Mmmmm!"; "Ahhhh!"; "Da-da!" List the sounds the infant does imitate so that they can be used in interaction, and new ones taught.

AREA: **12. Vocal Imitation**

BEHAVIOR: 12c. Shifts sounds—imitates sound in repertoire when made by caregiver

Position of Child: Any comfortable position
Materials: None

Teaching procedures	Steps for learning/evaluation
When the child vocalizes during play or caregiving activities, respond with sounds you have heard him or her make before. Pause long enough for child to attempt to alter his sounds in imitation of yours. Make certain the sounds are in the child's repertoire. Shift to other sounds you have heard the child make. Play a game of "imitation."	***Record*** + if the child: 1. Responds by imitating the sound made by caregiver. (Keep a record of the sounds the youngster readily imitates and shifts to.) ***Criterion:*** Child imitates (close approximations) sounds already in his or her repertoire; 3 of 4 trials on 2 separate days.

AREA: **12. Vocal Imitation**

BEHAVIOR: 12d. Imitates inflection (pitch)

Position of Child: Any comfortable position
Materials: None

Teaching procedures	Steps for learning/evaluation
As in skill 12c, present the child with 2-syllable sounds already in his or her repertoire. However, this time alter your *inflection* somewhat dramatically (e.g., "A-goo!"). Pause long enough for the child to imitate you. Reinforce with a smile, touch, and further vocalizations if the child imitates the *inflection* as well as the sound. If child imitates the sound but not the inflection, try again, further emphasizing 1 syllable.	***Record*** + if the child: 1. Recognizably changes the inflection (pitch) of his or her imitation. ***Criterion:*** Child imitates adult's novel inflection of sounds in child's repertoire; 3 of 4 trials on at least 2 separate days.

AREA: **12. Vocal Imitation**
BEHAVIOR: 12e. Attempts to match new sounds

Position of Child: Any comfortable position
Materials: None

Teaching procedures	Steps for learning/evaluation
During play or caregiving activities, initiate an imitation game. Use sounds *not* in the child's repertoire. Pause, wait for the child to imitate the sounds you make. If child does not imitate a new sound immediately, try shaping this by offering a sound that you know is in the child's repertoire, then one slightly varied, and finally an entirely new sound. The child may imitate a new sound more readily if the stage is "set" with familiar sounds. Make this a game. You imitate the child's sounds occasionally also.	***Record*** + if the child: 1. Imitates sounds not known to be in his or her repertoire previously. ***Criterion:*** Child approximates new sounds (not words) offered by caregiver 3 of 4 times on 2 separate days.

AREA: **12. Vocal Imitation**
BEHAVIOR: 12f. Imitates familiar 2-syllable words like "baba," "Dada," or "Mama"

Position of Child: Any comfortable position
Materials: None

Teaching procedures	Steps for learning/evaluation
During play or caregiving activities, initiate an imitation game. Use sounds *not* in the child's repertoire. Pause, wait for the child to imitate the sounds you make. Begin to verbalize simple and familiar words like "Dada," "Mama," and so forth. After each word, pause to allow the child a chance to imitate. Repeat each new word 4 or 5 times before attempting other new words. If child does not imitate a new word, work through a sequence of approximations based on sounds he or she knows to set the stage for imitation of new sounds and words. Make it a game!	***Record*** + if the child: 1. Imitates any 2-syllable words. (Record which words the youngster imitates.) ***Criterion:*** Child imitates 2-syllable words like "baba," "Dada," "Mama"; 3 of 4 trials on 2 successive days.

AREA: **12. Vocal Imitation**

BEHAVIOR: 12g. Imitates familiar 2-syllable words with syllable changes ("baby," "uh-oh," "all gone," etc.)

Position of Child: Any comfortable position
Materials: None

Teaching procedures	Steps for learning/evaluation
While playing an imitation game with the child, introduce simple and familiar 2-syllable words, then pause and wait for the child to imitate them. Make certain the words are very familiar or that they are words that have functional meaning in the child's life. When possible, incorporate this activity into the child's daily experiences (e.g., saying "all gone" as the child finishes a cracker). Use shaping procedures described in previous items in this area when necessary.	***Record*** + if the child: 1. Imitates familiar 2-syllable words with syllable changes. ***Criterion:*** Child imitates simple 2-syllable words; 2 of 3 trials on 3 consecutive days. Use at least 3 words that are familiar and useful to the child.

AREA: **12. Vocal Imitation**

BEHAVIOR: 12h. Imitates familiar words overheard in conversation

Position of Child: Any comfortable position
Materials: "Feely box"[a] and toys

Teaching procedures	Steps for learning/evaluation
Whenever working with a child, speak to him or her in short but complete sentences. If the child imitates any words or portions of these sentences, praise child immediately and enthusiastically. Work with a small group of children on labeling familiar items. Try using a large "feely box" filled with a variety of items. Have a child pull out 1 object. Say, "This is a_____. [child's name], what is this?" Encourage child to respond; model the correct phrase, such as say "This is a ball."	***Record*** + if the child: 1. Imitates familiar words overheard in conversation. (Record words the child imitates.) ***Criterion:*** Child spontaneously imitates familiar words overheard in conversation; 2 times on 2 consecutive days.

Note: Encouraging imitation should not be taken to such an extreme that it encourages echolalia. Functional labeling may help prevent this problem.
[a] A closed box with a hole in the top through which children can reach for objects that they cannot see.

AREA: 12. Vocal Imitation
BEHAVIOR: 12i. Imitates novel 2-syllable words

Position of Child: Any comfortable position that does not promote abnormal postures
Materials: Well-liked toys with 2-syllable names and a "feely box"[a]

Teaching procedures	Steps for learning/evaluation
This item can be worked on with individuals or in small-group situations. Present toys or objects whose names are 2 syllables long (table, baby, doggie, etc.). Name the object or toy and try to get child to imitate you by asking, "What is this?" When child names the item, reinforce child by giving him or her the item. Work with a small group of children and a "feely box." Have 1 child pull out a toy, tell him or her the name of the toy, and have the child repeat the name. Work individually with children on labeling action words: "Bouncing"—bounce ball when correctly imitated. "Bouncing"—bounce child on knee when correctly imitated. "Running"—take child's hand and run when word is imitated correctly. If child does not imitate, try saying, "Say ____."	*Record* + if the child: 1. Imitates novel 2-syllable words. (Record the words child imitates and the number of words imitated during a session.) *Criterion:* Child imitates (repeats) at least 3 novel 2-syllable words; 4 of 5 trials, 2 consecutive days.

Note: [a] A closed box with a hole in the top through which children can reach for objects that they cannot see.

AREA: 12. Vocal Imitation
BEHAVIOR: 12j. Imitates environmental sounds during play

Position of Child: Any comfortable position
Materials: A variety of toys (animals, cars, train, etc.) that have easy sounds associated with them

Teaching procedures	Steps for learning/evaluation
Play games with the child with toys and make sounds appropriate for those toys. Encourage child to imitate. (Example: car—"Varoom.") Label the sounds made (e.g., car's horn, whistle, siren). Take the child outside and expose him or her to sounds. Try imitating some of the sounds made. Label the sounds made. Encourage child to imitate these sounds. (Example: Caregiver and child hear a dog barking. Caregiver imitates sound, then says, "That is a dog. Dogs bark 'bow-wow'!" and imitates sound again. Or, "What does a (dog) say?" "Bow-wow!" "Say 'bow-wow.' ")	*Record* + if the child: 1. Imitates environmental sounds during play. (Record the sounds imitated.) *Criterion:* Child imitates at least 2 environmental sounds (with or without prompting); 4 of 5 trials on 2 consecutive days.

AREA: **12. Vocal Imitation**
BEHAVIOR: 12k. Imitates 2-word sentences

Position of Child: Any comfortable position
Materials: Puppets

Teaching procedures	Steps for learning/evaluation
During play encourage the child to imitate you. Use a puppet to model a short sentence, then ask if the child's puppet can say the same thing. Encourage short sentences whenever appropriate situations arise (e.g., "Daddy go" or "Want cookie?").	*Record* + if the child: 1. Imitates 2-word sentences. (Record any sentences the child imitates.) *Criterion:* Child will imitate at least 3 different 2-word sentences; 4 of 5 trials on 2 consecutive days.

AREA: **12. Vocal Imitation**
BEHAVIOR: 12l. Imitates 3-syllable words

Position of Child: Any comfortable position
Materials: Well-liked toys, foods, etc., with 3 syllables

Teaching procedures	Steps for learning/evaluation
Present the child with a toy, object, or food with a 3-syllable name (e.g., hamburger, telephone, strawberry, chocolate). Name the object or food and try to get the child to imitate you by asking the child, "What is this?" When the child names the items, praise child, by giving him or her the item. Try working with a small group of children and several objects. Encourage interaction. Praise close approximations of these words! They may be difficult at first.	*Record* + if the child: 1. Attempts to imitate a 3-syllable word (approximates the 3 sounds and the inflection pattern); and 2. Imitates a 3-syllable word so that it is understandable with careful listening; and 3. Imitates 3 or more 3-syllable words. (Record the words the child imitates and the number of words imitated during a session.) *Criterion:* Child imitates 3 different 3-syllable words; 3 of 4 trials on each word in 2 consecutive sessions.

13.

Vocal Communication

ITEMS IN THIS SEQUENCE are those most frequently included in curricula as "expressive language" items, beginning with the child's cries and coos—his or her earliest forms of communication—and ending with sentences. It is important throughout the sequence to remain cognizant of the child's "communicative intent" rather than focusing primarily on accuracy of pronunciation. A particular vocalization should be accepted as a word for a child if it is used consistently to refer to a specific object, person, or event, even if it bears only a faint resemblance to the actual word. Of course, accuracy cannot be neglected, since it determines how efficiently a child can communicate, but it should become the focus of intervention efforts only after the child has learned that his or her efforts to communicate will be rewarded by his or her caregivers.

13. Vocal Communication

a. Differentiates cries
b. Stops crying when sees (or touches) bottle or breast
c. Vocalizes to get attention
d. Vocalizes 5 or more consonant and vowel sounds
e. Laughs appropriately
f. Vocalizes 3 or more feelings
g. Repeats vocalizations that get reactions
h. Vocalizes to get return of object
i. Vocalizes repetitive consonant-vowel combinations
j. Indicates wants by vocalizing
k. Uses 2 or more word labels
l. Uses 3 or more word labels

m. Indicates wants with words
n. Uses 1 or more exclamations
o. Uses inflection pattern when vocalizing (babbling); no understandable words
p. Greets familiar people with some appropriate vocalization
q. Says "No" meaningfully
r. Names 5 or more familiar objects
s. Uses inflection pattern(s) in a sentence with 1 or 2 understandable words
t. Says familiar greetings and farewells at appropriate times
u. Names 3 or more pictures of familiar objects
v. Combines 2 or more words in sentences

AREA: **13. Vocal Communication**
BEHAVIOR: 13a. Differentiates cries

Position of Child: Any comfortable position
Materials: None

Teaching procedures	Steps for learning/evaluation
The caregiver must allow the child to experience a need. That is, it is important to avoid doing everything on schedule and/or so frequently that the child has no need to cry. It is equally important to respond to a cry quickly and to try to establish the reason for the cry, responding differently to different cries as soon as the difference can be identified.	Daily data are not necessary. The caregiver should be asked periodically to report when the child can distinguish different cries. *Criterion:* Caregiver reports that the child cries differently for different needs.

Note: This item is not a prerequisite for the development of subsequent behavior in this sequence, but is usually the first form of vocal communication observed in infants. For older handicapped infants, the item may be important primarily for teaching that the noise these infants make affects the social environment in a predictable way.

AREA: **13. Vocal Communication**
BEHAVIOR: 13b. Stops crying when sees (or touches) bottle or breast

Position of Child: Any appropriate position for feeding
Materials: Baby's bottle or mother's breast

Teaching procedures	Steps for learning/evaluation
Mother/caregiver should give the baby ample time to see the bottle/breast before feeding begins. Observe to see if the visually intact baby quiets when *sees* that he or she is about to be fed. Try to get attention by holding the bottle in the baby's line of sight briefly before presenting it. Wiggle the bottle within sight of the baby. For the *visually impaired* child, be sure to talk about the bottle or breast and touch it to the child's hand prior to putting it in his or her mouth.	*Record* + if the child: 1. Quiets upon *seeing* that he or she is about to be fed or (for *visually impaired*) upon feeling the bottle or breast touch his or her hand. *Criterion:* Infant stops crying upon seeing or touching bottle or breast; 3 of 3 trials per day on any 3 of 5 days.

Note: Criterion on this item is not a prerequisite for proceeding through the remainder of the sequence. This item is important primarily because it helps the child establish connections between his or her communicating a need (through crying), a person responding to that need, and the child's changing his or her communication (through ceasing to cry).

AREA: **13. Vocal Communication**
BEHAVIOR: 13c. Vocalizes to get attention

Position of Child: Any position
Materials: None needed

Teaching procedures	Steps for learning/evaluation
In a variety of situations, stop playing with or talking to the child, but listen to him or her. Return your attention to the child immediately when he or she initiates any vocalization other than crying. This does not require formal items to be taught so much as it requires a conscious effort on the part of the parent/caregiver to respond consistently to the infant's noncrying vocalizations. Vocalizations should be attended to consistently and fairly rapidly, facilitating association between the infant's actions and the adult's response.	***Record*** + if the child: 1. Makes a sound other than crying within 3 minutes after you have stopped attending to him or her; and 2. Makes sounds other than crying within 60 seconds after attention has been withdrawn. ***Criterion:*** Child vocalizes without crying within 60 seconds after attention has been withdrawn; 3 of 4 trials on 3 separate days.

Note: Speed of response may not be a critical element for some children. If the child busies himself or herself with contented play when the caregiver withdraws attention for several minutes, but then clearly bids for a new interaction by vocalizing (e.g., looks at caregiver, smiles, and then vocalizes), the child should be given credit at the second step.

AREA: **13. Vocal Communication**
BEHAVIOR: 13d. Vocalizes 5 or more consonant and vowel sounds

Position of Child: Any position that provides face-to-face interaction
Materials: None needed

Teaching procedures	Steps for learning/evaluation
Two of the best situations for increasing vocalizations are feeding and exercise or play. Face the child and interact naturally (talking, showing affection, etc.). Listen carefully to the sounds he or she makes. Write down all sounds heard during a particular observation.	***Record*** + if the child: 1. Makes 2 or more sounds in an eating or playing session; and 2. Makes 5 or more sounds in an eating or playing session. ***Criterion:*** Child makes 5 or more different sounds in an eating or playing session on 3 separate days.

Note: It is important to respond to all vocalizations by repeating them, by talking to the child, and so on. It is also vital to make vocalizing fun, a truly social event.

AREA: **13. Vocal Communication**
BEHAVIOR: 13e. Laughs appropriately

Position of Child: Any position that facilitates interaction
Materials: No materials are needed, but a variety of toys, hand puppets, and so forth, may be used

Teaching procedures	Steps for learning/evaluation
Situations where the baby experiences touching or noises are generally most effective in eliciting laughter at early ages (e.g., tickling child's face or stomach; making popping sounds with mouth in front of child). Toys that make noises, or using a hand puppet to tickle the child while making a variety of verbal noises frequently brings about laughing. Other things to try include: Blowing gently on child's face Making verbal sounds against child's tummy or back Playing with child's toes When child laughs, you laugh too and/or continue the stimuli that produced the laugh.	**Record** + if the child: 1. Laughs so that you can hear it and at appropriate times. **Criterion:** Child laughs in response to appropriate experiences; 3 of 5 trials in 2 separate sessions.

Note: Be sure to keep a record of the things that make the child laugh. They will change over time and will give you good clues as to how to play with the child most effectively.

AREA: **13. Vocal Communication**
BEHAVIOR: 13f. Vocalizes 3 or more feelings

Position of Child: Any position that facilitates interaction
Materials: None needed

Teaching procedures	Steps for learning/evaluation
Listen carefully to the child's vocalizations. Try to determine if they are different when he or she is showing enjoyment, distress, happiness/unhappiness, interest, and so forth. Provide feedback for such vocalization. If the child vocalizes dislike, say, "Oh, you don't like this; well, let's change it" or "Is that fun? Let's play with this one." It is important that the child learn through your actions that his or her vocalizations are being discriminated and are, therefore, affecting his environment. It may be helpful to artificially arrange a situation to "test out" perceptions of the child's vocalization. For example, when child is cooing and acting happy at mealtime, introduce a food you know he or she dislikes and continue to try to feed it to the child for several spoonfuls. Stop if child's protest is clear.	**Record** + if the child: 1. Vocalizes to show happiness, distress, interest, and so forth. **Criterion:** Caregiver can discriminate 3 or more feelings in the child's vocalizations (caregiver report plus 2 "tests").

AREA: **13. Vocal Communication**
BEHAVIOR: 13g. Repeats vocalizations that get reactions

Position of Child: Any position that facilitates face-to-face interaction
Materials: None needed

Teaching procedures	Steps for learning/evaluation
Observe the child, especially during feeding. As child begins to make sounds, respond by talking back to the child, giving him or her another spoon of food (saying, "Oh, so you want some more"), handing child a toy, repeating whatever you were doing when child made the sounds, and so forth. Give the message that you are listening and that you like for the child to "talk." Make frequent opportunities for vocal play where the child is likely to make sounds. This can be done while the child is lying on his or her back in a chair, on your lap, or in almost any position.	***Record*** + if the child: 1. Repeats sounds after caregiver reacts to child's original vocalization in a way noticeable to the child. (Record which sounds are repeated by the child.) ***Criterion:*** Child repeats vocalizations that caregiver reacts to; 3 of 3 trials on 3 separate days.

Note: At one stage of development, a child will stop vocalizing when you talk to him or her. Do not use that as a sign you should not talk to the child, however. Talk a little and then wait for child to vocalize again; let child continue to vocalize a little and then talk again. Gradually, he or she will learn to "take turns" and will not wait so long after you talk to begin vocalizing again.

AREA: **13. Vocal Communication**
BEHAVIOR: 13h. Vocalizes to get return of object

Position of Child: Any comfortable position
Materials: Small toy of interest to the child; bottle or finger food

Teaching procedures	Steps for learning/evaluation
When the child is actively involved in playing with a toy, watch what child does if he or she drops it and cannot retrieve it on his or her own. Return the toy immediately upon the onset of any vocalization on the part of the child except crying. *Or,* if the child has learned to hand you toys and expects you to give them back, wait momentarily before returning the toy, looking for a vocalization indicating child wants you to return the toy. Ask child, "Do you want the _____?"	***Record*** + if the child: 1. Vocalizes (other than crying) to get the return of object. ***Criterion:*** Child vocalizes to get an object returned; 3 times a day on 3 separate days.

Note: Do not wait too long to return objects; avoid making the child cry for them.

AREA: **13. Vocal Communication**
BEHAVIOR: 13i. Vocalizes repetitive consonant-vowel combinations

Position of Child: Seated, during feeding, or in any other position in which the child has been noted
to vocalize frequently
Materials: Spoon and strained or soft food, or toys that the child likes. Sometimes none will be
needed.

Teaching procedures	Steps for learning/evaluation
Listen carefully to the child's vocalizations. Note any consonant-vowel combinations he or she makes (e.g., "ba, da, ma, pa"). Talk back to child by stringing together repetitions of one of the child's frequent sounds (e.g., "ba, ba, ba, ba," using an interesting inflection pattern). Listen for child to repeat (he or she may repeat another sound rather than imitate you; at this stage it is the repetition that is important, not accurate imitation).	*Record* + if the child: 1. Repeats any consonant-vowel combination. *Criterion:* Child vocalizes repetitive consonant-vowel combinations; 3 times in 3 separate sessions.
If child does not begin to repeat any consonant-vowel combinations, you may stimulate during feeding child, saying "ma, ma, ma" as you introduce each bite. Wait between bites to see if child vocalizes.	
If child does not vocalize, apply gentle pressure at the child's lips with the spoon and again stimulate rhythmically with "ma, ma, ma."	
Always try to make vocalizing fun for the child. Make it into a turn-taking game and be excited when child takes his or her turn!	

AREA: **13. Vocal Communication**
BEHAVIOR: 13j. Indicates wants by vocalizing

Position of Child: Any position that facilitates communication
Materials: Several objects that are known to be of interest to the child

Teaching procedures	Steps for learning/evaluation
One at a time, place desired objects or toys out of the child's reach, but where they can be easily seen or heard.	*Record* + if the child: 1. Indicates his or her desire for an object by vocalizing, but without naming the object.
When child attends to an object, say or sign, "What do you want?" The child must make a sound other than a fuss or cry. When child does, give him or her the object. It is not necessary that the object be named!	*Criterion:* Child indicates 3 different objects that he or she wants by vocalizing with regard to them on 3 separate days.

(continued)

Teaching procedures	Steps for learning/evaluation
Prior to this, the child may be given the object when he or she points, gestures, or reaches persistently toward it. This response will need to gradually shaped into the response described above.	

Note: This kind of vocalization is frequently accompanied by gestures such as pointing and may initially sound like the beginning of a fuss (e.g., "uuhh"). As the child learns the sound produces results, the sound will be more relaxed and gradually can be shaped into words for the particular toys wanted.

AREA: **13. Vocal Communication**
BEHAVIOR: 13k. Uses 2 or more word labels

Position of Child: Any comfortable position
Materials: None needed

Teaching procedures	Steps for learning/evaluation
Observe to see if the youngster makes any attempt to approximate words ("Mama," "doggie," "Daddy," etc.). Try to shape the name of an object child wants by naming it, requiring some vocalization to get it, and then requiring a vocalization more closely approximating the name. Be sure to try to teach words containing sounds you have heard the child make frequently. When you recognize an attempt to say a word on the child's part, reinforce it by repeating the word and indicating what it stands for (for example, point to daddy). Be sure to use consistent labels yourself so as not to confuse the child. Use social reinforcement. Show your pleasure at the production of words!	*Record* + if the child: 1. Says any word with a clear symbol reference. (Record words used by the child.) *Criterion:* Child uses 2 or more words appropriately to label persons or objects.

AREA: 13. Vocal Communication
BEHAVIOR: 13l. Uses 3 or more word labels

Position of Child: Any comfortable position
Materials: Several toys the child likes

Teaching procedures	Steps for learning/evaluation
Label objects for the child whenever he or she is playing with them. Often child will name them spontaneously while playing a minute or longer after you have said the name. Write down words that are used appropriately. If words are slow to come, try more specific teaching. For example: Place a toy that the child likes within his or her visual field but out of child's reach. When child attends to the toy say, "What do you want?" When child approximates the name, give him or her the toy. If child does not try to name it, say the name for him or her and ask again. When a child wants to be picked up, ask child what he or she wants. Pick child up after he or she approximates "up." When the child wants to get down (from chair or being held) again, ask child what he wants. Put child down after he or she approximates "down." Consistently use the words "hi" and "bye" with the child in appropriate settings and combined with gestures.	***Record*** + if the child: 1. Uses 3 or more words consistently as labels. ***Criterion:*** Child uses at least 3 words as labels with meaning; 4 of 5 interactions on 3 separate days.

Note: Try to avoid frustrating a child by demanding words all of the time. Keep all talking activities as enjoyable and as natural as possible (i.e., it is better to give the child the ball or bounce the ball when he says "ball" than to clap your hands or say "good, you said ball").

AREA: 13. Vocal Communication
BEHAVIOR: 13m. Indicates wants with words

Position of Child: Any comfortable position
Materials: Several toys the child likes, snack food, juice, swing, rocking chair, wagon, and so forth

Teaching procedures	Steps for learning/evaluation
Always attend to the child's vocalizations, especially when it seems he or she wants something. If child points, say, "What is it you want? Do you want _____?" (if you have some idea of what the want might be). Look for an approximation of the word by the child before you give the object.	***Record*** + if the child: 1. Indicates a want with a word. ***Criterion:*** Child uses understandable words to indicate at least 2 different wants; 4 times on 3 separate days.

(continued)

Teaching procedures	Steps for learning/evaluation
Engage in an activity the child enjoys and label what you are doing. Stop and see if the child will repeat the label to get the activity to continue. (Example: Teacher says, "We will swing." Then swing the child. Stop swinging. Child should say "Swing." Continue the activity, verbally encouraging the child, "That's right, let's swing!")	
Encourage vocal responding by asking questions frequently. If the child does not respond within a short period of time, model the appropriate answer. (Example: "What do you want to do? Swing? Yes, let's swing!") Be sure to allow time for the child to respond before you answer.	

AREA: **13. Vocal Communication**
BEHAVIOR: 13n. Uses 1 or more exclamations

Position of Child: Any comfortable position
Materials: Puppets

Teaching procedures	Steps for learning/evaluation
Use exclamations frequently while playing with the child. For example, while swinging, say, "Oh!" and when you or the child go up high, say, "Uh-oh." When the child spills or drops something, again say, "Uh-oh!"	***Record*** + if the child: 1. Uses exclamations in imitation; and 2. Uses 1 or more exclamations spontaneously.
Perform silly antics for the child and use exclamations during the antics. (Example: walking into a wall, or falling, say, "Oh no!" or "Ouch!" or "Uh-oh!")	***Criterion:*** Child uses at least 1 appropriate exclamation; 1 time on 2 different days.
Play with puppets for the child and have the puppets become hurt or startled. Then have the puppets exclaim appropriately.	
Have the child work one puppet while you work another. Startle or bump into the child's puppet and have your puppet make an appropriate exclamation.	

AREA: **13. Vocal Communication**

BEHAVIOR: 13o. Uses inflection pattern when vocalizing (babbling); no understandable
words

Position of Child: Any that is comfortable for the child. Child may be engaged in play.
Materials: Puppets, children's books

Teaching procedures	Steps for learning/evaluation
Whenever a child vocalizes, wait for child to finish. Then repeat sounds similar to those child made but with greater inflection. Encourage a reciprocal babbling "conversation" between yourself and the child. Use different sentence types.	*Record* + if the child: 1. Babbles with inflection as if in conversation. *Criterion:* Child babbles, clearly showing inflection in the sounds made, when engaged in a "conversation"; 3 times in 3 separate sessions.
Same as above but using a puppet to talk to the child.	
Read a short, easy book to the child, using lots of inflection and tonal quality in the reading. Be sure to discontinue the activity when the child is not paying attention.	

AREA: **13. Vocal Communication**

BEHAVIOR: 13p. Greets familiar people with some appropriate vocalization

Position of Child: Any position
Materials: Puppets

Teaching procedures	Steps for learning/evaluation
Consistently greet the child with "hi" or "hello," every time you see him or her. Be sure to use the child's name in the greeting.	*Record* + if the child: 1. Greets familiar person with some appropriate vocalization. *Criterion:* Child greets familiar people appropriately on at least 2 occasions on 3 separate days.
Frequently greet other people with "Hi, [person's name]" or "Hello, [person's name]" in the child's presence. This could be a staged entrance by another person. Ask the child to say "Hi, [person's name]."	
Have puppets greet each other or greet the child.	
In all of the above activities reinforce child with attention and/or physical contact for appropriate greeting behaviors.	
In group sessions with children, begin the group by saying hello to each child. Sing group songs like, "Hello, my name is _____."	

AREA: **13. Vocal Communication**
BEHAVIOR: 13q. Says "No" meaningfully

Position of Child: Any position
Materials: Varied

Teaching procedures	Steps for learning/evaluation
Consistently say "No" when the child engages in inappropriate activity. Use a logical restraining action if necessary. If child repeats the word "No," whether or not with apparent meaning, cease your activity if at all practical and logical. Say "[Child's name] said 'No!' When engaging in activities with the child, ask the child questions like "More____?" or "No____?" If the child labels the activity, says "More," or says "Yes," continue the activity. If child says "No," stop the activity so the functional meaning of "No" can be learned.	***Record*** + if the child: 1. Says "No" in imitation; and 2. Says "No" spontaneously and meaningfully. ***Criterion:*** Child says "No" when he or she does not want (or does not want to do) something; 3 of 4 trials in 3 consecutive sessions.

Note: It will not always be appropriate for the child to have his or her way when using "No." It is probably good to verbalize a simple reason or "Yes" in these circumstances, even if the child does not understand the explanation. Many children will say "No," or "No-no," when they are about to do something they know is forbidden. This is an appropriate use of the word. Reinforce it by saying something like, "You're right, that is a no-no. Let's do this" (providing an alternative activity).

AREA: **13. Vocal Communication**
BEHAVIOR: 13r. Names 5 or more familiar objects

Position of Child: Any comfortable position that does not promote abnormal postures
Materials: Box with 5–10 different objects that the child likes

Teaching procedures	Steps for learning/evaluation
Individually or in a small group have the child pull 1 toy at a time from the box and tell you the toy's "name." If the child cannot tell the toy's name, let another child name it or you say its name. The first child should repeat its name. Place an object in the child's visual field but out of his or her reach. When child reaches for the toy or shows interest in it, say, "What do you want?" When child names the toy, give it to him or her and play a brief game with the toy. Progress to showing the child more than 1 toy and giving child the toy he or she labels. Teacher and caregiver should consistently label common items in the child's environment and items in which he or she shows an interest.	***Record*** + if the child: 1. Names a familiar object. (Keep a list of objects named during each session.) ***Criterion:*** Child correctly names at least 5 different objects each session in 3 separate sessions.

(continued)

Teaching procedures	Steps for learning/evaluation
In group activities, pass objects to each child and have the children repeat the object's name. Or pass 1 object around, with each child taking turns asking for the object. Try saying: ''What is this?'' ''This is a _____'' (pause and wait for the child to name it). ''What do you want?''	

AREA: 13. Vocal Communication

BEHAVIOR: 13s. Uses inflection pattern(s) in a sentence with 1 or 2 understandable words

Position of Child: Any position
Materials: Toy telephone, child's picture book, puppet

Teaching procedures	Steps for learning/evaluation
Model "talking" on the phone for the child. Allow him or her to play with the phone either alone, talking to "teacher," to another child, or to a puppet. When the child speaks, wait for him or her to finish, then take a turn in conversation. Use the words you recognized in the child's speech. Attempt to understand what the child meant; then respond appropriately, even if words are unclear. Read a simple picture book to the child. Be sure to hold the book so the child can see it. Many children will "attempt to read" or will "describe" what they see. Discontinue reading as soon as the child loses interest. Always speak to the child in short sentences. It is especially valuable to use "action descriptive" words and sentences to label objects. Make it fun!	*Record* + if the child: 1. Uses inflection pattern(s) in a sentence with 1 or 2 understandable words. *Criterion:* Child uses inflection patterns like sentences with 1 or 2 understandable words; 3 occasions on 3 separate days.

AREA: **13. Vocal Communication**
BEHAVIOR: 13t. Says familiar greetings and farewells at appropriate times

Position of Child: Any position
Materials: Puppets, toy telephone

Teaching procedures	Steps for learning/evaluation
Use verbal and gestural communication with the child consistently: Greeting: "Hello" or "hi" paired with name to greet child and to greet others in child's presence. Wave when saying "hello," or shake hands. Farewell: "Bye-bye" should be said to child every time he or she is leaving or someone is leaving child's presence—paired with a wave. Group-time activities with children: Greeting: Sing a "hello" song when the group meets, or say "hello" to each child individually. Have children say "hello" or "hi" to each other. Farewell: Sing "bye-bye, bye-bye" song and have children wave when persons leave the group. Have puppets greet each other and say "bye" to each other. Have puppets greet children and say "bye" to children. Have "conversations" on the phone with child. Always begin conversation with a familiar greeting and end conversation with a farewell.	*Record* + if the child: 1. Says a familiar greeting or farewell at an appropriate time in imitation; and 2. Spontaneously says a familiar greeting or farewell at an appropriate time. *Criterion:* Child appropriately greets and says farewell to familiar people on at least 2 occasions on 2 separate days. (Child does not have to greet and say farewell to the same person.)

AREA: **13. Vocal Communication**
BEHAVIOR: 13u. Names 3 or more pictures of familiar objects

Position of Child: Any comfortable position
Materials: Pictures of familiar objects the child likes (e.g., ball, doll, car, tree, etc.); some objects that match the pictures

Teaching procedures	Steps for learning/evaluation
Look at a picture book with the child. Frequently point out and name the pictures for the child. Then ask child "What is this?" Arrange 2 or 3 pictures of familiar objects on a table. Ask the child to find 1 of the pictures (e.g., "Show me the ball").	*Record* + if the child: 1. Names a picture (record which pictures are named); and 2. Names 2 pictures. *Criterion:* Child names at least 3 different pictures correctly; 4 of 5 trials in 3 separate sessions.

(continued)

Teaching procedures	Steps for learning/evaluation
If child correctly identifies pictures, ask "What is that?" while pointing to the picture. Continue to add more pictures of familiar objects for the child to name.	
If child does not correctly identify the object you asked for, remove all but 2 of the pictures and help child find the right one and name it.	

AREA: **13. Vocal Communication**

BEHAVIOR: 13v. Combines 2 or more words in sentences

Position of Child: Any position
Materials: Snack items

Teaching procedures	Steps for learning/evaluation
Whenever a child uses a single word to communicate (e.g., says "Daddy" when father comes through the door), expand the word to a short sentence (e.g., "Daddy's home"). Gradually, child should begin to make the 2-word combinations herself or himself. If child does not, make a special effort to apply 2–5-word phrases consistently to particular situations. For example, in all situations where someone is leaving, say, "Daddy's going now," "Mama is going to the store," "Grandma is going in the car." Encourage imitation.	*Record* + if the child: 1. Imitates a 2-word phrase or sentence; and 2. Spontaneously produces a 2-word phrase or sentence. *Criterion:* Child spontaneously uses at least 2 different 2-word sentences on 2 separate days.
Use prepositions in unfamiliar situations to promote the use of 2-word phrases. (Examples: Say, "On swing" when getting on swing; "Off swing" when getting off.)	
It may be necessary to become more specific, requiring imitation of 2-word phrases in order for the child to get something. For example, at snacktime have the child repeat "Want cookie," or "Want juice," and so on, after being asked, "Sally, do you want cookie?"	

14.

Social Skills

A CRITICAL ASPECT OF development is learning to engage in reciprocal social interactions with other people. Many handicapped children are very delayed in their ability to reinforce their caregivers and peers through smiling, laughing, game-playing, and the like. Deficiency in these skills often makes it difficult for a caregiver to maintain the personal motivation to work with a child in other areas.

In planning intervention the interaction between caregiver and child should be a primary focus. In the 0- to 12-month developmental period, one must be particularly aware of "orchestrating" interactions so that appropriate turn-taking occurs. For example, many handicapped children demonstrate long latencies between the time a caregiver makes a social overture and the time they smile, wave, or make some other appropriate response. In turn, the caregiver may turn away or begin another form of stimulation and miss or disrupt the response the child was preparing to give.

The interventionist's role may be one of helping the caregiver modify his or her rate or intensity of responses to fit the child's capabilities or, in the case of some severely motorically impaired children, of helping the caregiver identify a facial expression that constitutes a smile for his or her child, though it does not look like the smiles of other children.

In the 12- to 24-month developmental period, emphasis should shift to helping children initiate social interactions and respond to social overtures of peers and a broader range of adults.

14. Social Skills

a. Can be comforted by talking to, holding, or rocking
b. Smiles reciprocally
c. Smiles to auditory or tactile stimulation
d. Smiles at a familiar person
e. Smiles at mirror image (omit for significantly visually impaired children)
f. Tries to attract attention through smiling and eye contact or (if visually impaired child) through other body language

g. Responds differently to strangers versus familiar people
h. Participates in games
i. Repeats activity that is laughed at
j. Initiates game-playing
k. "Gives" things to others upon request (same as 9k)
l. Shares spontaneously with adults
m. Shows affection (hugs, kisses)
n. Tries to please others

o. Plays alongside other children—some exchange of toys

p. "Helps" in simple household tasks—imitates

q. "Performs" for others

r. Tries to comfort others in distress

s. Shares spontaneously with peers

AREA: **14. Social Skills**
BEHAVIOR: 14a. Can be comforted by talking to, holding, or rocking

Position of Child: Lying on back or stomach, or being held
Materials: None, although a small blanket may be helpful

Teaching procedures	Steps for learning/evaluation
When an infant shows distress and is crying, try comforting child by: First, talking softly to infant without touching him or her or picking child up. If child does not quiet in response to your talking: Touch child gently while continuing to speak softly to child. If child is still showing distress, pick child up and hold him or her gently, restraining child from a great deal of body movement—especially by holding child's arms folded in across his or her body. Some children respond well to being swaddled in a small blanket. If child is still not comforted, rock child while holding child in the aforementioned position.	*Record* + if the child: 1. Quiets and is comforted after use of any of the strategies given; and 2. Quiets in response to talking and touching at least 50% of the time. *Criterion:* Children are very different in the way they show distress and in the way they respond to comforting. There is no criterion to be met before other items can be worked on, but work on getting the child quiet with as little intrusion on your part as possible. Do respond to child's distress though!

Note: Be sure to try comforting child by doing things in the order in which they are presented in this item. The first ones offer minimal assistance to the child and allow child to assist in comforting himself or herself.

AREA: **14. Social Skills**
BEHAVIOR: 14b. Smiles reciprocally

Position of Child: Any position that promotes relaxation and good eye contact
Materials: None required

Teaching procedures	Steps for learning/evaluation
The first smiles of a child appear to be responses to internal events such as ''feelings of satisfaction,'' and so forth, rather than responses to social events. It is your smiling at the child and your response to the child when he or she smiles that creates social interchange. In all caregiving activities, is is very important to talk to the child and smile often. Try to maintain eye contact with child (even if child is diagnosed as ''cortically blind,'' since sometimes that diagnosis is in error) and provide physical contact (holding, stroking, etc.).	*Record* + if the child: 1. Smiles in response to seeing and/or hearing another person. *Criterion:* There is no criterion level for stopping with this item. Smiling in response to other people's smiles is almost always adaptive behavior. Work on items 14c and 14d when reciprocal smiles are occurring 3 or 4 times per day.

(continued)

Teaching procedures	Steps for learning/evaluation
When smiles begin to occur, take note of what activities you were doing that seemed to promote smiling and respond with enthusiasm to the smile! Make it clear to the child by a change in tone of voice, a hug, a bounce, and so on, that you like his or her smiling. Watch for the child to smile when he or she sees or hears you or any other person before offering any tactile stimulation or picking him or her up.	

Note: Work on items 14b and 14c simultaneously.

AREA: **14. Social Skills**

BEHAVIOR: 14c. Smiles to auditory or tactile stimulation

Position of Child: Any position that promotes relaxation and good eye contact
Materials: None required

Teaching procedures	Steps for learning/evaluation
Play with the child, making funny noises with your mouth, tickling child, blowing on his or her tummy, and so on. Do this as part of your normal caregiving routine as well as during special "play time" during the day. When child begins to smile, be sure to let him or her know you like the smile by changing your voice, facial, expression, or other stimulation. Continue this activity during caregiving at least up to the point that the child is initiating more complex game-playing.	*Record* + if the child: 1. Smiles in response to auditory and/or tactile stimulation. *Criterion:* There is no criterion level at which stimulation should be stopped. Look for smiling that appears to be contingent upon the stimulation given on a fairly regular basis.

Note: The frequency and intensity of smiling and laughing of individual children will be affected by their physical status and the characteristics of day-to-day interaction within their families as well as their level of cognitive functioning.

AREA: **14. Social Skills**

BEHAVIOR: 14d. Smiles at a familiar person

Position of Child: Any position that promotes relaxation and good eye contact
Materials: None required

Teaching procedures	Steps for learning/evaluation
This is a difficult item to teach, but it is an important marker of developmental progress. A good way to promote its development is to ensure	*Record* + if the child: 1. Smiles differently at a familiar person.

(continued)

Teaching procedures	Steps for learning/evaluation
that the child has a small number of primary caregivers who interact with him or her regularly and who consistently reinforce social responses. It is also important that the child has normal contacts with a variety of strangers (e.g., in the grocery store, at church, etc.) whenever feasible. The essence of the item is that the child discriminates—that he or she smiles in recognition of a familiar person and does not smile to a stranger. *Or* the child smiles in a clearly different fashion to strangers versus familiar people (e.g., child may smile equally often to both, but the smile in response to the stranger is preceded by a long pause in which child seems to "study" the person, whereas the smile to the familiar person is more spontaneous). Use naturally occurring situations (e.g., return of parent after babysitting) to score.	*Criterion:* Child smiles at a familiar person 3 times in different situations 2 of 3 trials in 3 different situations.

Note: For *sensory-impaired* children, it is important that the primary caregiver provide a great deal of tactile stimulation (stroking, cuddling, etc.) as well as talking and eye contact in order to increase the number of associations the child has with that person.

AREA: **14. Social Skills**
BEHAVIOR: 14e. Smiles at mirror image (omit for significantly visually impaired children)

Position of Child: Any position that promotes relaxation and looking at mirror
Materials: Mirror (4 × 6 inches or larger)

Teaching procedures	Steps for learning/evaluation
Place a mirror in front of the child in a position that allows child to see himself or herself, but not you. Observe child's reactions. If child does not smile upon seeing himself or herself in the mirror, do something with child in front of the mirror that usually elicits smiles (e.g., tickle, play peek-a-boo, look over top of the mirror, let child see your face (smiling) in the mirror too). Observe child's response to seeing himself or herself smile. Take the mirror away for a few seconds and then repeat the activity. Make a game of this with the child!	*Record* + if the child: 1. Smiles in response to seeing his or her mirror image when being tickled or played with; and 2. Spontaneously smiles upon seeing his or her mirror image. *Criterion:* Child smiles 2 of 3 times when shown his or her image in a mirror; 3 separate days.

Note: Delete for significantly *visually impaired* children.

AREA: **14. Social Skills**

BEHAVIOR: 14f. Tries to attract attention through smiling and eye contact or (if visually impaired child) through other body language

Position of Child: Any position that promotes relaxation and eye contact
Materials: None necessary

Teaching procedures	Steps for learning/evaluation
This response is most easily observed in natural settings, particularly in situations where adults are interacting with one another and a child might feel ignored. The child may look to the adults as they speak, and when one of the adults looks at the child, the child is likely to smile. When this occurs, reinforce child by smiling back and attending to him or her for a few minutes, *especially* if child is *physically handicapped* and cannot get attention in more active ways. After the child is smiling regularly in response to the smiles of her primary caregivers, deliberately approach the child with a neutral face and without talking, establishing eye contact but waiting for child to smile before interacting with him or her. After child smiles or attempts to attract your attention, smile in return and react naturally (e.g., ''Well, hi! How are you?''). For the *visually impaired* child, always respond to smiles with some kind of physical contact and talking. Say things like ''That is a beautiful smile'' as you hug him or her. Also watch for other ''body language'' that may indicate a desire to be picked up or attended to. Particularly pay attention to hand movements and respond in a consistent way.	***Record*** + if the child: 1. Smiles to attract attention in a natural setting. ***Criterion:*** There is no real criterion for this behavior. It should be reinforced and maintained whenever possible. It can be worked on along with other more advanced behaviors.

AREA: **14. Social Skills**

BEHAVIOR: 14g. Responds differently to strangers versus familiar people

Position of Child: Any position that promotes relaxation and good eye contact
Materials: None needed

Teaching procedures	Steps for learning/evaluation
This item is similar to 14d, but the child's behavior involves more than discriminative smiling. The child may reach toward the familiar person and turn away from the unfamiliar; stare soberly and	***Record*** + if the child: 1. Clearly responds differently to familiar versus unfamiliar people. (Record behaviors that indicate the distinction.)

(continued)

Teaching procedures	Steps for learning/evaluation
intently at the unfamiliar person while smiling at the familiar; cry when the unfamiliar person approaches, and so forth. These responses are developed by providing normal social contacts—emphasizing activities with regular caregivers that will make them important and identifiable persons to the child while also providing opportunities for the child to meet strangers in natural settings (shopping, visiting, etc.). Move about with the child, talking quietly to him or her. Approach persons child is not familiar with and play a game by saying, "Do you want to go with [person's name]?" Then pull child back and comfort him or her in a normal manner.	***Criterion:*** Child responds differently to unfamiliar and familiar people, although the overt behavior indicating the discrimination may vary from situation to situation; shows discrimination trials in any situation, 3 different days.

AREA: **14. Social Skills**

BEHAVIOR: 14h. Participates in games

Position of Child: Any position that facilitates relaxation and good eye contact
Materials: Any appropriate for the game to be played

Teaching procedures	Steps for learning/evaluation
During caregiving activities, play 1 or 2 games. Good games to begin with are peek-a-boo, "Here comes a little bug" ("walk" your fingers up the child's arm to child's tummy and then tickle him or her), "This little piggy went to market" (touching the toes), and so forth. As you begin playing a game, your first goal is to get the child to smile or laugh when you play with him or her. Once the child smiles during games, try to get him or her to become more actively involved. When you play "peek-a-boo," wait a few seconds to see if the child will try to pull off the cover of if he or she looks to one side to anticipate your reappearance. Stop other games partway through to see if the child will try to get you to continue them to completion.	***Record*** + if the child: 1. Laughs or smiles at any social interchange; and 2. Is actively involved in a game in some way beyond just smiling at it. (Record the game and the way the child is involved.) ***Criterion:*** Child actively participates in games; 2 times a day on 3 consecutive days.

Note: Continue this activity beyond criterion level just because it is fun! Introduce new games from time to time.

AREA: **14. Social Skills**
BEHAVIOR: 14i. Repeats activity that is laughed at

Position of Child: Any position that promotes good eye contact and social interaction
Materials: A variety of toys the child likes to play with

Teaching procedures	Steps for learning/evaluation
This item is something to work on during normal routines of the day, rather than at a specific time that has been set aside.	***Record*** + if the child: 1. Repeats any activity that is laughed at.
Whenever the child does something amusing, laugh at the child and watch to see if he or she repeats the activity.	***Criterion:*** Child repeats activities that are laughed at 2 of 3 times on 3 consecutive days.
If child does not spontaneously repeat an activity when you laugh at him or her:	
Try to get child to do it again by imitating what he or she just did or by physically assisting the child to repeat it.	
Combine your laughter with clapping or some other gesture to indicate pleasure with what the child has done.	

Note: If you are working with a *hearing-impaired* child, it is important to touch child or otherwise get his or her attention and then to clap along while laughing at his or her activity.

AREA: **14. Social Skills**
BEHAVIOR: 14j. Initiates game-playing

Position of Child: Any position that promotes play and social contact
Materials: None required

Teaching procedures	Steps for learning/evaluation
Watch for the child's efforts to start games you have previously played with him or her (peek-a-boo, "Ride-a-cock-horse," "This little piggy went to market") or new activities (child may hand you toys, showing that he or she wants you to play with him or her).	***Record*** + if the child: 1. Shows any effort to initiate social play.
	Criterion: Child seeks social play at least 3 times a day on 2 consecutive days.
You can increase the likelihood of the child's initiating social play by responding quickly to any of his or her efforts to draw you into play.	
Stopping to play for 30 seconds will make him or her more likely to seek you out again.	

Note: This item is important as the child begins to develop social interactions. However, a youngster may become too demanding and unable to entertain himself or herself after he or she learns the power of social play. It is important for caregivers to encourage independent play as well as social play, and to be aware of maintaining a balance between the two for the child.

AREA: **14. Social Skills**
BEHAVIOR: 14k. "Gives" things to others upon request (same as 9k)

Position of Child: Any position
Materials: Toys and objects available in the child's natural environment

Teaching procedures	Steps for learning/evaluation
When feeding or playing with the child, make a point of giving him or her things while saying, "Mommy *gives* it to [child's name]" (or words to that effect). Then say, "Give the ———— to Mommy" while holding out your hand. If child gives you the object, thank him or her and immediately give object back if it appears child wants it. If child does not give items, assist child in doing so by helping him or her to hold the item out toward yourself or others when he or she is asked to do so. Make a game of sharing food at mealtime, saying things like, "Give Mommy/Daddy a taste."	***Record*** + if the child: 1. "Gives" willingly, but only with assistance when asked for an item; and 2. "Gives" on verbal or gestured request. ***Criterion:*** Child "gives" items at least 3 or 4 times when asked to do so, on 2 consecutive days.

Note: Vary the words used (e.g., "give," "May I have") to increase generalization. Do not force the giving; prompt by gesturing with the outstretched hand. The issue here is not the communication of meaning but the pleasure of sharing.

AREA: **14. Social Skills**
BEHAVIOR: 14l. Shares spontaneously with adults

Position of Child: Any; feeding time is one natural time for this activity
Materials: Foods or toys the child enjoys

Teaching procedures	Steps for learning/evaluation
Young children frequently like to play a sharing game while eating or doing other things with caregivers. Offer the child a bite of cracker and then ask, "Do you want to give me a bite?" as you hand the child the cracker and lean toward him or her. Do similar things when playing with blocks (e.g., "Do you want to give me one?" after you have given several to the youngster). Wait long enough so that the child has a chance to offer items to you without being asked for them, but do ask and extend your hand for items if they are not offered. Make a game of this, saying, "Thank you," each time the child gives you something, and offering him or her some in return.	***Record*** + if the child: 1. Offers to share something with you when you suggest it and when you hold your hand out or lean forward with your mouth open; and 2. Offers to share something without being prompted to do so. ***Criterion:*** Child will "share" something with a caregiving adult spontaneously after a sharing game has been initiated; 3 times on each of 3 days.

AREA: **14. Social Skills**
BEHAVIOR: 14m. Shows affection (hugs, kisses)

Position of Child: Any position
Materials: None

Teaching procedures	Steps for learning/evaluation
Show affection to the child freely. Pat him or her gently, hug and kiss on occasion, and tell child you really like him or her! After a kiss, put your cheek close to the child's mouth and ask for a kiss; if necessary press your cheek against his or her lips and then act pleased and kiss child again. Place child's arms around your neck and ask for a hug. Help child hug you if necessary. Respond to child with another hug and/or a kiss.	***Record*** + if the child: 1. Hugs and kisses or shows affection in a reliable manner to peers in play or to a caregiving adult. ***Criterion:*** Child shows affection toward a familiar person at least once a day on 5 consecutive days. Continue to encourage this behavior, but stop recording at this point.

Note: There are family and personal differences regarding the type and amount of affection that is demonstrated. These should be respected in implementing this item. The issue is helping the child learn to both give and receive affection. Note other specific signs of affection offered by the child.

AREA: **14. Social Skills**
BEHAVIOR: 14n. Tries to please others

Position of Child: Any position
Materials: None

Teaching procedures	Steps for learning/evaluation
This behavior is a natural outgrowth of items 14k, 14l, and 14m. Watch the child for the following behaviors (or other similar behaviors): Child does an activity that has gotten a positive response earlier in the day or on previous days. Child looks to parents or others for approval after doing a task. Child hugs, kisses, pats, without the benefit of modeling or prompting. Always respond naturally and positively to these overtures by the child.	***Record*** + if the child: 1. Tries to please others by doing things he or she has done in the past and then looking for approval. ***Criterion:*** This item can be continued indefinitely. Stop recording after 15 "plus" responses have been recorded within any week.

AREA: **14. Social Skills**
BEHAVIOR: 14o. Plays alongside other children—some exchange of toys

Position of Child: Any position
Materials: Any toys that are attractive to the child

Teaching procedures	Steps for learning/evaluation
Give the child as many opportunities to be around other children as possible. Watch for: New and different behaviors (e.g., longer or shorter attention span, more looking around, etc.) in the presence of other children as opposed to when playing alone Positive responses to being with other children Play that is nondisruptive in the presence of other children (except for occasional but not deliberately hostile "toy snatching") Play alongside other children lasting 10–15 minutes Reinforce any of these activities, telling the child that he or she is playing nicely near others.	***Record*** + if the child: 1. Plays well alongside other children without disruptive behavior, but with some attention to the other children (parallel play). ***Criterion:*** Child plays alongside other children for periods of at least 10 minutes in 5 different play sessions.

Note: Deliberately disruptive behavior should be dealt with by removing the child from the situation momentarily, reintroducing him or her, and observing child carefully to see if the disruption continues. If it does, you need to determine its function. Is it a reaction to another child? If so, try to assess the appropriateness of the behavior of both children relative to the situation. Is it general discomfort in any group setting? If so, try to introduce child to a setting with just one other child. Is it primarily a bid for adult attention? If so, it may be helpful for the adult to try to engage that child and another in a joint activity. If nondisruptive behavior cannot be sustained without constant adult attention, it may be necessary to seek the help of a psychologist in setting up a behavior management program.

AREA: **14. Social Skills**
BEHAVIOR: 14p. "Helps" in simple household tasks—imitates

Position of Child: Any position appropriate to setting
Materials: Normal household equipment

Teaching procedures	Steps for learning/evaluation
When doing routine jobs in the house or yard, try to think of ways in which the child can "help." When cleaning up after meals let him or her try to wipe off his or her own tray or the table Let child have a few dishes in a pan to wash Let child pull flowers off dandelions Let child drop dirty clothes in the hamper, and so forth Always indicate pleasure at child's attempts to help, whether or not they are actually helpful, but work on developing competence whenever possible.	***Record*** + if the child: 1. Attempts to help on any task; and 2. Helps in simple household tasks. ***Criterion:*** Child helps with 2 different "household tasks" on 3 separate occasions.

Note: The degree of helping is not actually very important in this item. It is more important that the child imitate the actions of caregiving adults in learning to help with a variety of activities.

AREA: **14. Social Skills**
BEHAVIOR: 14q. "Performs" for others

Position of Child: Any position
Materials: None needed

Teaching procedures	Steps for learning/evaluation
Young children like to please adults and to "show off" for them. They will do this spontaneously and also upon request at times. They like, and should be encouraged, to: Sing songs Say short nursery rhymes Do tricks Generally show that they are developing skills and competencies that they are proud of When children do things, be sure to show excitement and to praise and applaud their efforts!	**Record** + if the child: 1. Engages in activities that allow him or her to perform for and "show off" to others. **Criterion:** Child "performs" for others on 5 separate occasions.

AREA: **14. Social Skills**
BEHAVIOR: 14r. Tries to comfort others in distress

Position of Child: Any position
Materials: None

Teaching procedures	Steps for learning/evaluation
Model "comforting" people in natural ways when they show distress (e.g., kissing hurt places, patting, or hugging the crying person). Request this kind of attention from the child (e.g., ask child to "kiss it better" when you hurt your finger). Suggest that the child comfort a hurt doll or stuffed animal. Children can comfort each other when they bump themselves, fall down, and the like during the day also. Reinforce them for doing this. Show that you appreciate the fact that they are showing concern for others.	**Record** + if the child: 1. Tries to comfort others when they are in distress. **Criterion:** Child attempts to comfort at appropriate times on 5 separate occasions.

Note: The most *physically handicapped* child can do this and should be encouraged to do so. Watch for any attempt to comfort another person, whether spontaneously, in imitation, on request, or in compliance with a prompt.

AREA: **14. Social Skills**
BEHAVIOR: 14s. Shares spontaneously with peers

Position of Child: Any position
Materials: Any toys or objects the child enjoys playing with, but especially a telephone, dishes, tools, and things that are better used with 2 people

Teaching procedures	Steps for learning/evaluation
Spontaneous sharing is most likely to occur when children are playing in an area with other children. When playing with dishes, pretend foods, clothes, and so forth, the child may take an item to another child and give it to or set it near the child—whether it is actually accepted or not. Reinforce the child for doing this (e.g., ''Good sharing!''; ''Is [person's name] having lunch with you?''; ''Are you letting [person's name] help you with the dishes?''). Children frequently use a great deal of verbal jargon while doing this kind of sharing—especially as they give things and later retrieve them. This behavior also offers a chance to work on early communication skills. This behavior can be facilitated by suggesting that ''——— might like to play'' or by guiding a child to share items and then commenting that others like such sharing.	***Record*** + if the child: 1. Gives objects to or places objects near a peer to be shared with the peer while playing. ***Criterion:*** Child gives objects to peers while playing. This should be observed 2 times on 2 separate occasions.

15.

Self-Direction

DURING THE DEVELOPMENTAL period from 12 to 24 months of age, it becomes increasingly important for a child to initiate and direct his or her own activities. This aspect of development is often overlooked in curricula where the emphasis is on adult-directed learning. In fact, self-initiated activity is sometimes regarded as negativism and a nuisance in intervention programs, rather than as a necessary component of active learning. The primary prerequisite for beginning the items in this sequence is some form of communication (at least an ability to indicate choices). Several items require motor responses that are necessary for active exploration and self-initiated movement away from the caregiver. If children are too handicapped to make these responses, the focus will have to be on helping these children separate comfortably from their primary caregiver and make choices between adult-determined alternatives regarding what is going to happen to them in all situations where this is feasible. For example, the child may be shown 2 pictures, one of the TV and the other of the swing, and asked if he or she wants to watch TV or go outside and swing (indicating the appropriate picture as the question is asked). Whichever picture the child touches or looks at determines the next activity.

Although not stressed in the items themselves, it should be recognized that learning to deal with rules is a part of self-direction. While encouraging independence, curiosity, and exploration, one should provide firm boundaries with clear consequences for transgressing them. Handicapped children frequently suffer from overindulgence and/or overprotection. Both tendencies should be avoided.

15.   Self-Direction

a.   Moves away from Mom in same room
b.   Moves away from Mom to nearby area
c.   Makes choices—has preferred toys, foods, and so forth
d.   Plays alone with toys for 15 minutes
e.   Explores different areas of own home
f.   Explores unfamiliar places with mother present

AREA: **15. Self-Direction**
BEHAVIOR: 15a. Moves away from Mom in same room

Position of Child: Any comfortable position that allows mobility
Materials: Toys or objects that are interesting or liked by the child

Teaching procedures	Steps for learning/evaluation
Set up the room so that there are interesting and enticing activities/toys in parts of the room away from where Mom (or familiar caregiver) and child are. Engage the mother in conversation while basically leaving the child alone but keeping an eye on him or her. If child does not move to engage in other activities, have another adult or child begin to interact with objects and/or encourage child to join in.	*Record* + if the child: 1. Moves from Mom when coaxed by another person; and 2. Moves away from Mom without coaxing. *Criterion:* Child moves away from Mom to play or explore on 5 different days.

Note: Be sure to adapt ways in which the *physically handicapped* child can effectively move (or indicate to a caregiver that he or she wants to move) to interesting activity. With a *visually impaired* child, try to attract him or her away from mother by activating a noisy toy in some part of the room, at first just a few feet away from Mom and then later further away. Ask Mom to talk to child as he or she plays, to assure child of the parent's continued presence.

AREA: **15. Self-Direction**
BEHAVIOR: 15b. Moves away from Mom to nearby area

Position of Child: Any comfortable position that allows mobility
Materials: Toys or items that are attractive to or liked by the child

Teaching procedures	Steps for learning/evaluation
Set up nearby area away from immediate space of mother and child (e.g., just inside the doorway to another room, in an alcove, on the other side of a room divider, etc.), so that it contains something of interest to the child. Engage the mother in conversation, while basically leaving the child alone. Do keep an eye on him or her, however. If child does not move to engage in activity away from mother, use another adult and/or child to act upon object(s) in nearby area in order to entice child to join in.	*Record* + if the child: 1. Moves to nearby area when coaxed; and 2. Moves without coaxing to an area outside of the room where mother is. *Criterion:* Child is observed to move from mother to nearby area on 5 different days.

Note: Be sure to make adaptations for the *physically impaired* child so that he or she can effectively move or indicate a desire to be moved to various activities. For a *visually impaired* child, it will be necessary for an adult to activate noisy toys some distance away from mother to make child aware that they are there. Have Mom continue to talk to the child as he or she moves away, to encourage child and help him or her to understand what he or she is doing.

AREA: **15. Self-Direction**
BEHAVIOR: 15c. Makes choices—has preferred toys, foods, and so forth

Position of Child: Any comfortable position that allows full movement of arms and legs
Materials: A variety of toys, foods, and so forth, that are attractive to or liked by the child

Teaching procedures	Steps for learning/evaluation
Allow the child many opportunities to make choices. Rather than just giving the child a toy, put 2 toys (or items of food) in front of the child and ask child which one he or she wants. Encourage child to respond in any way he or she can (visually, verbally, or physically). When child indicates a choice, be sure to let him or her have it, and repeat to child the choice he made (i.e., ''Oh, you want the _____''). It is possible to insist on a choice by simply waiting until the child looks at or reaches for one of the items, then giving that one to the child. To be sure child is actually choosing, however, select very distinct items to present (e.g., banana pudding and spinach), and after a series of such choices (8–10), jokingly offer the item not chosen.	**_Record_** + if the child: 1. Gives any clear indication of making a choice (visual, physical, or verbal). **_Criterion:_** Child regularly makes choices (at least 10 times a day) *and* either laughs or protests in some way when a nonchosen item is given to him or her.

Note: Adapt this item as appropriate for *visually impaired* children (i.e., help them to locate and feel or taste both items they are choosing between and then ask which one they would like).

AREA: **15. Self-Direction**
BEHAVIOR: 15d. Plays alone with toys for 15 minutes

Position of Child: Any comfortable position that allows free movement of arms
Materials: Toys or objects that are attractive to or liked by the child

Teaching procedures	Steps for learning/evaluation
Give the child opportunities to play with toys alone in a place where he or she can be checked every few minutes. Set up an area with a few toys or objects that are interesting to the child. Be sure he or she is comfortable (i.e., in a good position). Start child playing and then withdraw to the next room or become involved in another activity in the same room (e.g., reading, writing notes, etc.).	**_Record_** + if the child: 1. Plays for 5 minutes without requesting attention from the adult; and 2. Plays for 6–10 minutes without requesting attention; and 3. Plays for 11–14 minutes without requesting attention; and 4. Plays for 15 or more minutes without requesting attention.

(continued)

Teaching procedures	Steps for learning/evaluation
Watch for (see also caution below): New or different behaviors (e.g., longer or shorter attention span, looking around for mother or others) Actual play with toys rather than passive positioning and no interaction with objects Signs of distress. Intervene before the child gets fussy, and work up to 15 minutes of playtime alone.	***Criterion:*** Child plays 15 or more minutes alone on 5 different days in a 2-week period.

Caution: If self-stimulatory behaviors are observed to increase during free play, search for more responsive and interesting toys and, if necessary, increase adult interaction. The adult should give attention after a short period of non–self-stimulatory behavior, rather than at the point the self-stimulating behaviors occur.

AREA: **15. Self-Direction**

BEHAVIOR: 15e. Explores different areas of own home

Position of Child: Position that allows child free movement of arms and legs and mobility
Materials: Toys

Teaching procedures	Steps for learning/evaluation
After "child-proofing" the house to avoid a child's coming into contact with dangerous materials, encourage the child to explore by placing a favorite toy in an unfamiliar place or by putting particularly interesting new toys or materials in corners, under tables, in accessible drawers, or in other places the child usually does not go. At first show the child the object and where you are placing it; later, simply place it so it is partially visible and will invite exploration.	***Record*** + if the child: 1. Goes to unfamiliar places or drawers in a house and explores what is there after an adult has called his or her attention to something there; and 2. Goes to a place, drawer, or the like, and explores without having an adult call his or her attention to something in that place. ***Criterion:*** Child explores in his or her own home on 5 different days during a 2-week period (may be recorded by parental report).

Note: With *nonmobile children* who can use their hands, present them with a variety of containers, some familiar and some unfamiliar, with different toys in them. Credit them for choosing a new container and exploring the contents. For *blind* or *seriously visually impaired* children, more adult involvement will be necessary to encourage movement away from the familiar. Begin with exploring contents of boxes (clearly distinguishable by shape and texture), then go to a part of the room away from the child. Make noise with a toy and call to child. When child comes, help him or her feel and manipulate the toy and the environment while you talk about it (e.g., "This is the corner, feel how the walls come together. Now can you find the chair—reach behind you," etc.). Try to watch the visually impaired child as he or she begins to explore, so that you can talk about what he or she is experiencing and help him or her understand it.

AREA: **15. Self-Direction**
BEHAVIOR: 15f. Explores unfamiliar places with mother present

Position of Child: Any position that allows child as much free movement as he or she is capable of
Materials: Any present in new environment

Teaching procedures	Steps for learning/evaluation
Take the child with you when you shop, visit friends, or go into a new room or area. If child can crawl, or move about, encourage him or her to investigate the new environment (see caution below). If child cannot move independently, place him or her in one area near something of interest, and check back with him or her frequently. If necessary, help child explore the new environment; however, fade your presence as soon as possible.	***Record*** + if the child: 1. Explores after being encouraged by an adult; and 2. Explores independently. ***Criterion:*** Child explores 5 new environments without adult encouragement.

Note: Be sure to provide verbal exploration of the new experience for *visually impaired* children.
Caution: Be sure to be alert to potential hazards before allowing the child freedom to explore.

16.

Feeding

HANDICAPPED INDIVIDUALS SHOULD be encouraged to be independent in self-care activities to the greatest extent possible. This sequence is directed toward establishing appropriate feeding patterns and then toward independent eating. For many physically handicapped children, it will be critical to seek the services of a person knowledgeable about oral-motor problems (a communication disorders specialist, a physical therapist, or an occupational therapist) who can assist you in developing the best possible feeding patterns in the 0- to 9-month developmental period. As you begin to work on the development of self-feeding skills, it may be necessary to both devise and use adaptive equipment that facilitates self-feeding. Regardless of the adaptiveness of equipment, beginning feeders will usually be very messy. One of the major roles of the interventionist may be to persuade the caregiver that some mess is to be expected and must be tolerated in order for the child to learn self-feeding skills.

An occupational therapist should be able to offer many suggestions on how to adapt eating utensils for specific children.

16. Feeding

a. Sucks from nipple smoothly
b. "Roots" toward food or objects infrequently
c. Bites down on spoon infrequently
d. Gags infrequently, only when appropriate
e. Munches food (chewing up and down)
f. Development of tongue movements
g. Pulls food off spoon with lips
h. Holds own bottle (omit for breast-fed babies)
i. Drinks from cup held by adult
j. Tolerates junior or mashed table foods without gagging
k. Cleans lower lip with teeth
l. Chews with a rotary/side-to-side action
m. Finger feeding
n. Holds and drinks from cup
o. Brings spoon to mouth, gets food off
p. Scoops food from dish onto spoon
q. Chews well
r. No longer uses bottle or breast
s. Distinguishes between edible and nonedible substances

AREA: **16. Feeding**

BEHAVIOR: 16a. Sucks from nipple smoothly

Position of Child: Held in semiupright position in arms

Materials: Bottle or breast

Teaching procedures	Steps for learning/evaluation
Observe the child's reaction when a nipple is placed in his or her mouth. *Caution:* A child should be able to suck and swallow quite smoothly a few days after birth. This ability may be impaired by neurological immaturity, neurological damage, or prolonged periods of tube feeding. Because sucking problems are often early signs of neurological problems, they are frequently a sign that professional assistance is needed. Arrange for a physical therapist, occupational therapist, or pediatrician to see the child; use the procedures they prescribe for therapy.	*Record* + if the child: 1. Sucks and swallows smoothly. *Criterion:* Child is able to take liquids from bottle or breast without choking, withdrawing, or becoming tense; 3 meals for 3 days.

Note: No child should take a bottle in the back-lying position, particulary if his or her mobility is limited. Not only is choking more likely, but if the child's oral-motor function is abnormal, the milk may flow into the ear canals, causing infection.

AREA: **16. Feeding**

BEHAVIOR: 16b. "Roots" toward food or objects infrequently

Position of Child: Lying on back, head in midline. Test at a midpoint between feedings.

Materials: None

Teaching procedures	Steps for learning/evaluation
Touch the child lightly on the cheek and see if child turns head as if to find and suck on your finger. This movement is called the rooting reflex. It is present at birth and should begin to disappear by 3–4 months. It appears to be inhibited by hand-to-mouth activity, so if the child is bringing hands to mouth, no further intervention should be necessary. If child is not bringing hands to mouth, and if he or she has an active rooting reflex, hand-to-mouth activity should be promoted. Experiment with putting child in several positions to see which increases the probability of hand-to-mouth activity (often side-lying is best). Then you may physically guide the child's hand to his or her mouth, perhaps by putting a good-tasting substance on the hand.	*Record* + if the child: 1. Infrequently turns head in the direction of one of his or her cheeks when it is stroked lightly with a finger. *Criterion:* Child does not turn head after cheek is touched; 3 of 5 trials on 3 consecutive days.

(continued)

Teaching procedures	Steps for learning/evaluation
You may also use your own hands around the child's mouth, using first a firm and then a light touch. Do this several times a day. The rooting reflex will always be more easily elicited when the child is hungry and less easily elicited when he or she is sleepy or upset. Testing should be done with the baby alert and midway between feedings.	

Note: Some children cannot tolerate being touched around the mouth without arching their backs or becoming irritable. If this is the case, you should seek advice from a physical therapist, occupational therapist, or speech therapist with expertise in this area.

AREA: **16. Feeding**
BEHAVIOR: 16c. Bites down on spoon infrequently

Position of Child: Upright or semireclined
Materials: Baby food and spoon

Teaching procedures	Steps for learning/evaluation
Place a small amount of baby food on a spoon and place it on the baby's tongue, touching the bottom gums. Wait to see if the baby's jaws close tightly. This is called *bite reflex.* A normal baby will be able to open his or her mouth immediately. Inability to do so is a sign of neurological problems and indicates need for treatment by a therapist. The bite reflex normally fades as the child begins to munch on foods. Some techniques to use if the bite reflex is too strong are: Rub the gums with your finger prior to feeding. Use a smaller spoon. Use foods that encourage munching and chewing.	***Record*** + if the child: 1. Does not bite down on spoon when it is placed in his or her mouth. ***Criterion:*** Baby does not bite down on spoon; 3 of 5 trials on 3 consecutive days.

Note: If a child has a strong bite reflex, never place your fingers in his mouth! If a child is biting down hard on something and cannot release it, wait a few seconds for child to relax and release his or her bite. If child does not release bite, press your fingers on the muscles at the back of the jaw or hold child's nose (the physiological need for air will cause mouth to open). Do not pull the spoon from the mouth. This increases the bite reflex and could damage the child's mouth.

AREA: **16. Feeding**
BEHAVIOR: 16d. Gags infrequently, only when appropriate

Position of Child: When introducing solid foods, hold the child as upright as possible, giving appropriate firm head support and keeping the head in normal alignment with the trunk and slightly forward. Do not hold the child in a reclining position and pour food into the back of the mouth.
Materials: Baby/infant foods

Teaching procedures	Steps for learning/evaluation
Gradually introduce different tastes and textures of strained foods. If gagging occurs, dilute the foods a little, and choose those that are the smoothest. Gradually work back to the more textured material. Adding small amounts of baby cereal to strained food will increase the texture and stimulate adaptation. One technique that may reduce gagging is "tongue walking"—pressing firmly on the tongue with the tip of a small spoon, working from front to middle of the tongue.	**Record** + if the child: 1. Eats strained foods without gagging; and 2. Eats textured foods with minimal choking or gagging. **Criterion:** Child eats strained foods without gagging; 3 meals a day for 3 days.

Note: If a child gags frequently beyond 6 months of age *or* if he or she never gags on food in the back of the mouth before 6 months of age, consult a therapist.

AREA: **16. Feeding**
BEHAVIOR: 16e. Munches food (chewing up and down)

Position of Child: As upright as possible
Materials: Infant cereals and strained foods

Teaching procedures	Steps for learning/evaluation
Place food in the baby's mouth and observe reaction. If child pushes it out with tongue, try placing the next spoonful in the side of the mouth. Pushing food out of the mouth with the tongue may be reflexive at first and is not necessarily a rejection of the food being offered. Watch for the child to start moving jaws up and down while using the tongue to mash food against the roof of his or her mouth.	**Record** + if the child: 1. Moves jaw up and down while eating. **Criterion:** Child moves jaw up and down when solid food is in mouth; 3 meals a day on 3 different days.

Note: If a child persists in pushing food out of the mouth beyond 6 months of age, or has not developed a munching pattern, consult a therapist.

AREA: **16. Feeding**
BEHAVIOR: 16f. Development of tongue movements

Position of Child: As upright as possible
Materials: Regular meals; sticky foods such as oatmeal

Teaching procedures	Steps for learning/evaluation
Observe the child eating. Notice if child moves tongue to touch food at the sides and top of mouth or if child pulls tongue back while either eating or babbling. If you are not readily seeing tongue movement, try placing small amounts of sticky foods such as oatmeal or jam on the roof of child's mouth near the front, and between the cheek and gums. Observe the child's use of tongue to retrieve these foods. If you note difficulty, work on this for only a few minutes each feeding, placing preferred foods at the front of the mouth, requiring tongue action for retrieval.	*Record* + if the child: 1. Moves tongue to either one side or to the top of the mouth during 1 eating session; and 2. Moves tongue both to the side and to the top of the mouth during 1 eating session. *Criterion:* Tongue is seen to move both to side and to top of mouth; 3 eating sessions a day for 3 days.

Note: Peanut butter is frequently used to promote tongue mobility, but must be used very cautiously. Since it does not readily dissolve, there is some danger of aspiration.

AREA: **16. Feeding**
BEHAVIOR: 16g. Pulls food off spoon with lips

Position of Child: As upright as possible
Materials: Usual foods

Teaching procedures	Steps for learning/evaluation
Place a spoonful of food in the child's mouth, touching the lower lip only. Do *not* scrape the food off against the upper lip. Watch for the child to move his upper lip toward spoon to clean it off—move up a little, if necessary, to give child success in getting the food. If there are no lip movements, try: Alternately touching top and bottom lips with the spoon, waiting for lip closure; and using this method with the child's favorite sticky foods (fruit, pudding) Holding child's upper lip with your finger	*Record* + if the child: 1. Uses upper lips to pull some food off spoon; and 2. Uses lips to clean all food off spoon. *Criterion:* Child uses lips to clean food off spoon; 3 meals a day on 3 consecutive days.

Note: If a strong bite reflex is present, it may be triggered by the spoon touching the teeth. If this is a problem, use a very small spoon and avoid the teeth, pressing the spoon firmly on the front of the tongue. Pay special attention to keeping the child as relaxed as possible. (See "Handling" and "Positioning" subsections in Chapter 5.)

AREA: **16. Feeding**

BEHAVIOR: 16h. Holds own bottle (omit for breast-fed babies)

Position of Child: Held in arms or on pillow
Materials: Regular baby bottle or small preemie bottle like those in hospital nurseries

Teaching procedures	Steps for learning/evaluation
Present the baby with a bottle by placing the nipple in his or her mouth, but continue to hold onto it. Once baby is comfortably sucking on the bottle, gently place his or her hands on the bottle. Over time, child will take a firmer grip on the bottle. Hold the bottle a few inches from child's mouth and wait to see if he or she will reach out for it. As these skills improve, gradually release your hold on the bottle.	***Record*** + if the child: 1. Places hands on bottle during feeding; and 2. Reaches out for bottle and pulls it to mouth; and 3. Holds bottle without help for several seconds at a time; and 4. Holds bottle for entire feeding. ***Criterion:*** Baby holds bottle independently during feeding, 3 consecutive days.

Note: *Spastic* children frequently show difficulties with reach and grasp. Make sure these children are as relaxed as possible during feeding (see ''Handling'' and ''Positioning'' subsections in Chapter 5). You may have more success feeding handicapped babies by positioning them on a pillow in your lap, facing you directly. Be sure not to put a child in bed with his or her bottle. Let child drink first and then go to bed. Bottle drinking in bed is associated both with an increase in middle ear infection and with tooth decay.

AREA: **16. Feeding**

BEHAVIOR: 16i. Drinks from cup held by adult

Position of Child: Any position comfortable for feeding, but as upright as possible
Materials: Preferred liquids (avoid sugared beverages); several kinds of cups, small juice glass; plastic cup with weighted bottom; plastic cup with one side cut out so the top does not hit child's nose

Teaching procedures	Steps for learning/evaluation
Starts with a small amount of liquid in a cup. Bring the cup to the child's mouth and tip it slightly, waiting for the child to cooperate actively by closing lips around the cup. Hold the cup about an inch away from the child's mouth and wait for him or her to lean toward the cup. It is frequently helpful to start teaching cup drinking by using thicker liquids (e.g., milk or a mixture of milk and cereal), which are easier for the child to handle.	***Record*** + if the child: 1. Takes liquid from cup brought to mouth with some liquid running out of the mouth; and 2. Achieves some lip closure around the cup; a little liquid may escape at the sides. ***Criterion:*** Child leans head toward cup and drinks without excessive spilling or choking; 3 meals a day on 3 consecutive days.

Note: Spout cups are not very helpful in teaching the head and lip control needed for cup drinking.

AREA: **16. Feeding**

BEHAVIOR: 16j. Tolerates junior or mashed table foods without gagging

Position of Child: Any position that is comfortable for feeding
Materials: Smooth and textured foods (e.g., infant and junior baby foods, crackers)

Teaching procedures	Steps for learning/evaluation
Upon reaching 6–7 months of age, a child should be able to tolerate textures in food without gagging. This may be encouraged in children that age and older who refuse textured foods or gag on them, by very gradually increasing texture—adding a little baby cereal or wheat germ to strained foods and allowing adjustment to that before moving on to junior foods. Sometimes an overactive gag reflex can be modified by placing the spoon of food on the front of the tongue, lifting spoon slightly and placing it a little further back on the tongue, lifting and moving further back, and so on, to the point the child starts to gag—and then returning to the front to introduce the food. This might be done 2 or 3 times during each feeding.	***Record*** + if the child: 1. Eats several kinds of foods with texture without gagging during 1 meal. ***Criterion:*** Child eats junior or mashed foods at every meal without gagging for 3 days.

Note: If gag reflex remains strong enough so that child cannot tolerate junior foods after 9 months of age, seek professional help. *Spastic* children need to be in a relaxed state and in a proper sitting position to reduce the abnormal postures and reflexes that inhibit eating and promote gagging and teeth clenching. If the child is underweight, use mashed table foods, which have more calories as well as being less expensive than commercially prepared baby foods.

AREA: **16. Feeding**
BEHAVIOR: 16k. Cleans lower lip with teeth

Position of Child: As upright as possible
Materials: Usual, solid foods

Teaching procedures	Steps for learning/evaluation
Look for this "lip cleaning" to occur spontaneously as child is eating and food sticks to his or her lower lip. Do not routinely wipe the child's mouth after every bite. If the child is not starting to use his or her teeth to clean food off the lower lip, place favored sticky foods on the lip so that the child will have to retrieve them in order to get the taste. It may help to gently touch the lower lip with the spoon.	***Record*** + if the child: 1. Cleans lower lip to retrieve a specific food after his or her attention is called to it; and 2. Cleans lower lip with teeth spontaneously. ***Criterion:*** Child spontaneously cleans lower lip at least 3 times during each meal for 3 consecutive days.

AREA: **16. Feeding**
BEHAVIOR: 16l. Chews with a rotary/side-to-side action

Position of Child: As upright as possible
Materials: Variety of textured foods: junior baby foods, mashed table foods, thinly sliced meats, baby sausages, cheese strips, rice, spaghetti, cooked vegetables

Teaching procedures	Steps for learning/evaluation
Observe the child's response to textured foods and watch for adultlike chewing movements—rotary, side-to-side movements of the jaw. Frequently, just the stimulation of textured foods in the mouth is enough to trigger those movements, and no further intervention is needed. If the movements are not occurring, try placing favorite foods on one side of the mouth, between cheek and teeth.	*Record* + if the child: 1. Shows occasional rotary jaw movements during a feeding; and 2. Shows rotary movements at least half of the time during a feeding; and 3. Spontaneously and consistently shows rotary jaw movements for entire meal when chewing textured foods. *Criterion:* Child spontaneously and consistently shows rotary jaw movements when chewing textured foods; for all meals on 3 consecutive days.

AREA: **16. Feeding**
BEHAVIOR: 16m. Finger feeding

Position of Child: Seated, with appropriate support, in front of a tray
Materials: Sticky foods as well as easily grasped foods (e.g., pudding, bread sticks, crackers, bits of dry cereal)

Teaching procedures	Steps for learning/evaluation
Introduce the idea of self-feeding by placing sticky foods such as oatmeal or corn syrup on the child's fingers so child can lick them off. Provide a bowl of pudding so the child can place a hand in it and lick off the food. Progress to a food that is easy to grasp and does not require finger release to place in the mouth (e.g., bread stick or cracker). Gradually move to smaller items (e.g., cereal bits) that require hand opening to place in the mouth. As in all feeding items, new skills should be presented gradually, maintaining established ones.	*Record* + if the child: 1. Licks food from fingers after it has been placed on them; and 2. Places hand in bowl of food and licks food off his or her hand; and 3. Brings bread stick or cracker to mouth and bites independently; and 4. Picks up and eats small bits of food without help. *Criterion:* Child picks up and eats small bits of food without help; 3 meals a day on 3 consecutive days.

Note: Honey may be substituted for children over 12 months of age but should not be used for babies. There is an increased risk for infantile botulism when infants ingest honey.

AREA: **16. Feeding**
BEHAVIOR: 16n. Holds and drinks from cup

Position of Child: Supported in chair or highchair
Materials: Cup

Teaching procedures	Steps for learning/evaluation
Fill child's cup approximately one-third full with liquid and give to child when he or she is thirsty. If child cannot hold cup and bring it to mouth to drink, help child by placing both of child's hands on the cup and bringing cup to his or her mouth to drink. Gradually reduce your assistance and then return cup to the table. Give child plenty of opportunity to drink from a cup (during both feeding and pretend play). Be sure to allow some spillage and ample time.	*Record* + if the child: 1. Brings cup to mouth and drinks with assistance; and 2. Brings cup to mouth and drinks without assistance and with considerable spilling; and 3. Brings cup to mouth; drinks without assistance, with relatively little spilling, and returns cup to table. *Criterion:* Child drinks from a cup independently (step 3); at every meal for 3 consecutive days.

Note: Many cups are available on the market. Experiment to see which type of cup the child handles most easily (e.g., a cup with 1 or 2 handles, big handles or small, cups with cutouts for drinking).

AREA: **16. Feeding**
BEHAVIOR: 16o. Brings spoon to mouth, gets food off

Position of Child: Sitting supported in a highchair or other chair with tray
Materials: Spoon, dish, variety of foods for scooping

Teaching procedures	Steps for learning/evaluation
Place bowl with food in it in front of child. Fill the spoon and help child grasp it. Remove your assistance and tell child, "Eat your food." If child is unable to successfully bring spoon to mouth and eat the food, assist child by: Elevating child's elbow and reducing the effects of gravity (this is similar to the normal developmental process) Bringing your arm *under* child's arm and placing your hand on *top* of his or her wrist while standing or sitting behind the child. In this manner, you can assist child with added support and wrist guidance.	*Record* + if the child: 1. Brings spoon to mouth from a distance of 2 or 3 inches, cleans spoon, and eats; and 2. Brings spoon to mouth from dish, cleans spoon, and eats with minimal assistance; and 3. Brings spoon to mouth and eats without assistance. *Criterion:* Child brings spoon to mouth and eats without assistance; part of each of 3 meals on 3 consecutive days.

(continued)

Teaching procedures	Steps for learning/evaluation
At first, help child to get food into his or her mouth. Then assist only to the point that spoon is several inches from child's mouth and let child complete the task on his or her own. Gradually reduce all help until child can do it on his or her own.	

Note: Many children try to reach a spoon as they are being fed. This should be encouraged, regardless of how messy it is at first. Do not tire a child by insisting he or she feed himself all of every meal at first. Have child do the work when eating most preferred foods and those that best adhere to the spoon.

AREA: **16. Feeding**
BEHAVIOR: 16p. Scoops food from dish onto spoon

Position of Child: Sitting in highchair or other chair with tray
Materials: Spoon, dish, variety of foods easy to scoop

Teaching procedures	Steps for learning/evaluation
Place bowl of food in front of child. Have child grasp spoon, and encourage him or her to eat. If child brings spoon to mouth, but does not successfully scoop food onto the spoon, show child how to scoop food. If necessary, physically assist child to scoop food, but decrease your assistance as quickly as possible. Be sure to give child plenty of time and opportunity to practice. Start with foods that adhere well to the spoon (pudding, mashed potatoes, mashed bananas, etc.).	***Record*** + if the child: 1. Scoops food onto spoon with minimal physical assistance (sticky food); and 2. Scoops food onto spoon from dish without assistance (sticky foods); and 3. Scoops food onto spoon from dish without assistance (more difficult foods—e.g., lumpy vegetables, fruit). ***Criterion:*** Child scoops food from dish onto spoon without assistance; 3 meals a day on 3 consecutive days.

Note: Some physically handicapped children will only be able to scoop with adaptive equipment. Consult an occupational therapist for advice.

AREA: **16. Feeding**
BEHAVIOR: 16q. Chews well

Position of Child: Supported sitting in highchair
Materials: Variety of foods

Teaching procedures	Steps for learning/evaluation
Give the child the opportunity to eat a variety of foods containing lumps, foods of different or unusual textures, and foods of various consistencies.	***Record*** + if the child: 1. Chews a variety of foods during a meal well enough to avoid choking.

(continued)

Teaching procedures	Steps for learning/evaluation
Once the child begins to chew, try to encourage more mature chewing by giving child different solids between his or her back teeth. Try foods like long strips of hard cheese, semicooked carrots, and so forth. If necessary, hold one end, while letting child chew the other end. Move food to different placements in child's mouth to stimulate a combination of vertical, horizontal, and rotary jaw movements.	*Criterion:* Child chews a variety of foods; 3 meals a day on 3 consecutive days.

AREA: **16. Feeding**
BEHAVIOR: 16r. No longer uses bottle or breast

Position of Child: Any comfortable feeding position
Materials: Bottle, cup

Teaching procedures	Steps for learning/evaluation
As child learns to drink from a cup (item *n*), gradually reduce quantity of liquid given in a bottle or the time spent nursing. Substitute other cuddling behavior for the time normally spent holding the baby for bottle or breast feeding.	*Record* + if the child: 1. Drinks from bottle or breast no more than 2 times a day; and 2. Drinks from bottle or breast no more than once a day. *Criterion:* Child no longer drinks from bottle or breast.

AREA: **16. Feeding**
BEHAVIOR: 16s. Distinguishes between edible and nonedible substances

Position of Child: Any comfortable position
Materials: Edibles (foods) and nonedibles (objects)

Teaching procedures	Steps for learning/evaluation
Observe whether or not the child mouths nonedibles in his or her play. If child does, remove the nonedible and provide the child with something else to do. Offer child two similar items (one edible and one not). Praise the child when he or she eats the edible and plays with the nonedible.	*Record* + if the child: 1. Removes inedible substance from mouth after tasting it or after being told to remove it; and 2. Distinguishes between familiar edible and nonedible substances in training session; and

(continued)

Teaching procedures	Steps for learning/evaluation
If child still insists on putting nonedibles in mouth, make a face and verbally ask him to take it out while going through the motions. Get him to imitate you. If necessary, remove the nonedible yourself. Observe child's behavior when left playing alone. Ask child to remove nonedible from his or her mouth as necessary.	3. Distinguishes between familiar edible and nonedible substances during a 15-minute free-play observation. *Criterion:* Child distinguishes between familiar edible and nonedible substances in three 15-minute free-play observations.

17.

Grooming

T HE ACTIVITIES INCLUDED in this sequence are preparatory to actual "self-care." For the most part, they require that the child cooperate with the caregiver for the grooming activity, rather than that the child actively participate. If children have motor impairments that require their remaining dependent on others for their grooming and personal hygiene, it is critical to talk to these children about the grooming actitivies as they are taking place. Enlist their cooperation and help as possible, and provide information about the importance of these activities for their health and appearance. The handicapped person should not feel that someone is doing things *to* him but that someone is doing activities *with* him, and for specific benefits.

17.   Grooming

a.   Cooperates in hand-washing
b.   Cooperates in toothbrushing
c.   Washes own hands

d.   Wipes nose if given a handkerchief (or cooperates if cannot get hands to nose)

AREA: **17. Grooming**
BEHAVIOR: 17a. Cooperates in hand-washing

Position of Child: Standing/kneeling or comfortable position at sink that allows for trunk control
and full movement of child's hands
Materials: Soap and water

Teaching procedures	Steps for learning/evaluation
Before meals and at other appropriate times, tell the child it is time to wash his or her hands. Wash your hands to demonstrate how it is done. Encourage child to put his or her hands under the water. As you help child to wash and rinse and dry his or her hands, allow child to help as much as possible.	***Record*** + if the child: 1. Places hands in water upon verbal or gestured instruction to wash his or her hands; and 2. "Assists" while his or her hands are washed and dried (e.g., rubs hands together, rubs soap on hands, shakes water off before drying, etc.). Do not score a + if child protests if not allowed to continue playing in the water. ***Criterion:*** Child assists each time hands are washed for 4 consecutive days.

Note: Try finger painting with child, and then draw child's attention to the vanishing color when child helps you to wash his or her hands. Or, when child's hands are wet and child indicates to you to dry them, hand child a towel and help him or her to dry them, each time decreasing the amount of assistance you give.

AREA: **17. Grooming**
BEHAVIOR: 17b. Cooperates in toothbrushing

Position of Child: Standing/kneeling in front of mirror at sink or a position that allows good balance
and full movement of hands; physically handicapped child should be seated in a chair providing
good head support
Materials: Toothbrush, doll

Teaching procedures	Steps for learning/evaluation
Place the child in front of a mirror and tell child it is time to brush his or her teeth. Show child the brush and how you put toothpaste on it. Ask child to open his or her mouth, and then proceed to brush child's teeth (if child does not open his or her mouth, gently open child's lips manually and brush). Try to make the experience pleasant. If the child does not attempt to hold the toothbrush, physically asssist by placing the brush in child's hand and physically guiding it to his or her mouth.	***Record*** + if the child: 1. Allows toothbrushing without protest; and 2. Cooperates in toothbrushing by helping hold the brush, by opening mouth or turning head on command, or by demonstrating in any other fashion participation in the process of toothbrushing. ***Criterion:*** Child cooperates in toothbrushing at least once a day for 5 consecutive days.

Teaching procedures	Steps for learning/evaluation
If child cannot use his or her hands and arms well enough to assist in that fashion, teach child to turn her head, to open his or her mouth, to spit out the toothpaste (i.e., anything within the child's capabilities that increases independence and participation in the process).	

Note: Initially, it may be easier to use a damp washcloth with toothpaste on it to clean the child's teeth.

AREA: 17. Grooming
BEHAVIOR: 17c. Washes own hands

Position of Child: Standing/kneeling or any comfortable position for child at sink that allows full movement of child's hands
Materials: Soap and water

Teaching procedures	Steps for learning/evaluation
Tell the child it is time to wash his or her hands. Demonstrate to the child how to wash hands, using yourself as a model. Hand child the soap and encourage child to imitate you. If child cannot do this, physically assist child by helping him or her through the motions. Decrease your assistance until child is washing hands independently.	*Record* + if the child: 1. Washes hands independently (an adult may dry child's hands). *Criterion:* Child washes hands independently each time he or she is asked, for 4 consecutive days.

Note: Allow child lots of time to "experiment" with washing. You may play with activities (such as finger painting) in which the child's hands become obviously "dirty." Call child's attention to the disappearance of the color when child washes hands.

AREA: 17. Grooming
BEHAVIOR: 17d. Wipes nose if given a handkerchief (or cooperates if cannot get hands to nose)

Position of Child: Any comfortable position
Materials: Handkerchief

Teaching procedures	Steps for learning/evaluation
When the child has a runny nose or sneezes, tell child his or her nose needs wiping and hand child a handkerchief.	*Record* + if the child: 1. Cooperates in the wiping of his or her nose (does not struggle to avoid it); and

(continued)

Teaching procedures	Steps for learning/evaluation
If child makes no attempt to wipe his or her nose, physically assist child to do so. Gradually withdraw assistance on further trials. You may also demonstrate how to gently blow your nose. Encourage child to imitate. If child cannot get hands to his or her nose, work on getting child to hold still and to cooperate with your wiping his or her nose.	2. Wipes own nose when given a handkerchief and instructed to wipe nose. *Criterion:* Child wipes own nose on a regular basis when given a handkerchief and instructed to do so (precise criteria are difficult, since this item depends on the child's having a cold).

Note: Sometimes children learn this response better if also given opportunities to "play" at wiping a doll's nose, wiping Mom's nose, and so forth.

18.

Dressing

THE DRESSING AND UNDRESSING skills included in this sequence require some degree of motor facility, probably at least that represented by items *a* through *i* of sequence 19 (Reaching and Grasping). The intent of the sequence, however, is simply to promote as much independence in dressing and undressing as possible. Curriculum users are encouraged to be creative in adapting fasteners or in selecting particular types of clothing to encourage children to use what motor abilities they have in the dressing process. For severely motorically impaired children who may never be able to do anything beyond cooperating in the dressing process, it is important to talk about dressing. Make comments about color, about how nice particular articles of clothing make children look, and so forth, in order to engage these children in the task cognitively, even if they cannot participate actively in a physical sense.

18. Dressing

a. Cooperates in dressing and undressing
b. Removes loose clothing (socks, hats, untied shoes)
c. Unties shoes, hats, as an act of undressing
d. Unzips own clothing as appropriate
e. Puts on hat
f. Puts on loose shoes or slippers

AREA: **18. Dressing**
BEHAVIOR: 18a. Cooperates in dressing and undressing

Position of Child: Sitting (may be supported by adult) or any position that allows full movement of arms and legs
Materials: Child's clothes that are easy to put on/pull off

Teaching procedures	Steps for learning/evaluation
While dressing the child, name body parts as you move or touch them. Encourage child to move the appropriate parts. Place the child's arm or leg partially in or out of garment, and encourage child to assist you during dressing or undressing ("Push your leg through here!"; "Pull your arm out!"). Play peek-a-boo games with garments to encourage child to "help."	*Record* + if the child: 1. Cooperates by moving his or her limbs, lifting his or her head, holding still when asked to do so and so forth. *Criterion:* Child cooperates in dressing and undressing; each time child is dressed or undressed on 3 separate days.

Note: It may be necessary to use relaxation activities with certain children so they can make the most effective use of their limbs. Allow plenty of time for dressing.

AREA: **18. Dressing**
BEHAVIOR: 18b. Removes loose clothing (socks, hats, untied shoes)

Position of Child: Sitting or any position that allows full movement of arms and legs and visual attention to activity
Materials: Socks, hat, shoes that are loosened or easy to remove

Teaching procedures	Steps for learning/evaluation
Draw child's attention to what you are doing when you undress him or her by talking about it and showing child (or helping him or her feel it). Encourage child to participate. "Start" the process of removing clothing and have child finish it (e.g., pull a sock just past child's heel and then have child remove it the rest of the way). Try making a game of the activity—such as peek-a-boo—by pulling hat down over child's eyes and encouraging child to remove the hat. Assist child through the process, and then gradually fade your assistance. Use different pieces of clothing.	*Record* + if the child: 1. Completes removal of loose clothing when it is started by someone else; and 2. Removes loose clothing independently *Criterion:* Child removes loose clothing independently; 1 piece of clothing a day on 3 separate days.

AREA: **18. Dressing**
BEHAVIOR: 18c. Unties shoes, hats, as an act of undressing

Position of Child: Sitting or any comfortable position that allows child full movement of hands and
feet and visual focus on activity
Materials: Shoes (with ties), hat with tie, mirror

Teaching procedures	Steps for learning/evaluation
When you undress the child, always describe what you are doing. As you untie child's shoes say something like "Now, let's untie your shoes and take them off." Have the child watch as you untie one of his or her shoes (you may want to show child in the mirror when you untie his or her hat). Touch the child's hands to his or her shoe strings and help child untie the other shoe. Encourage imitation.	*Record* + if the child: 1. Touches own shoelaces and attempts to untie them; and 2. Unties own shoes as an act of undressing (when instructed or at another appropriate time and place). *Criterion:* Child unties shoes or hat as an act of undressing, each time he or she is undressed on 5 separate days.

Note: Adaptation may be made to ends of ties for children who are unable to grasp small strings; that is, plastic ring, bells, and so on, may be attached to make ends of laces easier to grasp. Shoes with velcro fasteners may be easier for some *physically handicapped* children. The focus of this activity is untying as a part of getting undressed, not just as a part of playing with the shoes.

AREA: **18. Dressing**
BEHAVIOR: 18d. Unzips own clothing as appropriate

Position of Child: Sitting, standing, or any comfortable position that allows child full movement of
hands and visual attention to activity
Materials: Coat, pants with zipper

Teaching procedures	Steps for learning/evaluation
Show the child how to unzip his or her coat or pants. Zip up the zipper and then ask child to unzip it. If the child cannot, or does not grasp the pull on the zipper, assist child by placing the metal pull in his hand. If child cannot maintain his or her grasp, then an adaptation to the pull may be necessary (i.e., larger plastic piece attached to it). If grasp is maintained, but child does not unzip, then assist by helping child to "start" the motion. Assist physically only as much as necessary, fading support as quickly as possible.	*Record* + if the child: 1. Unzips partway; and 2. Unzips own clothing all the way when asked to do so or when it is an appropriate time to be undressing. *Criterion:* Child unzips own clothing as appropriate on 5 separate days.

Note: For *physically handicapped* children, velcro fasteners may be substituted for zippers.

AREA: **18. Dressing**
BEHAVIOR: 18e. Puts on hat

Position of Child: Sitting/standing or any comfortable position that allows child full movement of
hands
Materials: Hat that is easy to pull on and easy to remove

Teaching procedures	Steps for learning/evaluation
Show child the hat. Then demonstrate by placing it on your head. Then have the child place the hat on his or her head. For a *visually impaired* child, place the hat in his or her hands and ask child to put it on his or her head. If child cannot, or does not put the hat on his or her head, gently guide child to do so. Be sure to allow ample time for child to respond. *Alternate approaches:* Use box of hats for child to choose from; use a mirror so child gets feedback from his or her actions. Good times to practice are during ''dress-up'' activities or when dressing up to go outside.	***Record*** + if the child: 1. Places hat on his or her head. ***Criterion:*** Child puts hat on; 3 times on 3 separate days.

AREA: **18. Dressing**
BEHAVIOR: 18f. Puts on loose shoes or slippers

Position of Child: Sitting position that allows child to easily obtain hand/foot movements and
visually focus on activity
Materials: Loose or slip-on shoes

Teaching procedures	Steps for learning/evaluation
Show the child how to put shoes on by putting on your shoes. Open up shoes as much as possible before giving them to child. Give them one at a time to child to put on. If the child does not, or cannot put shoes on, you may opt to have him or her try adult-size shoes (play ''dress-up''). If child cannot put shoes on by himself or herself, gently guide child to do so. Try smaller- and smaller-sized shoes.	***Record*** + if the child: 1. Puts on oversized shoes; and 2. Puts on his or her own loose shoes or slippers. ***Criterion:*** Child puts on his own loose shoes or slippers; each day on 3 separate days.

Note: Do not expect child to be able to differentiate right from left at this age. These same procedures can be used with *visually impaired* children if you hand them shoes, put them where they can easily find them, describe what they are to do, and prompt freely initially.

19.

Reaching and Grasping

T HE FINE MOTOR SKILLS represented in this sequence are those involved in picking up and releasing objects of various sizes. Although it is important to facilitate the development of good reaching and grasping patterns in both hands, it may be advisable to work through the sequence at a different rate for each hand when clearly asymmetric development is evident. Always record which hand is being used for a particular activity and devise means of getting the child to use the nondominant or nonpreferred hand for some activities.

The basic reaching and grasping patterns are established by 12 months (developmental level). Beyond that point, they are elaborated in a variety of manipulative skills. These are represented in the Object Manipulation sequences labeled I, II, III, IV, and V.

Although reaching and grasping skills are facilitated and motivated by the presentation of visual stimuli, they will develop adequately, although very slowly, in the absence of vision. In order to avoid a major delay in visually impaired children, it is important to be creative both in selecting and presenting toys. Some points to remember are: 1) Noisy toys that cease to make noise before the child reaches or as he or she reaches may cease to exist for the child cognitively unless he or she has achieved "object permanence," a concept generally late to develop in visually impaired children; 2) although most objects are presented at the midline for seeing children in order to maximize their use of vision in reaching, the midline is the most difficult place to localize a sound. Thus, it is extremely important to be aware of a child's auditory localization skills (sequence 2) in order to know the optimum placement for an object to be found by the child.

19. Reaching and Grasping

a. Moves arms actively when sees or hears object
b. Bats at object at chest level
c. Grasps object placed in his or her hand (not reflexive grasp)
d. Reaches out and grasps objects near body
e. Displays extended reach and grasp
f. Rakes and scoops small objects (fingers against palm)

g. Releases 1 object to take another

h. Grasps, using thumb against index and middle finger

i. Uses inferior pincer grasp (thumb against side of index finger)

j. Uses index finger to poke

k. Uses neat pincer grasp (thumb against tip of index finger)

AREA: **19. Reaching and Grasping**
BEHAVIOR: 19a. Moves arms actively when sees or hears object

Position of Child: Any position that allows free movement of arms
Materials: Objects or toys that are attractive (bright, shiny, or colorful)

Teaching procedures	Steps for learning/evaluation
Place the child in a comfortable position where he or she can easily see what you hold up, and so that his or her arms are free to move. Hold up a toy. Note whether child's arms begin to move or wave or swipe at the toy. Make sure child is looking at the object. As child waves his or her arms, move the object closer so child can touch it. You can make a mobile using an over-the-door hanger and tying toys to it. Place it on the child's crib or playpen with items hanging low enough for child to reach. If child looks at the object but does not initiate any arm/hand movement, occasionally physically assist arm movements that engage the hanging object. For the *visually impaired* child, search for objects that attract visual attention at an optimal distance from the eyes. Objects may need to be larger and shinier than for other children and should make noise. Side-lying may be the most effective position for children with motor impairments that prevent free use of the arms against gravity.	***Record*** + if the child: 1. Moves either or both hands upon presentation of an object. ***Criterion:*** Child moves either or both hands upon presentation of an object; 4 of 5 trials on 3 separate days.

AREA: **19. Reaching and Grasping**
BEHAVIOR: 19b. Bats at object at chest level

Position of Child: Any position to promote optimal hand use
Materials: Any attractive toy or objects, including some that make noise

Teaching procedures	Steps for learning/evaluation
Hold objects in front of the child at chest level and observe child's responses. If one or both arms move, bring the toy into range of the hands so that the object can be hit or touched. Also provide mobiles or other hanging toys for the child that are at the right distance to be hit or touched by the child.	***Record*** + if the child: 1. Makes 2 or 3 swipes at an object presented at chest level; and 2. Repeatedly bats at an object presented at chest level (4 or more directed hits at the object).

(continued)

Teaching procedures	Steps for learning/evaluation
If the child does not bat at the toys, bring the toys in closer so they touch one or both hands, such that any movement on the part of the child will make the toy move. As the child begins to hit at the toys under these circumstances, gradually move the toy away enough to promote active movement on the part of the child. If child does not try to bat at the toys with the above help, physically assist child to do so, but give no more help than is essential. For the *visually impaired* child, more physical assistance may be necessary to help the child locate the toy. Toys should have interesting noises. Many *physically handicapped* children will work best in a side-lying position.	*Criterion:* Child bats at an object presented at chest level 4 of 5 trials, 3 separate days.

AREA: **19. Reaching and Grasping**

BEHAVIOR: 19c. Grasps object placed in his or her hand (not reflexive grasp)

Position of Child: Any position to promote optimum hand usage
Materials: A variety of small interesting toys (rattles, jar rings, cubes, etc.)

Teaching procedures	Steps for learning/evaluation
Place an object in the child's hand and observe his or her reactions. If child immediately drops it, give it to child again or give him another toy of a different size, shape, weight, and so forth. Look for child's fingers to curve around the object and to hold it 10 seconds or more. There is little one can do to physically assist this response, but it may be possible to promote it by carefully varying the properties of objects given to the child and the way the object is placed in the hand. For *visually impaired* children, try both noisy objects and objects with different textures.	*Record* + if the child: 1. Grasps object placed in his or her hand for 10 seconds or more. *Criterion:* Child grasps object placed in his or her hand for 10 seconds or more; 4 of 5 trials, 3 separate days.

Note: Do not credit a purely reflexive grasp, that is, the automatic closing of the hand around any object that touches the palm of the hand. If you get this response, try giving the child toys that are large in diameter, are a different shape, and so forth. Make sure the child is as relaxed as possible.

AREA: **19. Reaching and Grasping**
BEHAVIOR: 19d. Reaches out and grasps objects near body

Position of Child: Any position to facilitate the use of arms and hands
Materials: Interesting toys

Teaching procedures	Steps for learning/evaluation
Place an interesting object within easy reach of the child and observe his or her attempts to pick it up. If child does not pick up the object, place it in child's hand for a few seconds to attract his or her attention to it and then take it and place it within reach again. If there is still no attempt to pick up the toy, physically assist the child to reach toward and touch the toy. The grasp at this point is usually "palmar" (i.e., fingers against palm of the hand). Be sure to vary toys so that the child will remain interested in the task. For *visually impaired* children, it may be necessary to touch the object to the child's hand so he or she will know where to reach, or to physically guide child's hand to touch the toy.	***Record*** + if the child: 1. Reaches out and grasps object in an uncoordinated fashion (undershoots or overshoots the object, fumbles while trying to pick it up, etc.); and 2. Reaches out and grasps object with coordination. ***Criterion:*** Child reaches out and grasps object in a coordinated fashion; 4 of 5 trials on 3 separate days.

Note: Some children with specific *motor impairments* will never be able to grasp with coordination, but should continue to practice. It is important to let such children work at picking up things with you, giving as little help as possible. Consult your therapist regarding positioning for this activity.

AREA: **19. Reaching and Grasping**
BEHAVIOR: 19e. Displays extended reach and grasp

Position of Child: Any position to facilitate the use of arms and hands
Materials: Toys of interest

Teaching procedures	Steps for learning/evaluation
Place a toy at a distance requiring the child to straighten his or her arm and/or to lean forward in order to reach it. If child does not reach and pick up the toy, move it a little closer until child does reach for it. Gradually present item further back until extended reach is obtained. For the hypertonic child, it may be necessary to facilitate extended reach by rocking and relaxing the child prior to trials. For a *visually impaired* child, hold a noisy toy at arm's length after having touched child with it. If necessary, hold toy close to or touching the child and move it away slowly as child is reaching (maintaining touch) to the extended position.	***Record*** + if the child: 1. Reaches for and picks up object at arm's length. ***Criterion:*** Child reaches for and picks up object at arm's length; 3 of 5 trials on 3 separate days.

AREA: **19. Reaching and Grasping**
BEHAVIOR: 19f. Rakes and scoops small objects (fingers against palm)

Position of Child: Sitting or supported sitting
Materials: Small objects (when you begin to work with very small objects, it is a good idea to use
edibles, because there is less danger when child puts them in his or her mouth)

Teaching procedures	Steps for learning/evaluation
Place small pieces of cereal such as Cheerios or Honeycomb on a table or tray in front of the child. Encourage child to get the food and eat it. If the child does not spontaneously pick up the small item: Place one in his or her hand and guide it to child's mouth (or simply feed the child one) and try again. Vary the size and shape of items (larger ones will be easier to pick up). Encourage picking up, and reduce the size of the items as the child masters picking up the bigger size. It may be hard for a *visually impaired* child to become interested in small objects. Focus on edibles and finger feeding and help child "feel" for the object on his or her food tray with an open hand.	**Record** + if the child: 1. Picks up any object as small as a Cheerio with a raking or scooping motion. **Criterion:** Child picks up 5 small objects each day, 3 separate days.

AREA: **19. Reaching and Grasping**
BEHAVIOR: 19g. Releases 1 object to take another

Position of Child: Any position that permits holding and reaching
Materials: Toys and objects of interest

Teaching procedures	Steps for learning/evaluation
When the child is holding an object, present another and encourage child to take it. (For a *blind* child touch him or her with the second object and talk about it.) If child does not take the second toy: Place it in his or her other hand and observe child's response. If child drops one of the toys, take back both toys and give the child the toy he or she dropped. Then present the other toy. If child does not take it, place it in his or her hand. Observe. Change toys and proceed with another trial, always following a failure with placing the toy in child's hands.	**Record** + if the child: 1. Releases one object when picking up another or when another is placed in his or her hands. **Criterion:** Child spontaneously picks up 5 or more items using thumb and forefingers in 1 hour on 3 separate days.

Note: In the normal developmental sequence, when a child first learns to reach for a second object, he or she usually drops the first. It is a more mature response for child to continue holding 2 objects.

AREA: **19. Reaching and Grasping**
BEHAVIOR: 19h. Grasps, using thumb against index and middle finger

Position of Child: Any position to promote optimal hand usage
Materials: 1-inch cubes; gradually decreasing sizes of objects (edibles are good for this activity)

Teaching procedures	Steps for learning/evaluation
Present objects to be picked up by the child on the thumb side of his or her hand. Encourage child to use his or her thumb and fingers to pick up the objects. If the child continues to pick up objects using fingers against his or her palm, try holding an object between your thumb and index finger so that the child cannot take it from you without using his or her thumb against his or her fingers. If child is not successful, do not frustrate the child—let child continue to pick up items with his or her fingers against palm for several more weeks and then try this activity again. With a *visually impaired* child, encourage "searching" for objects with an open hand, but, if necessary, physically guide the hand so that the object rests against the index and middle fingers. Encourage child to pick object up. Also work on child's taking something that you are holding between your thumb and fingers. Using food is often helpful.	***Record*** + if the child: 1. Picks up object using thumb against index and middle fingers when the object is held by someone else so that it cannot be "raked" with the fingers against the palm; and 2. Picks up object spontaneously using thumb against index and middle fingers. ***Criterion:*** Child spontaneously picks up 5 or more items using thumb and forefingers in 1 hour on 3 separate days.

AREA: **19. Reaching and Grasping**
BEHAVIOR: 19i. Uses inferior pincer grasp (thumb against side of index finger)

Position of Child: Any position to promote optimal hand usage
Materials: Small objects or finger foods

Teaching procedures	Steps for learning/evaluation
This grasp is a refinement of the grasp in 19h and is taught primarily by giving the child lots of experience picking up small objects. Give small objects to the child and observe how or she picks them up. Make it a game by having the child put objects through a hole into a container or, if child is cognitively able, by sorting items into various containers, and so forth. Varying the sizes, shapes, and colors of the objects maintains interest as does integrating this activity with other curriculum items.	***Record*** + if the child: 1. Picks up objects spontaneously using thumb against side of index finger. ***Criterion:*** Child picks up 5 items with thumb against side of index finger on 3 separate days.

Note: As children's hands develop, they will vary their use of different grasps. Within the course of 1 meal or training session, you may see a child pick up objects by raking his or her fingers against palm, by using thumb and forefingers, and by using thumb against index finger. What you should encourage is the most efficient grasp for the activity.

AREA: **19. Reaching and Grasping**
BEHAVIOR: 19j. Uses index finger to poke

Position of Child: Any to facilitate optimal hand usage
Materials: Busy box toy, empty pegboard, clay with holes poked in it and so on

Teaching procedures	Steps for learning/evaluation
Present busy box toy to the child. Demonstrate pushing button to get buzzing noise or "pop-up" reaction. Guide child to push the button with his or her index finger.	*Record* + if the child: 1. Spontaneously pokes button or other object with index finger or puts finger through small opening.
Cut a hole in a piece of wood or cardboard big enough for you to stick your finger through. Stick your finger through and "wave" it at the child, making a game of it. Child will probably reach for your finger. If so, withdraw it gradually, enticing child to come after it with his or her finger. If child gets finger through the hole, turn the board slightly so that child can see his or her finger wiggle.	*Criterion:* Child spontaneously pokes or places finger into openings; 3 times a session on 3 separate days.
Put honey or pudding in a jar with a small opening, demonstrate getting food out with finger.	
For a *visually impaired* child, help child explore holes with his or her finger. Interesting textures or sticky foods in the hole will reinforce the activity.	

Note: The point of this item is to get good separation of the index finger from the rest of the fingers. Watch for other activities where child does this spontaneously (e.g., pushing food or toys around with finger).

AREA: **19. Reaching and Grasping**
BEHAVIOR: 19k. Uses neat pincer grasp (thumb against tip of index finger)

Position of Child: Any to promote optimal hand usage
Materials: Small objects, finger foods

Teaching procedures	Steps for learning/evaluation
Give the child lots of practice picking up small objects, particularly small pieces of food at mealtime. Observe the grasp patterns child uses. If child persists in using a raking motion (fingers against palm) when other patterns would be more efficient, try handing the items to the child. Hold them between your thumb and index finger in such a way that child cannot get them with a raking movement. Also, continue to encourage poking activities or pushing objects with the index finger to increase the separation of that finger from the others.	*Record* + if the child: 1. Spontaneously picks up object using thumb against tip of index finger. *Criterion:* Child spontaneously picks up small object between thumb and tip of index finger; 5 of 5 trials on 3 separate days.

20.

Object Manipulation

DURING THE FIRST 12 months of life, the skills represented in this first part of the Object Manipulation section (items *a–i*) involve some degree of usable vision and are directed at developing visual motor coordinaion skills useful in reaching and manipulating.

At the 12-month developmental level, this sequence is expanded into five separate sequences (I–V), each of which involves youngsters in learning to manipulate particular kinds of materials. When utilizing these second-year sequences, vision is helpful and is relied upon by normal children. However, it is not essential, and visually impaired children can accomplish the tasks outlined by relying on tactile cues.

Thus, for children with visual impairments, mastery of the initial items (*a* through *i*) is not a prerequisite for beginning sequences I–V at the 12-month level. As soon as the visually impaired child is able to pick up and release items efficiently, efforts should be made to involve him or her with the materials used in these latter sequences. Of course, decisions will always have to be made as to which activities are most appropriate, considering the tactile skills and motor sophistication presented by individual children.

20. Object Manipulation

a. Looks at hand (or toy) to one side
b. Looks at or manipulates toy placed in hands at midline
c. Brings toy and hand into visual field and looks at them when toy is placed in hand (may move head or hand), or moves toy to mouth or midline (if a visually impaired child)
d. Watches hands at midline—actively moves and watches result
e. Plays with own feet or toes
f. Glances from 1 toy to the other when toy is placed in each hand, or plays alternately with the toys
g. Reaches out for toys and picks them up when both toys and hand are in visual field (modify for visually impaired children)
h. Reaches out for toys and gets them when toys, but not child's hands, are in child's visual field (modify for visually impaired children)
i. Looks toward object and visually directs reach or adjusts reach to get noisy object (if has no functional vision)

AREA: 20. Object Manipulation
BEHAVIOR: 20a. Looks at hand (or toy) to one side

Position of Child: Lying down with head turned to either side
Materials: Brightly colored ribbon; small bells on elastic bands or on loops of yarn or string

Teaching procedures	Steps for learning/evaluation
Tie ribbons to child's wrists; encourage child to look at them. Add bells and give child's hands a little shake so that the bells jingle. Sometimes just stroking or tapping child's hands will help to draw his or her attention to them. You may want to do this activity several times in succession, making sure there is a definite break between presentations (i.e., 5 or 6 seconds). Be sure to look at the child for signs of recognition or excitement when returning the ribbon, bell, or yarn to the child's hand or when gently shaking the toy. Look for the child's making eye contact with object. Any affective change (such as a smile) when the object is placed in the hand or shaken may indicate that child is looking at his or her hand (or the toy).	*Record* + if the child: 1. Looks at one of his or her hands in either side of midline. *Criterion:* Child turns head to look at his or her hand (or toy); 3 of 5 trials on 3 separate days.

AREA: 20. Object Manipulation
BEHAVIOR: 20b. Looks at or manipulates toy placed in hands at midline

Position of Child: Lying on back, reclining in infant seat, or on side (the latter if too physically handicapped to maintain head or hands in midline)
Materials: Bright, shiny objects that will gain the attention of the infant. Toys that will also emit a noise if shaken or squeezed are recommended.

Teaching procedures	Steps for learning/evaluation
Hold toy within reach of the child and try to gain the child's attention by shaking, rattling, or squeezing the toy. With your other hand bring the child's hand to midline to the toy. Once the child's hand is on the toy, shake or rattle the toy for him or her. Try to leave child holding the toy by himself or herself. Rather than holding toy for child, try merely supporting it lightly with 1 or 2 fingers to facilitate child's holding it.	*Record* + if the child: 1. Looks at toy even briefly after it is placed in his or her hands at midline; and 2. Looks at toy in hands at midline 5 or more seconds. *Criterion:* Child looks at toy placed in hands at midline 5 or more seconds; 3 of 5 trials on 3 separate days.

(continued)

Teaching procedures	Steps for learning/evaluation
You may alternate placing items in the hands with attaching brightly colored ribbons and bells to the hands or wrists to encourage child to bring hands to midline to look at them.	

Note: Present this item several times. With repetition, look for recognition (smiling, laughing) and motion toward the object by the infant.

AREA: **20. Object Manipulation**
BEHAVIOR: 20c. Brings toy and hand into visual field and looks
at them when toy is placed in hand (may move head or hand),
or moves toy to mouth or midline (if a visually impaired child)

Position of Child: Lying on back, reclining in infant seat, or lying on side
Materials: Toys or materials that are highly colored and/or that make a noise when manipulated by
the child

Teaching procedures	Steps for learning/evaluation
Hold the toy in the visual field of the child. Manipulate toy in a manner that will gain the child's attention. Place the toy in/on the child's hand, allowing child to bring toy back into his or her visual field by himself or herself. If child does not bring the toy into his or her visual field, move child's hand with the toy to midline or gently turn child's head toward the hand with the toy. Then manipulate the toy so that it creates a spectacle for the child. For the *visually impaired* child, choose noisy toys. Place one in child's hand and help child make the noise. Wait to see if child will then do it on his or her own.	**Record** + if the child: 1. Brings toy placed in his or her hand into visual field at midline or turns head toward the hand with the toy. **Criterion:** Child brings toy into visual field or turns toward it when it is placed in his or her hand; 3 of 5 trials on 3 separate days.

AREA: **20. Object Manipulation**
BEHAVIOR: 20d. Watches hands at midline—actively moves and watches result

Position of Child: Lying on back, in infant seat, or side-lying
Materials: None or, if necessary, a brightly colored mitten and bells

Teaching procedures	Steps for learning/evaluation
If the child does not watch or play with his or her hands: Place a mitten or bright ribbon or elastic to which bells are attached on child's hands or wrists. Help child bring hand into the midline and shake child's hand to gain attention to it (repeat several times).	***Record*** + if the child: 1. Watches his or her hands and actively moves them while watching them—10 seconds or more. ***Criterion:*** Child can be observed watching his or her hands at least 3 times during the day on 3 different days.

Note: Be sure to allow the child to work with both hands.

AREA: **20. Object Manipulation**
BEHAVIOR: 20e. Plays with own feet or toes

Position of Child: Lying on back or side
Materials: Ribbons, bells, or booties with bright colors or patterns

Teaching procedures	Steps for learning/evaluation
Place ribbons or bells on child's feet or shoes. If child does not play with his or her feet, gently shake child's feet to gain his or her attention. Call attention to the bells, ribbons, or "pretty shoes." Shake child's foot gently, saying, "Look at the ribbons, hear the bells!" *and/or* play "This little piggy went to market" while dressing the baby; wait to see if child then plays with his or her feet.	***Record*** + if the child: 1. Plays with own feet or toes while watching what he or she is doing after adult calls attention to child's feet; and 2. Spontaneously plays with own feet. ***Criterion:*** Child is observed playing with his or her feet or toes spontaneously on 5 separate occasions.

AREA: **20. Object Manipulation**
BEHAVIOR: 20f. Glances from 1 toy to the other when toy is placed in each hand, or plays alternately with the toys

Position of Child: Lying on back or supported sitting
Materials: 1-inch cubes, squeaky toys, rattles, and so forth

Teaching procedures	Steps for learning/evaluation
Place a toy in one of the child's hands. Get child to look at it and then place another toy in child's other hand. Encourage child to look at this toy. You can tap the toy or squeak it or do whatever will attract attention to it. Be sure to allow the child time to look at the first toy before adding the second toy. Sometimes an infant will drop the first toy as soon as a second one is placed in the other hand. Try placing objects in both hands several times and, perhaps, gently holding child's hands with the toys in them for a few seconds to encourage looking back and forth. Do not frustrate the child, however, who clearly wants to attend to 1 toy and ignore the other. Go on to the next item in the sequence. Help the *visually impaired* child play alternately with the toys.	***Record*** + if the child: 1. Looks from 1 toy to the other when toy is placed in each hand. ***Criterion:*** Child glances from 1 hand to the other when object is placed in each hand; 3 of 5 trials on 3 separate days.

AREA: **20. Object Manipulation**
BEHAVIOR: 20g. Reaches out for toys and picks them up when both toys and hand are in visual field (modify for visually impaired children)

Position of Child: Any position that encourages free hand usage. (Lying on the side may be particularly effective for children with motor problems.)
Materials: Any preferred toys that are easy to pick up. Very soft rubber squeaky toys are helpful for children who have trouble opening and closing their hands.

Teaching procedures	Steps for learning/evaluation
Place toy within easy reach of child, near one of his or her hands. Assure that child looks at the toy by moving it, making it produce noise, and so forth. If child does not grasp the toy: Touch the back of child's hand with the toy and then place it so that it is almost touching his or her fingers.	***Record*** + if the child: 1. Picks up toy (even if reach is initially inaccurate and movements awkward). ***Criterion:*** Child picks up toy on 3 of 5 trials on 3 consecutive days.

(continued)

Teaching procedures	Steps for learning/evaluation
Guide the child's hand to pick up the toy. If child has difficulty opening his or hand, it may help to stroke the back of child's hand several times to facilitate its opening so that the toy can be picked up. For seriously *visually impaired* children, first place the toy in child's hands. Then remove it and touch child's hand with it as you place it next to his or her hand to pick up. Choose noisy and highly textured toys.	

AREA: 20. Object Manipulation

BEHAVIOR: 20h. Reaches out for toys and gets them when toys, but not child's hands, are in child's visual field (modify for visually impaired children)

Position of Child: Any position to promote good hand usage. (Lying on the side may be effective for a child with motor problems.)

Materials: Any preferred toys that are easy to pick up

Teaching procedures	Steps for learning/evaluation
Place the toy within easy reach of the child but *not* near child's hand. The toy should be placed where the child cannot see his or her hand and the toy at the same time, and so that the child must move his or her hand to find the toy. For example, place the toy on the table while the child's hands are in his or her lap. If child does not pick up the toy, gently move child's hand into his or her visual field (preferably by moving the arm from the elbow or shoulder). Wait to see if the child then moves to pick up the toy. If not, facilitate further by moving child's hand closer to the toy. On subsequent trials try to increase the distance the child must move on his or her own. For a seriously *visually impaired* child, choose noisy toys. Allow child to feel a toy for a few seconds, then move toy 6–8 inches away from child's hand. Make a noise with toy until child locates and touches it.	*Record* + if the child: 1. Reaches out and gets toy. *Criterion:* Child picks up toy on 3 of 5 trials; 3 consecutive days.

AREA: **20. Object Manipulation**

BEHAVIOR: 20i. Looks toward object and visually directs reach or adjusts reach to get noisy object (if has no functional vision)

Position of Child: Lying on back, sitting supported, or lying on side
Materials: Toys, bottle, or food

Teaching procedures	Steps for learning/evaluation
When offering toys, a bottle, or food to the child, present them at midline and within easy reach. If child looks at toy and reaches for it directly, begin presenting items slightly away from midline in various positions. If child reaches without looking at what he or she is doing, try to attract child's attention to the object by tapping it, moving it up to eye level, and so forth.	***Record*** + if the child: 1. Looks at toys or objects when reaching for them. ***Criterion:*** Child looks at objects before reaching for them; 5 out of 5 trials on 3 separate days.

Note: Some handicapped children who have functional vision learn to ''grasp'' and pick up things without looking at them. This behavior will interfere with developing more advanced skills that require good coordination of visual and motor behaviors. Encourage visual attention to hand activities by careful placement of objects in visual field, by holding objects where they can be easily seen and not allowing child to get them until he or she looks at them, and so forth.

Object Manipulation: Form manipulation

20. Object Manipulation

I. Form manipulation

a. Places large round form in form board
b. Places square form in form board
c. Places round and square forms in correct holes when they are presented simultaneously
d. Places triangular form in hole

e. Places round, square, and triangular forms in form board when they are presented simultaneously
f. Completes simple puzzles
g. Places correct forms in form ball

AREA: **20-I. Object Manipulation: Form manipulation**
BEHAVIOR: 20-Ia. Places large round form in form board

Position of Child: Any position that maximizes use of upper limbs
Materials: A round form and a form board with 1 round cutout

Teaching procedures	Steps for learning/evaluation
Present the form board and the round form to the child. Encourage the child to use his or her fingers to feel the round shape of the object and the cutout in the form board. Ask child to put the objects in the hole. If child does it correctly, praise him or her. If child has difficulty, demonstrate placing the form and then ask child to try it. If necessary, physically help child put the form in the hole. Repeat the procedure, physically assisting if necessary. Praise the *motorically handicapped* child's close approximations. Assist as necessary or allow child simply to indicate where the form should go. Help the *visually impaired* child feel the object and the form board.	***Record*** + if the child: 1. Puts round form in form board with minimal assistance; and 2. Puts round form in form board independently. ***Criterion:*** Child puts round object in a hole; 3 of 3 trials on 3 separate days.

Note: If available form boards have several shapes in them, leave the other shapes in while working with the round one. The other shapes may even be taped in place initially.

AREA: **20-I. Object Manipulation: Form manipulation**
BEHAVIOR: 20-Ib. Places square form in form board

Position of Child: Any position that maximizes use of upper limbs
Materials: A square form and a form board with a square hole

Teaching procedures	Steps for learning/evaluation
Present the form board and the square form to the child. Encourage the child to use his or her fingers to feel the square shape of the object and the cutout in the form board. Ask child to put the object in the hole. If child does it correctly, praise him or her. If child has difficulty, demonstrate placing the form and then ask child to try it. If necessary, physically help child put the form in the hole.	***Record*** + if the child: 1. Puts square form in form board with minimal assistance; and 2. Puts round form in form board independently. ***Criterion:*** Child puts square form in a hole; 3 of 3 trials on 3 separate days.

(continued)

Teaching procedures	Steps for learning/evaluation
Repeat the procedure, physically assisting if necessary. Praise the *motorically handicapped* child's close approximations. Assist as necessary or allow child to simply indicate where the form should go. Help the *visually impaired* child feel the object and the form board.	

Note: If using a form board with only a square, follow mastery of this item with a few trials of alternating the board with the round hole and the board with the square hole. If using a board with both holes, alternate the shape you remove and ask the child to replace it.

AREA: 20-I. Object Manipulation: Form manipulation
BEHAVIOR: 20-Ic. Places round and square forms in correct holes when they are presented simultaneously

Position of Child: Any position that maximizes use of upper limbs
Materials: Round and square forms and a form board with both round and square holes

Teaching procedures	Steps for learning/evaluation
Present a form board and both the round and square forms to the child. Encourage the child to feel the shapes of the forms and holes. Ask child to put the forms in the holes. If the child has difficulty, demonstrate and place the blocks near the correct holes; then ask child to try again. If necessary, physically guide child's hand in placing the objects in the correct holes. Repeat the procedure, helping as necessary.	*Record* + if the child: 1. Places round and square forms in correct holes with minimal assistance; and 2. Places the round and square forms in correct holes independently. *Criterion:* Child places both a round and a square form in form board; 3 of 3 trials on 3 separate days.

AREA: 20-I. Object Manipulation: Form manipulation
BEHAVIOR: 20-Id. Places triangular form in hole

Position of Child: Any position that maximizes use of upper limbs
Materials: A triangular form and a form board with a triangular hole

Teaching procedures	Steps for learning/evaluation
Present the form board and the triangular form to the child. Encourage child to use his or her fingers to feel the triangular shape of the object and the cutout in the form board.	*Record* + if the child: 1. Puts triangular form in form board with minimal assistance; and 2. Puts triangular form in form board independently.

(continued)

Teaching procedures	Steps for learning/evaluation
Ask child to put the object in the hole. If child does it correctly, praise him or her. If child has difficulty, demonstrate placing the form and then ask child to try it. If necessary, physically help child to put the form in the hole. Repeat the procedure, physically assisting if necessary. Praise the *motorically handicapped* child's close approximations. Assist as necessary or allow child to simply indicate where the form should go. Help the *visually impaired* child feel the object and the form board.	***Criterion:*** Child puts triangular object in a hole; 3 of 3 trials on 3 separate days.

AREA: **20-I. Object Manipulation: Form manipulation**
BEHAVIOR: 20-Ie. Places round, square, and triangular forms in form board when they are presented simultaneously

Position of Child: Any position that maximizes use of upper limbs
Materials: A form board that has round, square, and triangular cutouts, along with shapes that fit into these spaces

Teaching procedures	Steps for learning/evaluation
If the child has difficulty placing 1 or more of the shapes, you demonstrate, then ask child to try again. If necessary, move the forms close to the appropriate spaces initially. If child still does not place the forms correctly, physically guide child to the right placement. Gradually reduce your help, praising child's efforts to place the forms without help. After placements are made, mix the arrangement of the forms in front of the child. *Variations:* Use boards with several holes for each shape to encourage generalization or use of simple "shape boxes" produced by many toy manufacturers.	***Record*** + if the child: 1. Places 2 of 3 different shapes (e.g., round and square) in correct holes with minimal assistance; and 2. Places round, square, and triangular forms in correct holes with minimal assistance; and 3. Places round, square, and triangular forms in correct holes independently. ***Criterion:*** Child places round, square, and triangular forms in correct holes; 3 of 3 trials on 3 separate days.

AREA: 20-I. Object Manipulation: Form manipulation
BEHAVIOR: 20-If. Completes simple puzzles

Position of Child: Any position that maximizes use of upper limbs
Materials: Large, simple puzzles with 4–5 pieces

Teaching procedures	Steps for learning/evaluation
Show the child a completed simple puzzle. While child watches, disassemble the puzzle and separate the pieces. Ask the child to put the puzzle (or picture) back together.	*Record* + if the child: 1. Puts 2 pieces in a simple puzzle; and 2. Completes a simple 4-piece puzzle; and 3. Completes 2 simple puzzles independently.
Assist the child if necessary. If the child has difficulty, place all the pieces in except 1. Help child put that one in. When child manages that, leave 2 pieces out, and so on.	*Criterion:* Child completes 2 simple puzzles; 3 of 3 trials on 3 separate days.
When child learns to complete the puzzle, change to another puzzle with more pieces than the first.	
Praise responses that are correct or close approximations requiring a little assistance. If child is incorrect or is having a great deal of difficulty, physically assist child in completing the puzzle, and work with simpler puzzles until child is able to do them easily.	
For the *visually impaired* child, use textured materials of familiar shapes.	

Note: Puzzles come in a large variety of sizes ranging from simple to difficult. Start with recognizable picture puzzles of familiar things that are easy to manipulate, and then increase the level of difficulty.

AREA: 20-I. Object Manipulation: Form manipulation
BEHAVIOR: 20-Ig. Places correct forms in form ball

Position of Child: Any position that maximizes use of upper limbs
Materials: Different-shaped objects (at least 6 different shapes) and a form ball with holes that match the objects

Teaching procedures	Steps for learning/evaluation
Present the child with several different-shaped objects and the form ball. Encourage the child to feel the shapes of the objects and the holes in the form ball. Ask the child to put the objects in the correct holes.	*Record* + if the child: 1. Places 1 form into the correct hole in a form ball; and 2. Places 2 forms into correct holes in a form ball with minimal assistance; and
If the child has difficulty, demonstrate the correct procedure.	3. Places 5–6 different forms in correct holes in form ball independently.

(continued)

Teaching procedures	Steps for learning/evaluation
Physically assist if necessary at first by holding the form ball so that most holes are covered by your hands, leaving only 1 or 2 holes open for child to attempt to place a form through. Gradually allow child to have more forms available and more choices (holes) available to place them into.	*Criterion:* Child places 5–6 different forms in a form ball; 3 of 3 trials on 3 separate days.

Note: It is important for the child to correct his or her own errors when possible. At this stage, many children do the task by trial and error rather than by good form discrimination. Give assistance primarily when the child is frustrated.

20-II.

Object Manipulation: Block patterns

20.   Object Manipulation

II. Block patterns

a. Imitates building a 2-block tower
b. Imitates building a 3-block tower
c. Imitates building a 6-block tower

d. Imitates building a "chair" with blocks
e. Imitates building 2 or more patterns of blocks

AREA: **20-II. Object Manipulation:** **Block patterns**
BEHAVIOR: 20-IIa,b,c. Imitates building 2-, 3-, and 6-block towers

Position of Child: Any position that facilitates use of upper limbs and provides stability of the trunk
Materials: 10–12 blocks of identical size

Teaching procedures	Steps for learning/evaluation
Let the child play with the blocks for several minutes. Tell child you're going to build a tower. Build a 4–6 block tower. Knock it down, start to build another, and ask the child to build a tower like yours. Begin with 2 or 3 blocks and work up to a 6-block tower as the child learns to stack the blocks. You may need to physically assist the child's getting 1 block on top of another. Provide lots of praise for child's attempts.	**Record** + if the child: IIa. 1. Attempts to place 1 block on another; and 2. Builds a 2-block tower without assistance. IIb. 1. Builds a 3-block tower without assistance. IIc. 1. Builds a 6-block tower without assistance. **Criterion:** Child imitates building a 2-, 3-, or 6-block tower; 3 successful trials on 2 separate days.

Note: Different sizes of blocks will be easier for children with different kinds of motor problems. Choose a size that is readily grasped and released. Help a *visually impaired* child to feel the blocks. It may be helpful to have child hold the bottom block(s) with one hand and place the top block with the other hand. Substantial physical assistance will be necessary at first.

AREA: **20-II. Object Manipulation:** **Block patterns**
BEHAVIOR: 20-IId. Imitates building a "chair" with blocks

Position of Child: Any position that maximizes use of upper limbs and provides trunk stability
Materials: 10 blocks of identical size

Teaching procedures	Steps for learning/evaluation
Place the blocks in front of the child. Tell the child you are going to make a "chair" with 3 of the blocks. Take 2 blocks and stack them and place the third block in front of the stack. Use your finger to show where one would sit in this chair. Show the child how to sit a small doll on the chair. Ask the child to build a chair. Demonstrate several times and physically assist if necessary. Help the *visually impaired* child feel the chair. You may want to substitute cloth blocks with velcro strips on them for wooden or plastic blocks, so that you are working on imitation of patterns and motor dexterity without the frustration of blocks falling over when there is poor aim.	**Record** + if the child: 1. Attempts to build "chair" but does not have proper placement of blocks; and 2. Builds "chair." **Criterion:** Child builds "chair" with blocks; 5 successful trials in 3 days.

Note: Vary this item with other simple block patterns (towers, rows of blocks, etc.) to keep the child's interest in playing with the blocks. The function of this item is to promote motor skill, imitation, and visual-motor coordination.

AREA: **20-II. Object Manipulation: Block patterns**
BEHAVIOR: 20-IIe. Imitates building 2 or more patterns of blocks

Position of Child: Any position that maximizes use of upper limbs and provides trunk stability
Materials: 10 blocks of identical size

Teaching procedures	Steps for learning/evaluation
While playing with blocks, create different, simple, single patterns, using 3–5 blocks (e.g., display ⊞ or ⊟).	**_Record_** + if the child:
	1. Imitates part of any pattern (e.g., ⊟); and
	2. Imitates the whole pattern; and
Make up names for each pattern and ask the child to try to make one, too. Physically assist child if necessary.	3. Imitates two or more simple patterns.
	Criterion: Child builds simple block patterns in imitation (in addition to the towers and chair of preceding items) 3 times per session in 3 consecutive sessions.
For the _visually impaired_ child, help child feel the shape of the blocks after each is added to the pattern. Talk about what you are doing as you place each block.	

Note: Vary the block patterns to maintain interest in the task and increase imitation skills. Also try imitaing patterns the child makes from time to time. Make this fun!

20-III.

Object Manipulation: Drawing

20. Object Manipulation

III. Drawing

a. Holds large writing utensil and marks with it
b. Scribbles spontaneously
c. Makes single vertical stroke in imitation
d. Shifts from scribble to stroke and back again in imitation
e. Imitates vertical and horizontal strokes
f. Imitates circular strokes

AREA: **20-III. Object Manipulation:**   **Drawing**
BEHAVIOR: 20-IIIa. Holds large writing utensil and marks with it

Position of Child: Any position that allows maximum use of hands/arms
Materials: Large crayon, pencil, magic marker (i.e., any thick writing utensil that is easily manipulated); several large pieces of paper

Teaching procedures	Steps for learning/evaluation

Show the child how to grab and hold the writing utensil. Make some slow, easy marks on the paper.
 	
    Place the utensil in the child's hand and guide it along the paper to make some "marks."
 	
    Take the utensil and hand it to the child and tell the child to make some of his or her own "marks."
 	
    Try this with different kinds of markers.
 	
    Praise any marking done by the child.
 	
    Imitation games can also be played while marking on paper.
	Record + if the child:
	1. Holds writing utensil with right end toward paper and attempts to write; and
	2. Makes marks with writing utensil.
	
	Criterion: Child grasps writing utensil and marks with it; 4 of 5 trials on 3 separate days.

Note: Motorically impaired children may need to have adaptive materials to hold the utensil in their hand. For example, Velcro tape may be placed around the hand to hold the pencil in place, or a pencil might be pushed through a small Styrofoam ball to provide something larger for the child to grasp. Seek help from a physical or occupational therapist.

AREA: **20-III. Object Manipulation:**   **Drawing**
BEHAVIOR: 20-IIIb. Scribbles spontaneously

Position of Child: Any position that facilitates maximum use of arms/hands
Materials: Two large writing utensils and large pieces of paper

Teaching procedures	Steps for learning/evaluation

Give the child many opportunities to play with a pencil (or other writing utensil) and paper. Show child how to scribble on the paper; physically assist child to scribble if necessary.
 	
    After child begins to scribble readily when you have demonstrated, begin each training or play session with just giving child the pencil and paper and observing what he or she does.
 	
    If child does not scribble spontaneously, demonstrate for the child and encourage child to scribble.
	Record + if the child:
	1. Scribbles after demonstration; and
	2. Scribbles spontaneously.
	
	Criterion: Child scribbles; 3 out of 4 trials on 3 separate days.

AREA: 20-III. Object Manipulation: Drawing
BEHAVIOR: 20-IIIc. Makes single vertical stroke in imitation

Position of Child: Any position that facilitates maximum use of arms/hands
Materials: Two large writing utensils and large pieces of paper

Teaching procedures	Steps for learning/evaluation
When the child is working on the paper, say, "Watch me" and make a quick vertical stroke on a piece of paper, making a noise like "whee" to call attention to the stroke. Ask the child to try it. If child continues to scribble, you demonstrate again, then physically assist if necessary. Work on both "up" and "down" strokes with the youngster.	*Record* + if the child: 1. Makes single line (in any direction); and 2. Makes vertical line. *Criterion:* Makes single vertical line in imitation; 4 of 5 trials on 3 separate days.

AREA: 20-III. Object Manipulation: Drawing
BEHAVIOR: 20-IIId. Shifts from scribble to stroke and back in imitation

Position of Child: Any position that facilitates maximum use of arms/hands
Materials: Two large writing utensils and large pieces of paper

Teaching procedures	Steps for learning/evaluation
When the child is marking on the paper, say, "Watch me" and make a quick vertical stroke on a piece of paper. Then say, "Can you do it?" If child imitates the stroke, say, "Good, now, do this" and scribble for the child. If the child then imitates the scribble, shift back again to the stroke. Make a game of it! If the child does not shift from scribble to stroke in imitation, physically assist child, but keep it fun!	*Record* + if the child: 1. Shifts from scribble to stroke and back again in imitation. *Criterion:* Child shifts from scribble to stroke and back again; 4 of 5 trials on 3 separate days.

Note: Try imitating whatever marks the child makes from time to time. This may increase child's interest in imitating you.

AREA: **20-III. Object Manipulation: Drawing**
BEHAVIOR: 20-IIIe. Imitates vertical and horizontal strokes

Position of Child: Any position that facilitates maximum use of arms/hands
Materials: Two large writing utensils and large pieces of paper

Teaching procedures	Steps for learning/evaluation
When the child is working on a paper, say, "Watch me" and make a hortizontal stroke across the paper. Say, "Can you do it?" If child makes a vertical stroke, demonstrate again. Physically assist child if necessary. Once child makes a horizontal stroke, say "Now do one this way" and make a vertical stroke. Alternate back and forth between vertical and horizontal strokes. Praise child for imitating your strokes. Make a game of it!	*Record* + if the child: 1. Imitates horizontal stroke; and 2. Alternates horizontal and vertical strokes in imitation. *Criterion:* Imitates vertical and horizontal strokes; 4 of 5 trials on 3 separate days.

Note: Finger painting or sand drawing with fingers can be used for children unable to grasp writing utensils. Different materials can be used for this activity to make it less repetitive (e.g., the use of texture—place a straw mat under the paper and draw vertical and horizontal lines over the mat; substitute different colors of paper; different utensils; etc.).

AREA: **20-III. Object Manipulation: Drawing**
BEHAVIOR: 20-IIIf. Imitates circular strokes

Position of Child: Any position that maximizes use of hands/arms
Materials: Two large writing utensils and several large pieces of paper

Teaching procedures	Steps for learning/evaluation
Show the child how to make free circular strokes. Talk about going "around" and making cirlces on the paper. Ask child to make a circle, guiding his or her hand if necessary. Play an imitation game as you make big and small circles and ask the child to "make one like this!"	*Record* + if the child: 1. Imitates circular motion (does not make a closed circle but makes ⊚ marks); and 2. Imitates a closed circle. *Criterion:* Child imitates circular strokes; 2 of 3 times on 4 separate days.

Note: Finger painting or sand drawing with fingers can also be substituted for the use of pencils or crayons.

20-IV.

Object Manipulation:
Placing pegs

20. Object Manipulation

IV. Placing pegs

a. Removes small round pegs from holes
b. Puts 1 large round peg in hole
c. Puts 2 or more large round pegs in holes
d. Puts 1 small round peg in hole

e. Puts 5–6 small pegs in holes (completes task)
f. Puts square peg in hole
g. Puts square pegs in holes (completes task)

AREA: **20-IV. Object Manipulation:**   **Placing pegs**
BEHAVIOR: 20-IVa. Removes small round pegs from holes

Position of Child: Any position that facilitates use of upper limbs
Materials: Small round peg (approximately ⅜ inch) and a pegboard

Teaching procedures	Steps for learning/evaluation
Present the child with a pegboard containing several small pegs. Space them far enough apart so they are easy to grasp. Ask the child to remove or take the pegs out. If the child removes a peg, praise him or her and encourage child to remove the others; repeat the trial by replacing the pegs in the holes. If child does not remove a peg, or has much difficulty, you remove the pegs, put them back in, and then ask child to do it. Physically assist the child through the movement if necessary. Use larger pegs if difficulty persists. Help the *visually impaired* child feel the holes with his or her finger when the pegs are out. It may be helpful to use the Montessori cylinders for this task. The cylinders drop into the holes so that the top surface is flush with the board, leaving only the knob to grasp.	*Record* + if the child: 1. Removes 1 large round peg from hole with minimal assistance; and 2. Removes 1 small round peg from hole with minimal assistance; and 3. Removes 1 small round peg from hole independently; and 4. Removes 3 or more small round pegs from a board. *Criterion:* Child removes 3 or more small round pegs from pegboard; 3 of 3 trials on 3 separate days.

AREA: **20-IV. Object Manipulation:**   **Placing pegs**
BEHAVIOR: 20-IVb. Puts 1 large round peg in hole

Position of Child: Any position that facilitates use of upper limbs
Materials: Large round peg (1 inch) and a pegboard

Teaching procedures	Steps for learning/evaluation
Present the child with a pegboard filled with pegs. Remove the pegs (or let child do it) and ask the child to put the pegs in the holes. If child does not put the pegs in the holes or has difficulty, you demonstrate placing the pegs, then repeat the instructions. Physically assist child if necessary to put 1 peg in.	*Record* + if the child: 1. Puts 1 large round peg in hole with minimal assistance; and 2. Puts 1 large round peg in hole independently. *Criterion:* Child puts 1 large peg in hole; 3 of 3 trials on 3 separate days.

AREA: **20-IV. Object Manipulation:**   **Placing pegs**
BEHAVIOR: 20-IVc. Puts 2 or more large round pegs in holes

Position of Child: Any position that facilitates use of upper limbs
Materials: 3 or 4 large round pegs (1 inch) and a pegboard

Teaching procedures	Steps for learning/evaluation
Present the child with several large pegs and a pegboard. Ask child to put the pegs in the holes. Encourage child to put all of the pegs in the pegboard. Physically assist the child if he or she is unable or unwilling to complete the task. Praise efforts and task completion.	*Record* + if the child: 1. Puts 2 or more large pegs in holes with minimal assistance; and 2. Puts 2 or more large pegs in holes independently. *Criterion:* Child puts 2 or more large pegs in holes; 3 of 3 trials on 3 separate days.

Note: Rather than several consecutive trials on this task, it may work better to do no more than 2, try some other activity, and then return to this one.

AREA: **20-IV. Object Manipulation:**   **Placing pegs**
BEHAVIOR: 20-IVd. Puts 1 small round peg in hole

Position of Child: Any position that facilitates use of upper limbs
Materials: One small round peg (approximately ⅜ inch) and a pegboard

Teaching procedures	Steps for learning/evaluation
Present the child with small round pegs and a pegboard. Ask child to put the pegs in the holes. If child does not put the pegs in the holes, or has difficulty, you demonstrate placing the pegs, then repeat the instructions. Physically assist the child if necessary to get 1 peg in.	*Record* + if the child: 1. Puts 1 small round peg in hole with minimal assistance; and 2. Puts 1 small round peg in hole independently. *Criterion:* Child puts 1 small peg in hole; 3 of 3 trials on 3 separate days.

Note: Go on to item 20-IVe if the child puts more than 1 peg in the holes.

AREA: **20-IV. Object Manipulation:**   **Placing pegs**
BEHAVIOR: 20-IVe. Puts 5–6 small round pegs in holes (completes task)

Position of Child: Any position that facilitates use of upper limbs
Materials: 5 or 6 small (⅜ inch) round pegs and a pegboard

Teaching procedures	Steps for learning/evaluation
Present the child with a pegboard full of pegs (no more than 6). Ask the child to put all of the pegs in the holes. If the child has difficulty, you demonstrate the task and repeat the command. If child fails to put all the pegs in the holes, encourage child to finish. If necessary, physically assist child in putting all the pegs in the holes. If child rapidly loses interest, it may be helpful to give child the board with some of the pegs in and encourage child to finish putting the pegs in; or, take turns with child in putting the pegs in. Gradually decrease the amount of help you provide.	***Record*** + if the child: 1. Puts 3 small pegs in holes with minimal assistance; and 2. Puts 3 small pegs in holes independently; and 3. Puts 5–6 small pegs in holes independently, completing the task given. ***Criterion:*** Child puts 5–6 small round pegs in holes; 3 of 3 trials on 3 separate days.

AREA: **20-IV. Object Manipulation:**   **Placing pegs**
BEHAVIOR: 20-IVf. Puts square peg in hole

Position of Child: Any position that facilitates use of upper limbs
Materials: Square pegs and a pegboard

Teaching procedures	Steps for learning/evaluation
Present the child with square pegs and a pegboard. Show child how to put the pegs in the holes and ask child to try it. Physically assist child if necessary.	***Record*** + if the child: 1. Places at least 1 square peg in hole. ***Criterion:*** Child places at least 1 square peg in hole; 3 trials in a row on 3 separate days.

Note: Go on to item 20-IVg if child places more than 1 peg in the board. Intersperse peg activities with other actitivies to avoid fatigue and/or boredom.

AREA: **20-IV. Object Manipulation:**   **Placing pegs**
BEHAVIOR: 20-IVg. Puts square pegs in holes (completes task)

Position of Child: Any position that facilitates use of upper limbs
Materials: 5–6 square pegs and a pegboard

Teaching procedures	Steps for learning/evaluation
Present the child with 5–6 square pegs in a pegboard. Remove the pegs and ask child to put all of them back in. Encourage and prompt as necessary at first. Make a game of it so that the youngster is having fun while placing the pegs.	***Record*** + if the child: 1. Places 2 or 3 square pegs in holes; and 2. Places all pegs (5 or 6) in holes. ***Criterion:*** Child places 5 or 6 square pegs in holes, completing the task provided; 3 of 3 trials on 3 separate days.

20-V.

Object Manipulation:
Putting in
and taking out

20. Object Manipulation

V. Putting in and taking out

a. Removes objects from container by reaching into container

b. Puts 1 or 2 objects in container

c. Puts many (6 +) objects into container (completes task)

d. Puts small objects through small hole in container

e. Puts many (6 +) small objects through small hole (completes task)

AREA: **20-V. Object Manipulation: Putting in and taking out**
BEHAVIOR: 20-Va. Removes objects from container by reaching into container

Position of Child: Any position that allows free movement of hands
Materials: A variety of containers and small objects

Teaching procedures	Steps for learning/evaluation
Give the child a container with several objects in it. Ask child to take out the objects. If child cannot or does not remove objects, then demonstrate how to remove them. If necessary, assist child by guiding his or her hand to take an object and helping child remove object from the container. Try placing a favorite toy or child's bottle into a container so child will want to take it out and will feel rewarded by being able to get it.	*Record* + if the child: 1. Removes 1 object from container; and 2. Removes all objects from container. *Criterion:* Child removes all objects from container by reaching through the opening; 4 of 5 trials on 3 separate days.

Note: To avoid having the child simply dump the objects, you may need to begin with a heavy container or put objects in the container that are likely to stay if it is turned over (e.g., have a box with a hole just big enough for the hand but not big enough for objects that are apt to land crosswise of the opening when it is turned over).

AREA: **20-V. Object Manipulation: Putting in and taking out**
BEHAVIOR: 20-Vb. Puts 1 or 2 objects in container

Position of Child: Any position that allows free use of hands
Materials: Several containers and a variety of small, easy-to-grasp objects

Teaching procedures	Steps for learning/evaluation
Give the child a small object, and take 1 for yourself. Show child how you drop your object into the container. Ask child to drop his or her object into the container. If child does not, or cannot put his or her object into the container, help child by holding his or her wrist and guiding child's hand over the container. Ask child to put object in. If child still does not, tap the top of child's hand until child lets go of the object. If that does not work, press gently on the back of child's hand, bending it foward until child releases the object. Praise his or her release! For *visually impaired* children, promote tactile exploration of the container and dropping 1 item in and retrieving it before working with several items. Choose noisy items to place in the container and a container that makes a good noise when the item is dropped into it.	*Record* + if the child: 1. Puts 1 object in container; and 2. Puts 2 (or more) objects in container. *Criterion:* Child places 2 objects into a container when handed them and told to "put them in"; 3 of 3 trials in 3 different sessions.

Note: This activity can be made more instructive by talking about items and their characteristics as they are put in or taken out.

AREA: **20-V. Object Manipulation:**   **Putting in and taking out**
BEHAVIOR: 20-Vc. Puts many (6 +) objects into container (completes task)

Position of Child: Any position that allows free use of hands
Materials: A variety of small objects and a container (oatmeal box, cookie jar, kettle, etc.)

Teaching procedures	Steps for learning/evaluation
Give the child 6 or more small objects (cubes, clothespins, bells, etc.). Demonstrate putting the objects in a container and dumping them out. Ask child to put all of the toys into the container. If child puts 1 or 2 in, and then stops, encourage him or her to go on until all are inside. You may need to hand child 1 item at a time until all are inside, and give child all the items back again and then dump them out. Make "dumping out and putting in" a game. Vary the task with different sizes of objects and containers. Challenge the child's motor skill (e.g., if child easily puts clothespins in a big container, try a container with a smaller opening like a milk jug).	***Record*** + if the child: 1. Places 3 or more objects in container; and 2. Places 6 or more objects in container with reminders to complete the task; and 3. Places 6 or more objects in container without reminders to complete the task. ***Criterion:*** Child places 6 or more objects in a container without reminders to complete the task; 3 trials on 3 separate days.

AREA: **20-V. Object Manipulation:**   **Putting in and taking out**
BEHAVIOR: 20-Vd. Puts small objects through small hole in container

Position of Child: Any comfortable position (i.e., sitting or kneeling) that allows child to freely
      move arms and hands
Materials: Shoe box with a slot and poker chips; piggy bank and coins; bottle and clothespins, and
      so forth

Teaching procedures	Steps for learning/evaluation
Demonstrate putting a small object through a hole or slot into a container, such as poker chips or money into a piggy bank or clothespins into a bottle. Reward the child's close approximations if child cannot put object in independently. Help child to put object in by physically guiding him or her through the motions. Add extra visual, tactile, or auditory cues as necessary (e.g., small bells dropped into tall metal cylinder, poker chips covered with aluminum foil, etc.). You may need to gradually change object size from larger to smaller.	***Record*** + if the child: 1. Puts 1 small object through hole in container. ***Criterion:*** Child puts 1 small object through a small hole in container; 4 of 5 trials on 3 separate days.

Note: If child puts more than 1 object through the hole, move immediately to item 20-Ve.

AREA: **20-V. Object Manipulation:**   **Putting in and taking out**
BEHAVIOR: 20-Ve. Puts many (6 +) small objects through small hole (completes task)

Position of Child: Any comfortable position that allows free use of hands
Materials: Narrow jars, box with slot in top, pop bottle, and so on; small objects to drop in

Teaching procedures	Steps for learning/evaluation
Give the child several (6 +) small objects (e.g., bells, poker chips, blocks, etc.) to put into a container that has a small opening (e.g., small hole cut into plastic cover). Ask child to put all the objects into the container. If necessary, demonstrate how to put the item into the container. If child does not put all of the items in, hand child 1 item at a time until all are placed inside. Give all the items back to the child, and ask child to do it again. Reward the child's approximations, and physically guide child when necessary.	*Record* + if the child: 1. Puts 2 or 3 small objects through small hole into a container; 2. Puts 6 or more small objects through small hole into container (completes the task). *Criterion:* Child puts 6 or more small objects into a container; 4 of 5 trials on 3 separate days.

21.

Bilateral Hand Activity

THE ACTIVITIES IN THIS sequence were separated from the other fine motor activities because they all involve the use of two hands. They begin with activities in which both hands do essentially the same thing and progress to activities in which each hand is performing a different function to accomplish a single task (e.g., one hand holds a bead while the other pushes a string through). The activities also progress from rather unrefined movements to those requiring considerable coordination. It is extremely important for curriculum users to recognize that not all activities are appropriate for all children. For example, the child with athetoid cerebral palsy might actually be able, with a great deal of effort, to put beads on a string (item 21n), but such an activity would never be functional for him or her. The activity would teach the child more about frustration tolerance than it would be a useful fine motor skill, even though the latter is the item's intent. The more handicapped a child is, the more important it is to seek the advice of a physical and/or occupational therapist in choosing those activities which will be functional and enjoyable for him or her.

21. Bilateral Hand Activity

a. Bats at objects at chest level
b. Raises both hands when object is presented—hands partially open
c. Brings hands together at midline
d. Places both hands on toy at midline
e. Transfers object from hand to hand
f. Claps hands
g. Plays with toys in midline; one hand holds toy and the other manipulates
h. Pulls pop beads or balls apart at midline
i. Holds dowel in one hand and places ring over it
j. Puts pencil through hole in piece of cardboard
k. Removes loose wrappers
l. Unscrews small lids
m. Puts loose pop beads together
n. Strings 3 large beads

AREA: **21. Bilateral Hand Activity**
BEHAVIOR: 21a. Bats at objects at chest level

Position of Child: On back, head supported in midline if necessary (side-lying may be necessary for
    children unable to raise their arms)
Materials: Mobiles or objects attached to strings

Teaching procedures	Steps for learning/evaluation
Dangle brightly colored noisemaking objects at chest level, or arrange a crib mobile so that it is at chest level and close enough so that child can hit it if child waves his or her arms. Observe the arms, watching for signs of excitement (e.g., batting of the arms in the direction of the object[s]). Be sure to select a mobile or dangling object that moves or makes noise when only touched lightly, so that the baby's efforts to hit it are rewarded. You can encourage movement of the *physically handicapped* child by jiggling the object yourself whenever slight movement is made in the direction of the object. It may be necessary to physically assist hand-batting in *visually impaired* children in order for them to know an object is present.	*Record* + if the child: 1. Increases movement of arms upon presentation of object at chest level; and 2. Bats at objects at chest level (hands may be fisted). *Criterion:* Child bats at objects at chest level; observed twice on 3 separate days.

AREA: **21. Bilateral Hand Activity**
BEHAVIOR: 21b. Raises both hands when object is presented—hands partially open

Position of Child: Lying down on back or in infant seat (side-lying may be necessary for some
    children)
Materials: Any attractive toys or objects that the child favors

Teaching procedures	Steps for learning/evaluation
Hold or dangle an object at chest level. Observe the child's reactions. If child does not reach up with his or her hands, try lowering the toy until it briefly touches one hand and then raise it slightly, returning to midline. If the child is too *physically impaired* to raise hands while on his or her back, place child on his or her side and try to encourage reaching movements with both hands. Encourage reaching and batting movements even if hands remain fisted.	*Record* + if the child: 1. Raises or reaches with both hands spontaneously; hands partially open. *Criterion:* Child raises or reaches with both hands spontaneously toward an object, hands partially open; 3 of 5 trials, 3 separate days.

Note: Consult a physical therapist if the child's thumbs remain entrapped in his or her hands beyond a 2-month level.

AREA: **21. Bilateral Hand Activity**
BEHAVIOR: 21c. Brings hands together at midline

Position of Child: Any position that allows free arm movement (side-lying may be best for many
    neurologically impaired children)
Materials: Stick-on bows, Silly Putty, pop beads

Teaching procedures	Steps for learning/evaluation
If this behavior is not observed in general free play, put something colorful and easy to remove on one of the child's hands or wrists (e.g., a stick-on bow, a yarn bracelet). Observe to see if child brings the other hand to it to touch it. If child does not, physically guide the two hands to the midline (by gently pushing the shoulders and upper arms). For the *visually impaired* child, hold noisy, textured toys at the midline, physically guiding child's hands to a position to find the toy. Also, when holding the child on your lap, encourage child to find his or her own hands by gently guiding child's hands together.	***Record*** + if the child: 1. Brings hands together at midline. ***Criterion:*** Child brings hands together at midline 3 times on 3 separate days.

AREA: **21. Bilateral Hand Activity**
BEHAVIOR: 21d. Places both hands on toy at midline

Position of Child: Any position that allows free arm movement
Materials: Any attractive toys; rattles and other things that make noise may be especially
    attractive

Teaching procedures	Steps for learning/evaluation
Hold a toy at midline within reach of the child. Try to get child to look at it. If child does not reach for it, place his or her hands on it. Repeat this activity with various toys at different times. Be sure to use a noisemaking toy if you are working with a *visually handicapped* child.	***Record*** + if the child: 1. Spontaneously places both hands on toy at midline. ***Criterion:*** Child spontaneously places both hands on toy at midline; observed 3 times in 1 hour on 3 separate days.

AREA: **21. Bilateral Hand Activity**
BEHAVIOR: 21e. Transfers objects from hand to hand

Position of Child: Any position that permits free use of hands
Materials: Masking tape; plastic ring; jar or key ring (at least 3 inches in diameter); and other
easy-to-grasp toys

Teaching procedures	Steps for learning/evaluation
Make "circles" of tape with sticky side out. Place a "circle" on one of the child's hands. Encourage child to pull it off with his or her other hand. Also give child a metal jar ring (as used on canning jars) to hold. As child plays with it, see if he or she will take hold of both sides and let go with one hand and then the other, thus transferring. Look for other easy-to-grasp objects that are likely to promote transfer (e.g., large yarn pom-poms, lightweight toys with several "handles"). With a *visually impaired* child, it may be necessary to provide much more physical assistance (i.e., guiding child's hands to the object to facilitate transfer). Look for or make toys with interesting textures (e.g., cover a small embroidery hoop with pieces of fabric or yarn, making some smooth and some rough places).	*Record* + if the child: 1. Spontaneously transfers any objects from one hand to the other. (Record which objects are transferred.) *Criterion:* Child transfers 3 different objects from one hand to another in 1 day; 3 separate days.

AREA: **21. Bilateral Hand Activity**
BEHAVIOR: 21f. Claps hands

Position of Child: Any position to facilitate use of both hands
Materials: None

Teaching procedures	Steps for learning/evaluation
Frequently clap your hands to show approval of the child's accomplishments. Also play lots of clapping games (e.g., "pat-a-cake"). Sing clapping songs in which the child can observe you clapping and in which you can physically guide child's hands to clap. Gradually reduce the amount of physical assistance you provide.	*Record* + if the child: 1. Claps hands after caregiver has helped him or her start the movement; and 2. Claps hands without assistance (may be in imitation or spontaneously). *Criterion:* Child claps hands without assistance; 2 times a session in 3 separate sessions.

AREA: **21. Bilateral Hand Activity**
BEHAVIOR: 21g. Plays with toys in midline; one hand holds toy and the other manipulates

Position of Child: Any position to facilitate use of both hands
Materials: Toys with moving parts

Teaching procedures	Steps for learning/evaluation
Select toys carefully to fit the sensory and motor capabilities of the child. Observe as toys are held at midline. Watch for holding with one hand and patting, feeling, pulling, and so forth, with the other. The point is that both hands are being used, but each is doing something different. You may stimulate the child's play by demonstrating what can be done with the toy, but it is more likely that the characteristics of the toys themselves will stimulate the activity.	*Record* + if the child: 1. Plays with toy in midline, one hand holding toy, and the other manipulating. *Criterion:* Child plays with toys in midline, one hand holding toy and the other manipulating. Observed with 2 different toys on 3 separate days.

AREA: **21. Bilateral Hand Activity**
BEHAVIOR: 21h. Pulls pop beads or balls apart at midline

Position of Child: Any position to facilitate use of 2 hands
Materials: "Pop beads," small balls with Velcro strips on them

Teaching procedures	Steps for learning/evaluation
Show the child a string of pop beads. Pull them apart and put them back together. Give them to the child. Physically assist child, if necessary, to pull them apart. (Different brands of pop beads require differing degrees of strength to pull apart. Select carefully for characteristics of the child. Gradually increase difficulty as child gets stronger.) Balls with Velcro strips on them may also be attached to each other and pulled apart by the child. This requires less strength than the pop beads.	*Record* + if the child: 1. Pulls balls or beads apart at midline. *Criterion:* Child pulls pop beads or balls apart; 3 in one session on 3 separate days.

AREA: **21. Bilateral Hand Activity**
BEHAVIOR: 21i. Holds dowel in one hand and places ring over it

Position of Child: Any position to facilitate use of both hands
Materials: Several ½-inch dowels, 5–10 inches long; wooden or plastic rings or "donuts" of different sizes

Teaching procedures	Steps for learning/evaluation
Sit down with the child and a container of dowels and rings of different sizes. Let child explore the materials on his or her own for several minutes, and comment on what he or she does. If child makes no attempt to put a ring on a dowel, show him or her how to do it. If child lacks the coordination to get the dowel through a hole only slightly larger than the diameter of the dowel, select rings with larger holes. Physically assist child to perform the task if necessary. As child becomes more adept, reduce your assistance and introduce rings with smaller holes again.	*Record* + if the child: 1. Places ring with a larger hole (1–3 inches larger than diameter of the dowel) over a dowel; holds dowel in one hand and uses other to place the ring; and 2. Places close-fitting ring over a dowel; holds dowel in one hand and uses other to place the ring. *Criterion:* Child places a close-fitting ring over a dowel while holding dowel in one hand and using other to place the ring; 3 times in 1 session on 3 separate days.

AREA: **21. Bilateral Hand Activity**
BEHAVIOR: 21j. Puts pencil through hole in piece of cardboard

Position of Child: Any position to facilitate use of both hands
Materials: Pencils, Tinker Toys, or dowels the size of a pencil; 4 × 4-inch squares of cardboard or Masonite with various size holes in them

Teaching procedures	Steps for learning/evaluation
Give the materials to the child and let him or her explore them. Have some of the holes large enough so that you could put child's finger through them, others small enough so that there is just room for the pencil. Play with child and show him or her how you can stick your finger through the hole, put the pencil through, and so forth. If child makes no effort to do the task spontaneously or in imitation, physically assist child to do it. Help the *visually impaired* child feel the holes in the board and put his or her finger through. Assist child in pushing the pencil slowly back and forth over the board until it goes into one of the holes.	*Record* + if the child: 1. Puts finger through hole in cardboard; and 2. Puts pencil or ⅜-inch dowel through hole in cardboard. *Criterion:* The child puts pencil or ⅜-inch dowel through a small hole in a piece of cardboard; 3 times per session on 3 separate days.

AREA: **21. Bilateral Hand Activity**
BEHAVIOR: 21k. Removes loose wrappers

Position of Child: Any position to facilitate use of both hands
Materials: Small toys, gum, cereal, crackers, all in loose paper wrappers

Teaching procedures	Steps for learning/evaluation
Give the child a box of 6–10 objects wrapped loosely in paper (i.e., wrapped around with ends twisted). If child does not unwrap an item spontaneously, you unwrap one and say (and sign) "Look what I found. Let's see what you can find." Observe child's efforts to unwrap. You may have to assist by loosening the wrappings for him or her, adjusting the task to the child's motor coordination. The point of the item is to use two hands. The wrapper should not be so loose that the item can be shaken out with only one hand; however, it should be loose enough to allow successful unwrapping. Physically assist the *visually impaired* child to unwrap favorite toys or edibles.	***Record*** + if the child: 1. Removes a loose wrapper using both hands. ***Criterion:*** Child removes loose wrappers from 4 objects using both hands on 3 separate days.

AREA: **21. Bilateral Hand Activity**
BEHAVIOR: 21l. Unscrews small lids

Position of Child: Any position to facilitate use of both hands
Materials: Various small jars with "easy-to-screw" lids, small toys, or edibles. (Select jars to fit the size of the child's hands. Baby food jars are appropriate for many children, but may be too large in diameter for very small hands.)

Teaching procedures	Steps for learning/evaluation
Present the child with several jars, each of which has an interesting item inside. Let child explore the lids. If child makes no attempt to unscrew the lids, show him or her how it can be done. Remove the object from the jar, return it, and replace the lid very loosely (so that one-quarter to one-half turn will get it off). Give jar to child to try. Physical assistance may be used but will probably be less effective than making the task easier and letting the child master the unscrewing on his or her own. For the *visually impaired* child, present an empty jar to explore; talk about it and then place a noisy toy or food inside and put the lid on. Talk about what you are doing. Give the jar to the child. Physically assist child to remove the lid and get the contents. Repeat. Frequently use the terms "unscrew," or "screw," "turn," and so forth.	***Record*** + if the child: 1. Unscrews a lid partially loosened for her (one-quarter to one-half turn); and 2. Unscrews a lid independently (1–2 full turns). ***Criterion:*** Child unscrews lids from small jars; 3 lids per session on 3 separate days.

AREA: **21. Bilateral Hand Activity**
BEHAVIOR: 21m. Puts loose pop beads together

Position of Child: Any position to facilitate use of both hands
Materials: Loose-fitting pop beads; adjust size and looseness to motor capabilities of the child

Teaching procedures	Steps for learning/evaluation
Give the child a box of pop beads that are not connected to one another. Allow child to explore them. If child makes no effort to put them together, show child how to do it; begin making your "necklace" and encourage child to make one. Physically assist child if necessary. Praise efforts as well as success. This activity may be inappropriate for a *visually impaired* child, unless the pop beads are large and constructed so that it is easy to feel the hole as well as the "knob" that is to be inserted in it.	***Record*** + if the child: 1. Puts 2 loose pop beads together; and 2. Puts 3 loose pop beads together. ***Criterion:*** Child puts loose pop beads together; 4 beads connected on 3 separate days.

AREA: **21. Bilateral Hand Activity**
BEHAVIOR: 21n. Strings 3 large beads

Position of Child: Any position to facilitate use of both hands
Materials: Large kindergarten beads of various shapes and colors; string—slightly longer than the length of the beads—knotted at one end and with a stiff tip at the other end

Teaching procedures	Steps for learning/evaluation
Present the child with a container of beads and a string. With a second string show child how to make a necklace, stringing slowly so child can observe the process of putting the tip of the string through the bead and then pulling it from the other side. Carefully observe child's efforts to imitate what you have done. Offer physical assistance or verbal instruction as necessary to help child accomplish the task.	***Record*** + if the child: 1. Pushes tip of the string through the bead, but needs help getting the bead further back on the string; and 2. Pushes tip of the string through the bead *and* independently puts bead further back on the string in preparation for another bead. ***Criterion:*** Child independently strings 3 large beads; 3 separate days.

22.

Gross Motor Activities: Prone (On Stomach)

IN THE PROCESS OF physical development, the skills children develop as they lie on their stomachs and lift or extend their bodies against gravity are critical for adequate motor performance in other positions. Development proceeds from the head toward the legs (in the cephalo-caudal direction) and from the center of the trunk toward the fingers and toes. As children lie on their stomachs and work against gravity, they first learn to raise their heads. Following that, the arms and later the legs are used to bear weight and move forward. The rib cage is expanded and stabilized to allow for deeper respiration. As you work through the sequence, strive for symmetry in the back muscles and equal ability in the right and left limbs. If the child does not develop good patterns in the prone position he or she will not have the strength or automatic postural responses to be competent in sitting, standing, and walking.

A good way of working on deficient prone skills is to position the child on his or her stomach while working on other curriculum items and during play periods. Parents should be encouraged to carry this through at home. It is particularly important to work and play with blind infants in the prone position, although they often object to this position (working against gravity is difficult and the blind child lacks the motivation normally provided by visual stimuli). Many other children will also object to being placed on their stomachs because it is difficult for them to lift their heads and look around. Suggestions for dealing with this are included in the appropriate items of the curriculum.

It is important to recognize the difference between good motor patterns in the prone position and incomplete or abnormal ones. Compare the way a child looks with normal children you know and with the pictures provided in the motor development chart (Figure 3, Chapter 5). Please note that there is a picture in the motor development chart to go with each item below. Be sure to consult a physical therapist if you have questions.

22.   Gross Motor Activities: Prone (On Stomach)

Note: Each of the following items corresponds to a picture in the motor development chart (Figure 3) on pages 34 and 35.

a.   Lifts head, freeing nose; arms and legs flexed

b.   Lifts head to 45° angle, with arms and legs semiflexed

c.   Extends arms, legs, head, and trunk in prone position

d.   Bears weight on elbows in prone position

e.   Rolls from stomach to back

f.   Reaches while supported on one elbow

g.   Supports self on hands with arms extended and head at 90°

h.   Pivots in prone position

i.   Pulls forward on stomach

j.   Pulls self to hands and knees

k.   Rocks forward and backward in all-fours position

l.   Plays with toys in an asymmetrical half-sitting, half–side-lying position

m.   Moves forward (creeps) on hands and knees

n.   Raises one hand high while on hands and knees

o.   Crawls up stairs

p.   Crawls down stairs, backward

AREA: **22. Gross Motor Activities: Prone**
BEHAVIOR: 22a. Lifts head, freeing nose; arms and legs flexed

Position of Child: Lying on stomach (prone) on a supporting surface
Materials: Brightly colored or shiny toys; noisemaking toys

Teaching procedures	Steps for learning/evaluation
Place the child on his or her stomach and encourage head-lifting by placing toys on the floor in front of child. Shake or otherwise activate the toy when the child's head comes up, so as to provide motivation and reinforcement. The muscles at the base of the skull may be stimulated manually, using a *firm,* not light, stroke. The activity may be preceded by holding or swinging the child upside-down for 5–10 seconds. This helps facilitate all extensor muscle actions. Head-lifting can also be elicited by placing the child on your stomach and chest while you are lying on your back with head raised talking to the child. Raising the elevation of your shoulders (making the baby slightly more upright) will make it easier for the child to raise his or her head. As child becomes more competent, lie flatter so that the effect is the same as being on a flat surface.	***Record*** + if the child: 1. Lifts head briefly and turns it to the side; and 2. Lifts head and holds it up for 1–2 seconds; and 3. Lifts head with arms and legs flexed for 5 seconds. ***Criterion:*** Child lifts head and holds it up with arms and legs flexed; 5–7 seconds, 3 times per session in 3 consecutive sessions.

Note: For *spastic* children, relaxation techniques should be used prior to and during the activity. If the child consistently maintains an open mouth or tightened arms or legs, consult a therapist.

AREA: **22. Gross Motor Activities: Prone**
BEHAVIOR: 22b. Lifts head to 45° angle, with arms and legs semiflexed

Position of Child: Lying on stomach on a supporting surface
Materials: Dangling toys or mirrors, or teacher's face

Teaching procedures	Steps for learning/evaluation
When the child is able to lift his or her head independently, hold toys up and raise them so that child must lift his or her head to a 45° angle from the supporting surface to maintain a view of them. You may give some assistance initially, in elbow placement.	***Record*** + if the child: 1. Lifts head to 45° angle for 5–10 seconds; and 2. Lifts head to 45° angle with arms and legs semiflexed for 10–20 seconds (see drawing *b* in prone motor sequence, Figure 3, Chapter 5).

(continued)

Teaching procedures	Steps for learning/evaluation
The muscles of the neck and back may be stimulated manually using *firm*, not light, strokes.	*Criterion:* Child lifts head to 45° angle; 20–30 seconds; 5 out of 8 trials in 3 consecutive sessions.

Note: For a *spastic* child, relax the child as much as possible before beginning this item. Turn the knees out slightly to keep the legs from thrusting. If shoulder position looks abnormal, loosen the arms by passively moving the shoulder blades. If the arms are extremely tight, place a bolster or rolled towel under the shoulders to bring the upper arms forward. If these measures are unsuccessful, consult your therapist. *Hypotonic* children may hold their legs in "frog" position. This should be corrected by holding their legs together.

AREA: **22. Gross Motor Activities: Prone**
BEHAVIOR: 22c. Extends arms, legs, head, and trunk in prone position

Position of Child: Lying on stomach
Materials: Favorite toys, therapy ball, towel roll

Teaching procedures	Steps for learning/evaluation
With the child in a prone position on the floor, over a therapy ball, or on your lap, gently pull child's shoulders up, allowing time for child to lift his or her head and trunk. Release your hold when you feel the child staying up independently, and resume it when you feel the child losing control. Provide visual interest and motivation with toys. Swinging the child gently in an upside-down position is often helpful to prepare for this activity. Practice items 22c and 22d together, alternating between them.	*Record* + if the child: 1. Lifts head, trunk, and arms briefly and slightly, elbows held higher than hands, and legs resting on the surface; and 2. Lifts head, trunk, and arms a few inches from the surface and holds for 3–5 seconds. Elbows level with hands; legs straight and lifted slightly off the surface (see drawing *c* in prone motor sequence, Figure 3, Chapter 5). *Criterion:* Child lifts head, trunk, arms, and legs of the surface and holds at least 5 seconds with hands held higher than elbows; at least 3 times in 1 session.

Note: This item is extremely important in terms of building postural stability. Prone extension should be incorporated into much of the handicapped child's daily routine. *Spastic* children can easily get "stuck" in step 1 and be held back from further gains. They should be positioned with a towel roll under the arms to keep their elbows forward. Do not practice item 22h unless the child has mastered at least step 2. Your therapist will give you guidance.

AREA: **22. Gross Motor Activities: Prone**
BEHAVIOR: 22d. Bears weight on elbows in prone position

Position of Child: Lying on stomach
Materials: Favorite toys, mirror, music

Teaching procedures	Steps for learning/evaluation
Elicit head-lifting and head-turning with toys, mirror, musical radio, or your face. Initially, you may position the child's shoulders, giving some downward pressure on them. Practice items 22c and 22d together, alternating between them.	*Record* + if the child: 1. Lifts head and upper trunk, bearing weight on forearms that are semiflexed under the chest. Head is at 90°; and 2. Lifts head and upper trunk, bearing weight on forearms, with elbows directly under the shoulders. When turning the head, one arm may become more flexed. The fingers may be curled. *Criterion:* Child lifts the head and upper trunk, bearing weight on forearms with hands open. The head is at 90°, the elbows positioned under the shoulders. Arm position remains the same during head-turning. Child can stay in this position at least 30 seconds, 3 times per session in 3 consecutive sessions.

Note: This item is particularly important for children with *spastic* and *athetoid* patterns, as it builds postural stability, helps diminish the effects of the asymmetric tonic neck reflex, and helps the hands tolerate tactile stimuli. With *spastic* children, precede work with relaxation and use a towel roll under the shoulders if necessary to prevent pulling back of the arms. With all children, make sure the head is not tipped back excessively ("stacking"). If you see this, try attracting the child's gaze downward. Work on item 24a should also be stressed a this time.

AREA: **22. Gross Motor Activities: Prone**
BEHAVIOR: 22e. Rolls from stomach to back

Position of Child: Lying on stomach on a supporting surface
Materials: Toys that the child enjoys; a blanket

Teaching procedures	Steps for learning/evaluation
Entice the child to roll by dangling a toy in front of child's face, then move it to the side and behind child's line of sight. If child does not roll, place child on a blanket and tilt him or her slightly, making it easier for child to roll; or place child on a slight incline to make it easier to roll. You can also initiate rolling by starting child in side-lying position and gently guiding his or her	*Record* + if the child: 1. Turns head and partially raises one side of body; and 2. Turns from stomach to back by extending back without trunk rotation; and 3. Turns from stomach to back, leading with the shoulder and rotating the trunk (shoulder goes first, then hip, and finally foot).

(continued)

Teaching procedures	Steps for learning/evaluation
shoulder until child is on his or her back. Once child rolls readily from side to back, begin in the prone position again. Always guide movements from the shoulders and/or hips, allowing child to control his or her head.	*Criterion:* Child rolls from stomach to back, leading with a shoulder or hip and showing trunk rotation; 5 times per session in 3 consecutive sessions.

Note: For a *spastic* child, it is important to guard against mass thrusting movements in the rolling pattern. Make sure child is relaxed, and do the movements slowly, allowing time for child to respond.

AREA:　**22. Gross Motor Activities: Prone**
BEHAVIOR:　22f. Reaches while supported on one elbow

Position of Child:　Lying on stomach, supported on elbows
Materials:　Interesting toys that can be "batted" (e.g., suspended balloons, soft balls)

Teaching procedures	Steps for learning/evaluation
When the child is lying on his or her stomach, supported on elbows, suspend an interesting toy out in front at one side, encouraging child to reach for it. If necessary, assist child in maintaining balance while reaching, by placing your hand over child's buttocks. Withdraw this assistance as child becomes more stable.	*Record* + if the child: 1. Reaches straight out for a toy; weight is shifted to the opposite arm and leg, and the supporting arm collapses slightly; and 2. Reaches slightly above shoulder level for a toy; hips stay flat on floor, and the supporting arm does not collapse (see drawing *f* in the "On Tummy" sequence of the motor development chart, Figure 3, Chapter 5); and 3. Reaches high for a toy; supporting shoulder does not collapse, and the upper trunk is rotated against the lower trunk. *Criterion:* Child reaches high for a toy; supporting shoulder does not collapse, and the upper trunk is rotated against lower trunk; 3 times per session in 3 separate sessions.

Note: With *spastic* children, precede the activity with relaxation, and position their legs to avoid a thrusting pattern. With *hypotonic* children, keep their legs straight, not in a "frog" position.

AREA: **22. Gross Motor Activities: Prone**
BEHAVIOR: 22g. Supports self on hands with arms extended and head at 90°

Position of Child: Prone on supporting surface
Materials: Favorite toys, large ball, bolster

Teaching procedures	Steps for learning/evaluation
Present a favored toy in front of the child's face, then raise it, encouraging child to push up on his or her arms.	*Record* + if the child:
	1. Bears weight on hands when pushed forward over ball or bolster; and
If child cannot push up, place child over a ball or bolster and roll child forward, experimenting with different speeds, until child places his or her hands on the floor with weight on hands. When child regains strength, try getting child to push up from floor again.	2. Pushes up and stays 5–10 seconds; and
	3. Pushes up and stays 10–20 seconds; and
	4. Pushes up and stays 30 seconds or more.
	Criterion: Child, lying on stomach, pushes up to a fully extended arm position, supporting on hands, with the head upright, for 30 seconds; 3 times per session in 3 consecutive sessions.
It may be helpful to "gear the child up" for this activity by swinging, bouncing, and so forth. Upside-down positioning for 5–10 seconds is also helpful in building up extensor tone.	

Note: If child is *spastic* and shows a thrusting pattern in this position with shoulders turned in, arms crossed, or tightly clenched fists, *do not persist* in the activity since it will only reinforce undesirable patterns, and lead to W-sitting and bunny-hopping. Rather, use relaxation techniques on the arms and work on items 22c, 22d, and 22f.

AREA: **22. Gross Motor Activities: Prone**
BEHAVIOR: 22h. Pivots in prone position

Position of Child: Lying on stomach
Materials: Favorite toys; bottle

Teaching procedures	Steps for learning/evaluation
Attract the child with a bottle or favorite toy. Encourage child to pivot in a circle in order to get the toy. It is usually best not to have other toys in sight and to use a toy the child particularly likes.	*Record* + if the child:
	1. Pivots several inches, in both directions, pushing with 1 arm and reaching with the other; and
If the child has trouble making a full pivot, reward attempts of half-pivots, and continue working.	2. Pivots in a half-circle in both directions; and
	3. Pivots in a full circle in both directions.
	Criterion: Child pivots 360° in both directions; at least 3 times in 1 session in 3 consecutive sessions.

AREA: **22. Gross Motor Activities: Prone**
BEHAVIOR: 22i. Pulls forward on stomach

Position of Child: Prone on supporting surface (floor with rug or mat)
Materials: Toys the child enjoys

Teaching procedures	Steps for learning/evaluation
Place a toy that the child is interested in just out of child's reach. Get down on the floor facing the child and call child to you while "showing" the toy. Encourage parents to place toys just out of reach at home. Initially you can help the child by moving him or her passively through the activity. At first, use of a prone scooter board may help give the child a sense of movement, but continue to work for progress in pulling forward on the floor. This activity is important in developing abdominal strength.	***Record*** + if the child: 1. Pulls forward a few inches, using both arms together, without legs; and 2. Pulls slowly forward at least 2 feet using arms *and* legs; and 3. Pulls forward spontaneously, 5 feet or more, using arms and legs, with stomach close to floor. ***Criterion:*** Child pulls forward 5 feet or more, using arms and legs, with stomach close to floor; 3 times in 1 session on 3 separate days.

Note: With *spastic* children, the arm position must be watched carefully. If the child shows a strong tendency to keep the arms flexed and tucked under the body, using the pulling motion will only reinforce abnormal patterns. Go back and work on relaxation items, then look for any improvement in the pattern. Consult your therapist for help with mobility patterns.

AREA: **22. Gross Motor Activities: Prone**
BEHAVIOR: 22j. Pulls self to hands and knees

Position of Child: Prone, on a supporting surface
Materials: Favorite toys to elicit movement; low obstacles such as bolsters, pillows, large foam wedge

Teaching procedures	Steps for learning/evaluation
Encourage the child to belly-crawl over a variety of low obstacles. This will strengthen the muscle groups needed for assuming the hands-and-knees position. Belly-crawling up a slight incline will also be beneficial. Place your hand under the child's stomach while child is pushing up on his or her hands. Gently start moving child into the all-fours position and wait for child to start participating actively in assuming this position. If the child's back sags in all-fours, give gentle pressure at the shoulders and hips, alternating right and left sides.	***Record*** + if the child: 1. Uses arms to push backward while lying on stomach; and 2. Brings legs into a flexed position under the trunk while pushing backward; and 3. Pulls to hands and knees spontaneously and maintains the position for several seconds. ***Criterion:*** Child pulls to hands and knees spontaneously and maintains position for several seconds; at least 3 times in 1 session.

Note: This position may not be recommended for *spastic* and *athetoid* children. If the legs show too much flexing and pulling in, or if excessive neck extension is being used to reflexively maintain an all-fours position, the child should skip this posture entirely, as it will lead to W-sitting and bunny-hopping.

AREA: **22. Gross Motor Activities: Prone**
BEHAVIOR: 22k. Rocks forward and backward in all-fours position

Position of Child: All-fours position on a supporting surface
Materials: Tilt board and music

Teaching procedures	Steps for learning/evaluation
With the child on hands and knees, place your hand under the abdomen and initiate the forward-backward rocking movement. Do this until the child begins to rock alone. Play music while the child is on all fours, and encourage child to move to the music. You may also try placing child on a tilt board and rocking child back and forth slowly to give the sensation of this motion.	***Record*** + if the child: 1. Pulls to all fours and makes minimal forward-backward movements; and 2. Rocks back and forth with a stiff awkward movement; and 3. Rocks back and forth smoothly with head turning freely. ***Criterion:*** Child spontaneously rocks back and forth several times in succession while on all fours, with the head turning freely from side to side; at least 3 times in 1 session in 3 consecutive sessions.

AREA: **22. Gross Motor Activities: Prone**
BEHAVIOR: 22l. Plays with toys in an asymmetrical half-sitting, half–side-lying position

Position of Child: Start with child on stomach
Materials: Any toys or other object the child likes to hold and play with; pillows

Teaching procedures	Steps for learning/evaluation
Place toys on the floor next to the child at the level of the lower rib cage. Physically guide child, if necessary, onto his or her side and into the half-sitting position as shown in drawing *l* in the "On Tummy" sequence of the motor development chart (Figure 3, Chapter 5). Gradually release your hold as the child is able to maintain the position. Placing pillows behind the child may also help to stabilize the position.	***Record*** + if the child: 1. Holds a half-sitting, half–side-lying position for several seconds after being placed; and 2. Initiates movement into the position; and 3. Moves into the position and holds it several seconds. ***Criterion:*** Child assumes a half-sitting, half–side-lying position independently and uses it for play; at least 1 time a session for 30 seconds in 3 consecutive sessions.

Note: This is an excellent play position for children not yet safe in sitting. It builds head, trunk, and shoulder control and helps rotational patterns.

AREA: **22. Gross Motor Activities: Prone**
BEHAVIOR: 22m. Moves forward (creeps) on hands and knees

Position of Child: On hands and knees
Materials: A favorite toy

Teaching procedures	Steps for learning/evaluation
While the child is on all fours, hold up a favorite toy slightly above eye level and entice the child to crawl forward to reach it. Crawling (on stomach) up a few stairs or over low obstacles may be a beneficial preparatory activity. Children may learn to do this more easily in very shallow water (e.g., in an infant pool or bathtub). Children may creep more readily on grass or carpet than on a smooth floor. For a *hypotonic* child, you may see sagging of the belly in the all-fours position. You can help counteract this by giving gentle, firm pressure at the rib cage and hips simultaneously, first on one side, then on the other. Children with Down syndrome should be watched for this.	*Record* + if the child: 1. Assumes all-fours position and moves forward a few inches before returning to stomach; and 2. Moves forward slightly by advancing first an arm, then the opposite leg; and 3. Moves forward several feet by advancing an opposite arm and leg simultaneously. *Criterion:* Child creeps briskly for long distances, using this as a form of locomotion.

Note: With *spastic* or *spastic/athetoid* children, crawling may not be advised. Look at the position of the legs. If you see an abnormal amount of bending and pulling in, do not have the child crawl. Ask your therapist for advice.

AREA: **22. Gross Motor Activities: Prone**
BEHAVIOR: 22n. Raises one hand high while on hands and knees

Position of Child: On hands and knees
Materials: Favorite toys

Teaching procedures	Steps for learning/evaluation
With the child supporting on both hands in the all-fours position, dangle a toy to one side and encourage child to reach up and get it. Initially, you may assist the child physically in shifting weight to one arm by holding at the hips or trunk.	*Record* + if the child: 1. Reaches for toy below shoulder level with weight shifted to opposite arm and leg, and a bent supporting arm; and 2. Reaches for toy at shoulder height with weight equal on both legs, and supporting arm remains straight and firm; and 3. Reaches high for toy; supporting arm does not collapse, and the upper trunk is rotated against the hips (see drawing *n* in the "On Tummy" sequence of the motor development chart, Figure 3, Chapter 5).

(continued)

Teaching procedures	Steps for learning/evaluation
	Criterion: Child reaches high for a toy with strong supporting arm and upper trunk rotated; 3 times per session in 3 consecutive sessions.

AREA: **22. Gross Motor Activities: Prone**
BEHAVIOR: 22o. Crawls up stairs

Position of the Child: On hands and knees
Materials: Set of 6–10 stairs, approximately 6 inches high, 3 feet long, and 6–8 inches deep, and toys

Teaching procedures	Steps for learning/evaluation
Place a favorite toy on the steps, initially just 1 or 2 steps above the child. Assist by physically placing the child's arms and legs in the proper position and helping child pull up. Gradually withdraw assistance.	***Record*** + if the child: 1. Places hands on the bottom step but does not climb up; and 2. Crawls up the stairs with physical assistance; and 3. Crawls up stairs independently. ***Criterion:*** Child crawls up stairs without physical assistance; 1 time on 3 separate days.

AREA: **22. Gross Motor Activities: Prone**
BEHAVIOR: 22p. Crawls down stairs, backward

Position of the Child: On stomach
Materials: Set of 6–10 stairs, approximately 6 inches high, 3 feet long and 6–8 inches deep

Teaching procedures	Steps for learning/evaluation
Place the child on his or her stomach and physically assist arm and leg movements as child descends the stairs, gradually withdrawing assistance. Stay close and praise efforts.	***Record*** + if the child: 1. Attempts placement of arms/legs on a lower step but withdraws; and 2. Crawls down the stairs with physical assistance; and 3. Crawls down stairs backward. ***Criterion:*** Child crawls down the stairs without physical assistance; 1 time on 3 separate days.

Note: Some children may find it less threatening to descend stairs by sitting facing forward and lowering themselves to the next stair.

23.

Gross Motor Activities: Supine (On Back)

T HE ITEMS IN THE SUPINE sequence develop stabilizing functions in the front of the neck, trunk, shoulders, and hips. This stability allows the child to lift his or her arms and legs, bringing them into the visual field and using them for play. Items *a* through *e* develop the basic capabilities necessary for self-feeding, and should be integrated into feeding programs.

For children with abnormal muscle tone, however, a completely supine position is frequently inappropriate, either for exercise or for general positioning. Hypotonic children cannot act against gravity; thus, they lie on their backs with their arms and legs passively on the floor. They naturally prefer this position over being on their stomachs, as it allows them to observe their environment more readily. However, it is the least preferred position for promoting muscle development. Children with spasticity will often show increased muscle tone when lying on their backs, thus inhibiting the development of more functional patterns.

In order to establish the functions represented in this sequence, the use of side-lying and semi-reclining positions are frequently more appropriate for children with abnormal tone. Some children will progress to performing items while on their backs; others will never achieve this. A good rule of thumb is to always position the child in the manner in which he or she can function most effectively while still providing some neuromuscular challenge. A physical or occupational therapist can provide valuable guidance regarding the best positioning of children with motor development problems.

23. Gross Motor Activities: Supine (On Back)

Note: Each of the following items corresponds to a picture in the motor development chart (Figure 3) on pages 34 and 35.

a. Turns head from side to side in response to visual and/or auditory stimuli while in supine position
b. Bends and straightens arms and legs
c. Brings hand to mouth

d. Maintains head in midline position while on back
e. Reaches out with arm
f. Feet in air for play
g. Rolls from back to stomach

AREA: **23. Gross Motor Activities: Supine**
BEHAVIOR: 23a. Turns head from side to side in response to visual and/or auditory stimuli while in supine position

Position of Child: Lying on back (supine)
Materials: Any visual and/or auditory stimuli that holds the infant's attention

Teaching procedures	Steps for learning/evaluation
Position the child comfortably and engage child's attention with his or her head in the midline position. Move your face to one side so that the child will have to turn his or her head to continue seeing you. *And/or* With the child's head in midline, talk to child from his or her right or left side, encouraging child to turn to your voice. It may help to touch the child's cheek on the side that you wish the child to turn toward. Be sure to do this on both sides and vary the stimuli you use in trying to get the child to turn his or her head. (This item is similar to 2c and 5a. The aim here, however, is not getting the child to respond to particular sensory stimuli.)	*Record* + if the child: 1. Looks in the direction of the stimulus; and 2. Looks in the direction of the stimulus and partially turns toward it. *Criterion:* Child turns head completely from side to side in response to visual and/or auditory stimuli while in supine position; at least 5 times in a session.

Note: Children with high muscle tone often have difficulty performing voluntary movements while lying on their backs. A supported sitting position may be more effective. This is especially true if head-turning tends to evoke a neck reflex motion that the infant cannot break out of, or if the infant tends to stiffen or arch his or her back in the supine position. If these patterns are present, keep the child relaxed and hold child's arms across his or her chest.

AREA: **23. Gross Motor Activities: Supine**
BEHAVIOR: 23b. Bends and straightens arms and legs

Position of Child: Lying on back
Materials: Bells on ribbons or elastic that fits over wrists/ankles

Teaching procedures	Steps for learning/evaluation
Put bells on the child's wrists and/or ankles so that when child kicks or moves his or her arms he or she will hear a sound. Passively move the child's arms and legs in an alternating movement. Wait for the child to start doing it independently. Stroking the child's chest and stomach may help elicit the movements.	*Record* + if the child: 1. Moves arms/legs after they have been moved passively by caregiver; and 2. Bends and straightens arms/legs spontaneously. *Criterion:* Child bends arms/legs and straightens them spontaneously; at least 5 times per session in 3 separate sessions.

Note: Children with increased muscle tone tend to become stiffer when lying on their backs. If you see this happening, use relaxation techniques before working on this item. You may want to initiate the movements in a side-lying position. In any event, make sure that you are not eliciting stiff, thrusting movements.

AREA: 23. Gross Motor Activities: Supine
BEHAVIOR: 23c. Brings hands to mouth

Position of Child: Lying on back
Materials: Peanut butter, honey, pudding; bracelets or mittens; feeding bottle

Teaching procedures	Steps for learning/evaluation
Put a small amount of honey, peanut butter, pudding, or other age-appropriate food on the child's thumb and hold it close to his or her mouth. Show child what you are doing and let child smell the food. Encourage child to lick the food off his or her thumb. Place colorful bracelets or mittens on the child's hands. Place the child's hand on the bottle during feeding times. From time to time withdraw the bottle and wait for child to pull it back. A few light finger strokes on the child's mouth may help elicit the movements.	*Record* + if the child: 1. Keeps hand close to face after it is placed there; and 2. Moves hand a few inches toward the face; and 3. Brings either hand to his or her mouth. *Criterion:* Child spontaneously brings hands to mouth; at least 3 times per session in 3 separate sessions.

Note: It may be easier for some children, particularly for *spastic* children, to begin this activity in a side-lying position. If a child bites down strongly on objects placed in the mouth, avoid placing child's fingers inside his or her mouth. Consult a therapist regarding how to deal with this problem.

AREA: 23. Gross Motor Activities: Supine
BEHAVIOR: 23d. Maintains head in midline position while on back

Position of Child: Lying on back, head in midline
Materials: Favorite toys or legs a pillow

Teaching procedures	Steps for learning/evaluation
Engage the child's visual attention with his or her head in the midline position or legs maintain it there. If the child is having difficulty, place your hor legss on his or her cheeks, hold child's head in position, or legs continue attempts to engage child visually. Hold a favorite toy above the child's face to engage him or her visually. You want the child to hold his or her head still, so do not move the toy very much. It may be easier for some children to begin this exercise by having a soft pillow under the head.	*Record* + if the child: 1. Maintains head in midline while lying on back for a minimum of 5 seconds, 10 seconds, or legs 20 seconds. *Criterion:* Child maintains head in a midline position while lying on back for 30 seconds; 3 times per session, 3 separate sessions.

(continued)

Teaching procedures	Steps for learning/evaluation
For the *visually impaired* child: Talk to the child, guiding his or her head back to midline when it turns. This skill is often more difficult for a visually impaired child to learn than for a sighted child. A longer period of holding the head in midline may be necessary.	

Note: For many children with *spasticity,* the back-lying position is not optimal. Observe the child. If you see neck arching or tightening of the arms and/or legs, which do not respond to relaxation techniques, the child should be taken out of the back-lying position. If child consistently responds in this manner, he or she should be kept out of back-lying positions as much as possible.

AREA:	**23. Gross Motor Activities: Supine**
BEHAVIOR:	23e. Reaches out with arm

Position of Child:	Lying on back (supine) on a supporting surface
Materials:	Objects that make noise (e.g., bells, rattles); brightly colored objects

Teaching procedures	Steps for learning/evaluation
Hold a noisy object (rattle, bell) in front of and above baby's face where he or she can see it. Shake it so that it makes noise. If the child does not reach out, bring the object closer; briefly touch it to the baby's hand.

A mobile can be suspended above the child. Choose one that will move if the child touches it. Also, be sure to check the view of the mobile from the child's perspective. Many of the commercial ones look interesting only from above, not from where the baby sees it. Make sure the youngster can reach the mobile to activate it.

For the *visually impaired* child, be sure to continue the noise for a longer period and guide the child's hand to the toy while it is making noise. Look for or make toys to hand over the crib that will make a noise if the baby waves his or her arms and touches them. Begin with positioning toys very close to the baby's chest and gradually move higher as he or she learns to reach. | ***Record*** + if the child:
1. Moves arm purposefully in an attempt to "reach" object presented; and
2. Reaches with poor direction for an object held above his or her face.

Criterion: Child reaches up in the right direction for an object held above his or her face; at least 5 times per session in 3 separate sessions. |

Note: Both *spastic* and *hypotonic* children frequently have more difficulty reaching out when they are on their backs. Thus, side-lying or supported sitting may be better. Precede this activity with a period of relaxation to increase such children's control and ability to reach if necessary.

AREA: **23. Gross Motor Activities: Supine**
BEHAVIOR: 23f. Feet in air for play

Position of Child: Lying on back (supine) on a supporting surface
Materials: Brightly colored booties, bells, or bracelets

Teaching procedures	Steps for learning/evaluation
Put brightly colored booties, bells, or bracelets on the child's feet and make sure he or she sees them. Passively bring child's feet up and place his or her hands on them. Release your hold when you feel the child holding. Lightly stroking the abdomen may help the child bring his or her legs up. Holding your hand on the abdomen or lifting the hips will help the child maintain the position. (This item is similar to 20e, but the goal here is for the child to raise arms and legs and touch his or her feet, not visual attention to playing with the feet.)	***Record*** + if the child: 1. Initiates flexion movement of legs; and 2. Raises legs several inches off the floor and reaches to his or her knees with the hips remaining on the bed or floor; and 3. Raises legs off the floor and reaches feet with his or her hands; hips lifted off the floor. ***Criterion:*** Child raises legs off the floor and reaches feet with his or her hands, hips off the floor; 3 times a day on 3 separate days.

Note: It may be easier to initiate this movement in side-lying or semi-reclining positions. This item is important for trunk stability. If the child is not making progress with it, consult your therapist for alternative methods of strengthening abdominal muscles.

AREA: **23. Gross Motor Activities: Supine**
BEHAVIOR: 23g. Rolls from back to stomach

Position of Child: Lying on back on a supporting surface
Materials: Blanket or wedge; interesting toys

Teaching procedures	Steps for learning/evaluation
Elicit head-turning by placing something interesting on one side of the child or by having another person call to the child on that side. Bend the child's leg and pull it across his or her stomach; wait for child to complete the roll. If the child is having difficulty, try starting from a side-lying position, then move the starting position further back. If necessary, the child can be placed on a slight incline to make the rolling movement easier. The same effect can be obtained by placing child on a blanket and pulling up on the side of it.	***Record*** + if the child: 1. Rolls from back to side; and 2. Rolls from back to stomach on an incline or when helped with a blanket; and 3. Rolls from back to stomach without help, first turning his or her head, then bringing leg across, using rotation of the trunk. ***Criterion:*** Child rolls onto stomach by first turning his or her head, then bringing a leg across his or her body, using rotation of the trunk; 3 times a session on 3 separate days.

Note: Some children with increased muscle tone will roll over by using a complete arching movement of neck and back. This is very *abnormal* and must be prevented. If you see this pattern, use relaxation techniques prior to this activity. Should this not help, the child should be kept out of the back-lying position and a therapist consulted.

24.

Gross Motor Activities: Upright

EFFICIENT FUNCTIONING IN an upright position is the ultimate goal of motor programming and is the product of adequate development in the prone (on stomach) and supine (on back) positions. For overall program planning, it is important to distinguish between the use of upright positioning for motor development and the usefulness of this positioning to facilitate cognitive and social development, although these purposes frequently overlap.

Sitting, for example, is a motor skill involving muscle strength and balance. The motor goal activities in the prone position are used to strengthen the muscles, and activities in the sitting position are used to increase balance. Sitting is also, however, an important position for facilitating cognitive and social development, since it provides children with a wider view of the world around them, different experiences with object manipulation, and greater opportunity for social interaction. Sitting serves these functions, however, only if the head can move freely and the hands are free for play and are not used for support. Children who must use their hands for support should be placed in appropriate seating devices for social and cognitive activities. A therapist will advise you on the most appropriate devices and positions for different activities for each child.

Likewise, many children will never achieve independence standing or walking, but they need experiences in the fully upright position. A therapist can provide advice on the use of prone-standers or other types of equipment that allow children to be as upright as possible while providing sufficient support to make the position functional for school or play activities.

24. Gross Motor Activities: Upright

Note: Each of the following items corresponds to a picture in the motor development chart (Figure 3) on pages 34 and 35.

a. Head steady when held
b. Holds trunk steady when held

c. Moves to sitting position from stomach or all-fours position

d. Sits alone
e. Pulls self to standing position
f. Steps sideways holding a support
g. Stoops to pick up toy while holding on to a support

h. Removes hands from support and stands independently
i. Takes independent steps
j. Moves from hands and knees, to hands and feet, to standing

AREA: **24. Gross Motor Activities: Upright**
BEHAVIOR: 24a. Head steady when held

Position of Child: Held at the shoulder of an adult and supported at the upper trunk
Materials: Wall or door mirror

Teaching procedures	Steps for learning/evaluation
Hold child so that child can see himself or herself in a mirror over your shoulder. *And/or* Have someone else stand behind you and talk to the child so as to attract and hold his or her attention. *Important:* Instruct parents in carrying and positioning techniques that supply only the minimum necessary head support.	***Record*** + if the child: 1. Lifts head momentarily; and 2. Holds head steady for 5–10 seconds; and 3. Holds head steady for 10–15 seconds; and 4. Maintains head erect and steady as the adult sways gently back and forth for 15–20 seconds; and 5. Maintains head erect and steady and turns from side to side; 30 seconds. ***Criterion:*** Child holds head erect and steady while in an upright position and can turn head from side to side; 2 minutes or more for 3 consecutive sessions.

Note: Head control is basic to the development of further postural control and is important in the development of visual-motor coordination. There are some children for whom the acquisition of head control will be an extremely slow process. These children require careful attention to positioning so that their heads are supported for activities requiring visual attention.

AREA: **24. Gross Motor Activities: Upright**
BEHAVIOR: 24b. Holds trunk steady when held

Position of Child: Held by an adult supported at hips
Materials: None required

Teaching procedures	Steps for learning/evaluation
Hold the child at the hips. Provide trunk support with your hand as needed and withdraw it whenever you can. Sway back and forth while holding the child in this position, gradually increasing the demands upon the child's trunk musculature. It is frequently helpful to hold the child so that he or she is facing away from you and is forced to use the back muscles to stay up. Instruct the parents in carrying techniques that supply only the minimum necessary support. Once a child is fairly steady, carrying over the shoulders is fun and beneficial.	***Record*** + if the child: 1. Holds trunk steady without support momentarily; and 2. Holds trunk steady without support for 10 seconds; and 3. Holds trunk steady without support for 20 seconds; and 4. Holds trunk steady without support for 30 seconds; and 5. Holds trunk steady and occasionally rotates from side to side. ***Criterion:*** Child holds trunk erect and steady and can rotate from side to side; 3 minutes or more for 3 consecutive sessions.

Note: *Hemiplegic* children should be carried with the affected side *away from* your body. This will encourage reaching out with the affected arm.

AREA: **24. Gross Motor Activities: Upright**
BEHAVIOR: 24c. Moves to sitting position from stomach or all-fours position

Position of Child:　On stomach or all fours
Materials:　Any toy for which the infant shows a preference

Teaching procedures	Steps for learning/evaluation
With the child in a prone or all-fours position, offer an attractive toy. Move it in a direction so that child will turn to one side and push up with his or her arms into a side-sitting and then full-sitting position (see drawing *c* in upright motor sequence of motor development chart, Figure 3, Chapter 5). Initially, you may assist the child to push up by exerting gentle pressure on his or her hips. Reduce the amount of help you give as child learns to move himself or herself into the sitting position. Ask a therapist to demonstrate this technique to you.	*Record* + if the child: 1. Initiates an attempt to move from a stomach or all-fours position into sitting position; and 2. Moves about halfway into sitting position but returns to starting position or gets to sitting with help; and 3. Moves into upright sitting position without help. *Criterion:*　Child moves from a prone or all-fours position into upright sitting without assistance; 3 times in 1 session.

AREA: **24. Gross Motor Activities: Upright**
BEHAVIOR: 24d. Sits alone

Position of Child:　Sitting, with support or assistance
Materials:　Toys small enough to hold; large ball

Teaching procedures	Steps for learning/evaluation
With the child in a sitting position, provide toys that can be held or that have a mobile or other interesting visual display at eye level to attract the child's attention and encourage reaching. If necessary, provide support at the trunk as the child reaches out to play with the toys. Seat the child on a ball or on your lap and tilt slowly from side to side, forward and backward. This helps develop balance reactions. At first the child may extend the arms to catch himself or herself; later the child will simply pull himself or herself up using trunk muscles. When working on the floor, placing toys at the shoulder level (e.g., on a low shelf, rather than on the floor) will encourage straighter sitting.	*Record* + if the child: 1. Sits alone for 5–10 seconds with back curved slightly, hands resting on legs, and head held steady; and 2. Sits straight with slight support at the waist for 30–60 seconds, with head steady and hands free for play; and 3. Sits up straight with no help for at least 60 seconds, with head steady and hands free for play; and 4. Sits up straight without help with hands free for play and head and trunk able to freely rotate from side to side. *Criterion:*　Child sits up straight unassisted with hands free for play and head and trunk able to rotate from side to side for 5 minutes, 2 times per session (or 10 minutes at 1 time).

Note:　If the child is unable to perform these steps adequately, more experience in the prone position should be provided, and supportive seating should be provided for play. Signs of inadequate trunk development include loss of balance, consistent prop-sitting, W-sitting, and legs held stiffly extended. If you see these positions, correct them manually and consult a therapist for additional exercises and seating arrangements.

AREA: **24. Gross Motor Activities: Upright**
BEHAVIOR: 24e. Pulls self to standing position

Position of Child: All fours or sitting position
Materials: Any favorite toys

Teaching procedures	Steps for learning/evaluation
Place toys on a couch or low chair. Show the child the toys and where you are placing them. Encourage child to pull up to a standing position in order to see and touch the toys. If child is unable to pull to stand, encourage child to reach up from a kneeling position to grasp things while remaining on his or her knees. Gradually put toys a little farther out of reach. Help child grasp something to help pull self up. Reduce help and encourage child to reach for the toy. Make a game of it!	***Record*** + if the child: 1. Pulls on support and partially straightens legs; and 2. Pulls to standing by straightening both legs at once; and 3. Pulls to standing by first bending one leg, placing that foot flat on the floor, and then straightening the leg to come to standing, remaining standing for 30 seconds (see drawing *e* in the "Upright" sequence of the motor development chart, Figure 3, Chapter 5). ***Criterion:*** Child pulls self up independently by first bending one knee and placing the foot flat on the floor, then pulling to stand and remaining for 30 seconds; at least 5 times per session for 3 consecutive sessions.

Note: Observe the child's leg and foot position while standing. A *spastic* child should not be left on tiptoes with the knees pulled together. If you see this, correct it manually. A therapist should be consulted regarding correct standing positions.

AREA: **24. Gross Motor Activities: Upright**
BEHAVIOR: 24f. Steps sideways holding a support

Position of Child: Standing at edge of chair or table
Materials: Any favorite toys

Teaching procedures	Steps for learning/evaluation
After the child has pulled to a standing position, move his or her toys a few inches out of reach and to the side. Encourage child to step sideways to get them. Do this to both sides, gradually increasing the distance at which the toys are placed. Make sure you are using toys the child likes to play with and will want to reach.	***Record*** + if the child: 1. Takes a few sideways steps, moving only one extremity at a time, leaning his or her trunk on the support; and 2. Takes several sideways steps, moving an arm and leg on one side at the same time, leaning his or her trunk very little on the support; and 3. Takes a series of 10–12 sideways steps in quick succession without leaning trunk on the support; and

(continued)

Teaching procedures	Steps for learning/evaluation
	4. Steps freely along furniture and around the corners, using one hand and rotating the trunk. *Criterion:* Child steps freely along furniture and around the corners, using one hand and rotating the trunk; 3 times in 2 consecutive sessions.

AREA: **24. Gross Motor Activities: Upright**
BEHAVIOR: 24g. Stoops to pick up toy while holding on to a support

Position of Child: Standing holding on to a support
Materials: Toys the child is interested in and likes to play with

Teaching procedures	Steps for learning/evaluation
While the child is standing holding on to a support, offer toys on one side. At first offer them slightly below the level of the support. Gradually offer them lower, until they can be retrieved from the floor.	*Record* + if the child: 1. Maintains one hand on the support and stoops one-third of the way to the floor; and 2. Maintains one hand on the support and stoops two-thirds of the way to the floor; and 3. Picks up object from floor and returns to standing, maintaining support with one hand. *Criterion:* Child picks up an object from the floor and returns to standing position, maintaining support with one hand; at least 5 times per session.

Note: This item should be combined with language or cognitive games such as finding objects, putting them in containers, stacking, sorting, and so forth.

AREA: **24. Gross Motor Activities: Upright**
BEHAVIOR: 24h. Removes hands from support and stands independently

Position of Child: Standing with support
Materials: Favorite toys

Teaching procedures	Steps for learning/evaluation
When the child is standing holding onto a support, offer a large toy that must be grasped with both hands, or suspend on array of toys in front of the child. Present the toy close to the child at first to allow use of the support for leaning. As the child's balance and standing improve, require the child to move away from the support to get the toy. Play hand-clapping games while the child is standing at a support.	*Record* + if the child: 1. Releases hands momentarily, leaning trunk on support; and 2. Releases hands for at least 5 seconds with no trunk support; and 3. Stands alone for 10–20 seconds; and 4. Stands alone for 30 or more seconds. *Criterion:* Child maintains erect standing position for 30 seconds; at least 3 times in a session.

Note: Children stand independently when they are physically ready for it. Be sure that a child is competent in all prone and supine activities before working on this item. To be certain, check with a therapist.

AREA: **24. Gross Motor Activities: Upright**
BEHAVIOR: 24i. Takes independent steps

Position of Child: Standing with or without a support
Materials: Any favorite toys

Teaching procedures	Steps for learning/evaluation
With the child in a standing position, entice child to take a few steps toward you, using toys and verbal encouragement. Place favorite toys or food on chairs placed a few feet apart and encourage child to go back and forth to get the items.	*Record* + if the child: 1. Takes a few steps, leaning forward toward the outstretched arms of an adult; and 2. Takes several steps with trunk upright and arms held up. *Criterion:* Child takes several independent steps in an upright position; 3 times on 3 different days.

Note: It is very important not to force walking prematurely. Children walk when they are physically ready for it. If the child seems fearful or resistant about walking, do not force him to do so or frustrate him with too much coaxing.

AREA: **24. Gross Motor Activities: Upright**
BEHAVIOR: 24j. Moves from hands and knees, to hands and feet, to standing

Position of Child: On hands and knees
Materials: Favorite toys

Teaching procedures	Steps for learning/evaluation
Place the child in a clear space on the floor and entice child to stand by offering your hands or a toy. Give as much assistance as is needed until child is able to do it alone. Demonstrate the movement, then ask the child to do it. Give only as much assistance as is needed!	*Record* + if the child: 1. Moves from all fours to hands and feet; and 2. Lifts hands off floor briefly when in a hands and feet position; and 3. Moves upright from hands and feet position and remains steady for a few seconds. *Criterion:* Child comes to standing position independently and maintains a steady upright position from an all-fours position; at least 5 times per session.

24-I.

Gross Motor Activities: Upright Stairs

24. Gross Motor Activities: Upright

I. Stairs

a. Walks up stairs with railing
b. Walks down stairs with railing
c. Walks up stairs without railing, placing both feet on 1 step at a time

d. Walks down stairs without railing, placing both feet on 1 step at a time

AREA: **24-I. Gross Motor Activities: Upright   Stairs**
BEHAVIOR: 24-Ia. Walks up stairs with railing

Position of Child: Standing, at bottom of stairs
Materials: Steps (at least 3) and a railing

Teaching procedures	Steps for learning/evaluation
Position yourself close to the child at first, giving support at the hips and withdrawing it as the child becomes more secure.	*Record* + if the child: 1. Faces the railing and grasps it with both hands while ascending the stairs sideways; and 2. Uses one hand on the railing and faces forward while ascending, both feet on 1 step; and 3. Uses one hand on the railing and ascends the stairs in alternating fashion. *Criterion:* Child uses one hand on the railing and ascends the stairs in alternating fashion; 2 times on 3 separate days.

AREA: **24-I. Gross Motor Activities: Upright   Stairs**
BEHAVIOR: 24-Ib. Walks down stairs with railing

Position of Child: Standing, at top of stairs
Materials: Steps with railing

Teaching procedures	Steps for learning/evaluation
Position yourself in front of child and give support at the hips, withdrawing it as the child becomes more secure.	*Record* + if the child: 1. Faces railing and holds on with both hands while descending sideways, both feet on 1 step; and 2. Uses one hand on the railing and faces forward while descending the stairs, both feet on 1 step; and 3. Uses one hand on the railing and descends steps in alternating fashion. *Criterion:* Child uses one hand on the railing and faces forward while descending stairs in alternating fashion; 2 times on 3 separate days.

AREA: **24-I. Gross Motor Activities: Upright   Stairs**
BEHAVIOR: 24-Ic. Walks up stairs without railing, placing both feet on 1 step at a time

Position of Child: Standing, at bottom of stairs
Materials: Steps (at least 3), with or without railing

Teaching procedures	Steps for learning/evaluation
Place the child away from the railing. Position yourself behind the child and give support at the hips, withdrawing it as the child becomes more secure. A favorite toy or food can be placed on the top step.	*Record* + if the child: 1. Walks up the steps, sometimes placing hands on the next step for support; and 2. Walks up the stairs without hand support but is slow and unsteady; and 3. Walks up stairs without railing, both feet on 1 step. *Criterion:* Child walks up stairs efficiently and quickly, both feet on 1 step; 2 times on 3 separate days.

AREA: **24-I. Gross Motor Activities: Upright   Stairs**
BEHAVIOR: 24-Id. Walks down stairs without railing, placing both feet on 1 step at a time

Position of Child: Standing, at top of stairs
Materials: Steps with or without railing

Teaching procedures	Steps for learning/evaluation
Place the child away from the railing. Position yourself in front of the child and give support at the hips, withdrawing it as child becomes more secure.	*Record* + if the child: 1. Walks down the steps, sometimes reverting to a sitting or crawling position; and 2. Walks down the steps in upright position, but is slow and unsteady; and 3. Walks down stairs without railing, placing both feet on 1 step at a time. *Criterion:* Child walks down the steps, both feet on 1 step; 2 times on 3 separate days.

24-II.

Gross Motor Activities: Upright Balance

24. Gross Motor Activities: Upright

II. Balance

a. Stands on one foot while hands are held

b. Walks with one foot on the walking board and one foot on the floor

c. Stands on one foot without help

d. Walks on line independently, following the general direction

AREA: **24-II. Gross Motor Activities: Upright   Balance**
BEHAVIOR: 24-IIa. Stands on one foot while hands are held

Position of the Child: Standing
Materials: Music, shoes, socks, pants, ball

Teaching procedures	Steps for learning/evaluation
When dressing and undressing the child, have child hold on to you with his or her hands. Have child lift his or her legs to help in putting on pants, shoes, and socks. Hold the child's hands while playing music. Demonstrate how to march and dance. Show the child how to kick a ball placed on the floor.	*Record* + if the child: 1. Shifts weight and attempts to raise one leg but does not clear the floor; and 2. Raises one foot off the floor briefly; and 3. Stands on one foot for a few seconds while hands held. *Criterion:* With hands held, child is able to raise one foot off the floor and hold it for 2–3 seconds; 3 consecutive days. (Record right and left feet separately.)

AREA: **24-II. Gross Motor Activities: Upright   Balance**
BEHAVIOR: 24-IIb. Walks with one foot on the walking board and one foot on the floor

Position of the Child: Standing
Materials: Walking board 72 inches long, 2½ inches wide, 4 inches high; books

Teaching procedures	Steps for learning/evaluation
Demonstrate the activity by placing a board on the floor and stepping onto it. Then have the child step onto it. Remove the supporting blocks from the walking board to place it closer to the floor. Give the child physical assistance, withdrawing when possible. Repeat above procedure with supporting blocks in place. Place books on the floor and have the child practice placing one foot.	*Record* + if the child: 1. Places one foot on the board but does not take any steps; and 2. Walks at least one-half the length of the board; and 3. Walks with one foot on the walking board and one foot on the floor the length of the board. *Criterion:* Child walks full length of the board with one foot on the board and one on the floor; 3 times on 3 consecutive sessions.

AREA: **24-II. Gross Motor Activities: Upright   Balance**
BEHAVIOR: 24-IIc. Stands on one foot without help

Position of the Child: Standing
Materials: Music, shoes, socks, pants, ball, books, ropes

Teaching procedures	Steps for learning/evaluation
Use the activities listed under 24-IIa, withdrawing hand support and requiring longer periods of balance. Construct an obstacle course that requires the child to step over books or ropes placed at graduated heights.	***Record*** + if the child: 1. Attempts to lift one foot but does not clear the floor; and 2. Lifts one foot briefly; and 3. Stands on one foot without help for a few seconds. ***Criterion:*** Child is able to lift one foot off the floor and hold it for 3–4 seconds; 4 times each session on 3 consecutive sessions.

AREA: **24-II. Gross Motor Activities: Upright   Balance**
BEHAVIOR: 24-IId. Walks on line independently, following the general direction

Position of the Child: Standing
Materials: 10-foot line painted or taped on floor; fabric, 45 inches wide; 2 boards, 72 inches long; or other designs placed on floor

Teaching procedures	Steps for learning/evaluation
Start by teaching the child to walk on a length of fabric 45 inches wide. Gradually fold the material into smaller widths. Show the child how to follow footprints or designs on the floor. Place 2 boards on the floor and have the child walk between them, gradually moving them closer together. Pull a toy along the painted or taped line; encourage the child to follow it.	***Record*** + if the child: 1. Follows the line for 1 or 2 steps, then wanders off; and 2. Follows the line for at least half its length; and 3. Walks on line independently, following the general direction. ***Criterion:*** Child walks the entire length of the line independently; 3 trials on 3 consecutive sessions.

24-III.

Gross Motor Activities: Upright Jumping

24. Gross Motor Activities: Upright

III.   Jumping

a.   Jumps off floor with both feet   b.   Jumps off step with both feet

AREA: **24-III. Gross Motor Activities: Upright   Jumping**
BEHAVIOR: 24-IIIa. Jumps off floor with both feet

Position of Child: Standing
Materials: Bed or trampoline; rope; music

Teaching procedures	Steps for learning/evaluation
Hold the child by the trunk, later by the hands, as he or she bounces on a bed or trampoline. Hold child by the hands and practice jumping to music. Release your hold when possible. Tie a rope between two table legs. First let it lie on the floor then raise it slightly. Make a game of jumping over the rope.	*Record* + if the child: 1. Attempts to jump but his or her feet do not clear the floor; and 2. Jumps by raising one foot at a time; and 3. Clears the floor with both feet once. *Criterion:* Child jumps 5 times consecutively, clearing the floor with both feet simultaneously; 3 consecutive sessions.

AREA: **24-III. Gross Motor Activities: Upright   Jumping**
BEHAVIOR: 24-IIIb. Jumps off step with both feet

Position of Child: Standing
Materials: Step, 6 inches high (boards or books of varying thicknesses)

Teaching procedures	Steps for learning/evaluation
Start by having the child jump off a board or book 1 inch thick as you hold his or her hands. When child can jump off without hands held, use 2 inches height and repeat the procedure. Work up to 6 inches.	*Record* + if the child: 1. Walks off 6-inch step; and 2. Jumps off 6-inch step with one foot leading and landing before the other; and 3. Jumps off step with both feet. *Criterion:* Child jumps off 6-inch step with both feet moving together and landing at the same time; 5 times in 3 consecutive sessions.

24-IV.

Gross Motor Activities: Upright Posture and locomotion

24. Gross Motor Activities: Upright

IV.   Posture and locomotion

a. Walks sideways
b. Walks backward
c. Squats in play

d. Runs stiffly
e. Runs well

AREA: **24-IV. Gross Motor Activities: Upright**   **Posture and locomotion**
BEHAVIOR: 24-IVa. Walks sideways

Position of the Child: Standing
Materials: Tables, ball, toys

Teaching procedures	Steps for learning/evaluation
Have the child push a small car along a table. Have child hold a large ball and carry it along a table. Hold child's hands and walk sideways to music. Hold one of the child's hands and put a pull-toy in the other; guide the child in walking sideways. Give physical assistance at first, withdrawing it when possible.	*Record* + if the child: 1. Takes a few sideways steps with physical assistance; and 2. Takes a few sideways steps independently in a training situation; and 3. Walks sideways spontaneously. *Criterion:* Child is noted to spontaneously take several sideways steps while playing; 3 times on 3 different days.

AREA: **24-IV. Gross Motor Activities: Upright**   **Posture and locomotion**
BEHAVIOR: 24-IVb. Walks backward

Position of the Child: Standing
Materials: Pull-toys, large mirror

Teaching procedures	Steps for learning/evaluation
Present the child with a pull-toy and place both of child's hands on the string. Initially guide child through the backward walking pattern, withdrawing as soon as possible. Play a game of walking toward and away from a mirror.	*Record* + if the child: 1. Takes backward steps with physical guidance; and 2. Takes a few backward steps independently in a training situation; and 3. Walks backwards spontaneously. *Criterion:* Child is observed to spontaneously take several backward steps during play; 3 times on 3 different days.

AREA: **24-IV. Gross Motor Activities: Upright**   **Posture and locomotion**
BEHAVIOR: 24-IVc. Squats in play

Position of the Child: Standing
Materials: Small and medium-sized toys; xylophone, drums, tables, large tunnel tubes

Teaching procedures	Steps for learning/evaluation
Place toys on the floor and have the child squat to pick them up. Place xylophone, drums, or similar interactive toys on the floor and guide child into a squatting position to play. Play a game in which the child walks under tables or through tunnels.	***Record*** + if the child: 1. Initiates a squatting movement; and 2. Assumes a squatting position for a few seconds at a time; and 3. Squats easily in play. ***Criterion:*** Child squats down and remains in that position for 10–15 seconds while playing; on 3 separate days.

Note: "Squatting" refers to a position in which the hips and knees are bent to a little over 90°; the child is actively contracting leg muscles to maintain the position.

AREA: **24-IV. Gross Motor Activities: Upright**   **Posture and locomotion**
BEHAVIOR: 24-IVd. Runs stiffly

Position of the Child: Standing
Materials: Ball, small-wheeled toys

Teaching procedures	Steps for learning/evaluation
Roll a ball or push a small-wheeled toy across the floor and demonstrate running after it. Accompany this with hand-clapping and verbal encouragement. Entice the child to chase you by playing hide-and-seek.	***Record*** + if the child: 1. Takes a few quick steps in a training situation; and 2. Consistently takes 5–10 stiff running steps in a training situation; and 3. Runs spontaneously but stiffly. ***Criterion:*** Child is observed to spontaneously run several feet with the legs held stiffly and the feet widely spaced; 3 different times on 3 separate days.

Note: While running, the arms may be held up and out to the side.

AREA: **24-IV. Gross Motor Activities: Upright   Posture and locomotion**
BEHAVIOR: 24-IVe. Runs well

Position of the Child: Standing
Materials: Ball, small-wheeled toys

Teaching procedures	Steps for learning/evaluation
Teach as in item 24-IVd, using longer distances as tolerated by the child. Mature running emerges with practice and improved balance.	***Record*** + if the child: 1. Begins to use a reciprocal arm movement and narrows his or her base of support while walking; and 2. Runs short distances, with fairly good balance. ***Criterion:*** Child has good reciprocal arm swing and maintains a narrow base of support while running; on 3 separate days.

Index

322   Index

Seizure disorders, 37
Self-direction, 203–207
  explores different areas of own home, 206
  explores unfamiliar places with mother present, 207
  makes choices—has preferred toys, foods, and so forth, 205
  moves away from Mom to nearby area, 204
  moves away from Mom in same room, 204
  plays alone with toys for 15 minutes, 205–206
Social skills, 189–201
  can be comforted by talking to, holding, rocking, 191
  "gives" things to others upon request, 197
  "helps" in simple household tasks—imitates, 199
  initiates game-playing, 196
  participates in games, 195
  "performs" for others, 200
  plays alongside other children—some exchange of toys, 199
  repeats activity that is laughed at, 196
  responds differently to strangers versus familiar people, 194–195
  shares spontaneously
    with adults, 197
    with peers, 201
  shows affection, 198
  smiles
    at a familiar person, 192–193
    to auditory or tactile stimulation, 192
    at mirror image, 193
    reciprocally, 191–192
  tries to attract attention through smiling and eye contact or other body language, 194
  tries to comfort others in distress, 200
  tries to please others, 198
Spastic cerebral palsy, characteristics of, 36
Spatial concepts, 99–109
  looks or moves in the right direction for objects that fall and roll or bounce to a new location, 104
  looks or reaches for or toward objects
    in sight that touch body, 101
    out of sight that touch body, 102
    that fall from view quietly, 103
    that fall from view while making a noise, 102–103
  moves self around barrier to get object, 107
  pulls string to get object from behind barrier, 106
  puts objects away in correct places, 108–109
  reaches object from behind barrier, 106–107
  retrieves objects from usual locations in another room, 108
  retrieves toys dropped in container through hole in top, 105

  searches for objects out of visual field or away from midline, 104–105
  shifts attention from 1 object to another, 100
  uses "tools" to deal with spatial problems, 109
Special purpose chairs, 40
Symbolic play, see Objects and symbolic play, functional use of
Symmetric tonic neck reflex (STNR), 29
  abnormal, 33

Tactile integration and manipulation, 65–72
  explores objects with fingers, 68
  finds object hidden in textured material, 69
  permits hands, feet, or body to be moved over rough-textured surfaces, or moves them spontaneously, 67
  permits soft, smooth textures to be rubbed on hands, feet, or body, or moves own body over such textures, 66
  plays in water, 68
  plays or pokes with clay, 71–72
  plays with soft-textured materials, 69–70
  reacts to tactile stimulation with movement, 67
  responds differently to warm/cold, rough/smooth, 66
  spreads firmer materials with hands, 71
  spreads soft materials with fingers, 70
Tactile stimulation, 65
Teaching principles of the Carolina Curriculum, 7–10
Tension athetosis, 36
Thumbs, entrapped, 33
Tilting reactions, 31
Toe grasp reflex, 30
  abnormal, 33

Visual problems, 37
Visual pursuit and object permanence, 81–89
  continues to look at caregiver when caregiver's face is covered with a cloth, 85
  gaze lingers where object disappeared, 84
  looks at cover under which object disappeared, 85
  looks at or to the correct place for toy
    after seeing toy covered in 3 places successively, 87–88
    when object is hidden in 1 of 3 places, 86–87
    when object is hidden in 1 of 2 places, 86
  looks successively at 2 covers until toy is found, 88
  looks systematically at 3 covers until toy is found, 89
  visually fixates for at least 3 seconds, 82